BEST ROAD TRIPS
NEW YORK
& THE MID-ATLANTIC

ESCAPES ON THE OPEN ROAD

AMY BALFOUR

Contents

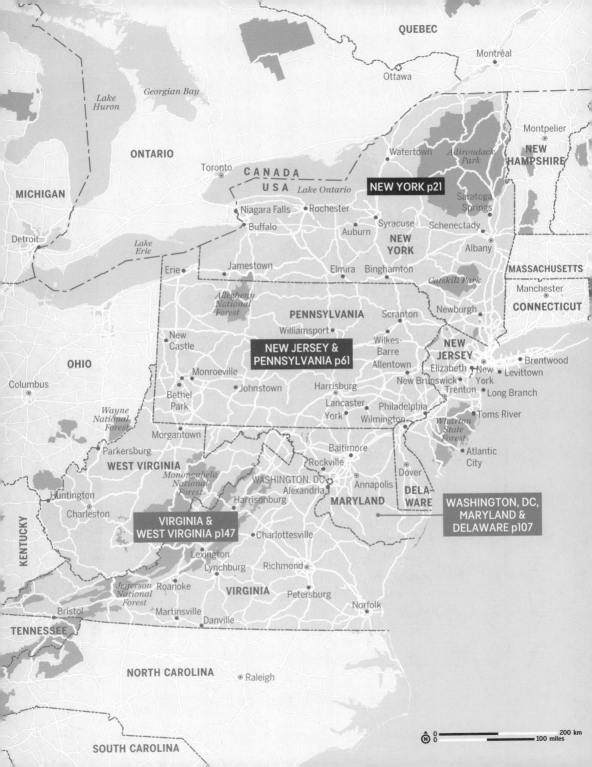

Welcome to New York & the Mid-Atlantic

The best road trips through New York and the Mid-Atlantic deliver spectacular scenery and compelling history – and often the unexpected. Tucked between the Appalachian Mountains and the Atlantic Ocean, the region is home to iconic byways like Skyline Drive and the Blue Ridge Parkway, as well as low-key back roads that swing past wildflowers and sand dunes.

But it's not just the drives that are compelling. It's also the stops along the way. Our trips brake for some pretty cool sights, from weathered crab shacks beside the Chesapeake Bay to the architectural splendors of Fallingwater to the gravity-defying weirdness of the Mystery Hole. History, spotlighting the founding of the United States as well as its visionary but complicated leaders, is also front and center.

If time is limited, make sure to drive one of our eight Classic Trips, which take you to the very best of New York and the Mid-Atlantic.

The Adirondacks (p46)
SELMA KREHIC/SHUTTERSTOCK ©

Our Picks

BEST ROUTES FOR SPECTACULAR VIEWS

Big views in the Mid-Atlantic don't make you fear for your life. Instead, you feel like you're part of the beauty, whether driving a federal byway along mountain ridges or cruising past windswept dunes. Pretty stops include lakeside vineyards, shimmering marshes, a grand limestone arch, ancient river valleys, bountiful farmlands and the PA Grand Canyon. And, of course, the gobsmacking Niagara Falls.

TOP TIP

Wildlife abounds on the 105-mile Skyline Drive and the 469-mile Blue Ridge Parkway. There are no stoplights, so watch your speed.

Blue Ridge Parkway

Sunsets in western Virginia turn the gentle Blue Ridge a stunning shade of cobalt.

P.174

Down the Delaware

Ditch the car for the Delaware River, where perspectives are ever-changing.

P.76

Niagara Falls & Around

150,000 gallons of water plunge 1000ft per feet second: it's a glorious sight to behold.

P.52

Through the Wilds Along Route 6

Stroll the Kinzua Bridge skywalk to views of the valley 225ft below, followed by stargazing.

P.100

Maritime Maryland

Salt breezes and steamed crabs enhance waterfront views of the Chesapeake Bay.

P.120

ZACK FRANK/SHUTTERSTOCK ©

Blue Ridge Parkway (p174)

Our Picks

BEST HISTORY ROUTES

Explore the story of the United States, stopping at destinations that played a pivotal role in the country's formation. The Mid-Atlantic is dotted with historic homes and seats of power, many of them linked to the Founding Fathers. Battlefields from the French and Indian War, the Revolutionary War and the Civil War share the stories of soldiers and generals. And music accompanies the history on Virginia's Crooked Road.

TOP TIP

Ghost tours are a fun way to learn about a city's history while enjoying a few scares along the way.

The Civil War Tour

From Antietam to Appomattox, destinations analyze key events in the nation's most important conflict.

P.162

Bucks County & Around

Explore the spots outside Philadelphia where George Washington maneuvered during the Revolutionary War. **P.70**

Crooked Road sign, Floyd (p169)

Maryland's National Historic Road

One of the most diverse states in America, Maryland has a history that is both painful and progressive.

P.110

Adirondack Peaks & Valleys

Forts built in the 1700s delve into the French and Indian War and the Revolutionary War.

P.46

The Crooked Road

From Bristol to the Carter Family Fold, the Crooked Road celebrates the roots of country music.

P.168

Antietam (p162)

Our Picks

BEST OUTDOOR ADVENTURE ROUTES

Outdoor adventures run the gamut in the Mid-Atlantic, and they're typically backdropped by a beautiful landscape, from the Blue Ridge Mountains to the Atlantic Ocean. Our trips pause for hiking on the Appalachian Trail (AT), cycling along the Potomac River and holding tight on a wheeled luge at Lake Placid. Water adventures also get their due, with kayaking, sailing and whitewater rafting opportunities in abundance.

TOP TIP

For a stargazing event, bring a red-light flashlight, which is less likely to interfere with your night vision.

Skyline Drive

Steep hikes to waterfalls, horseback rides past epic vistas and cavern tours through underground wonders.
P.150

The Appalachians & the AT

Hike along America's most famous trail and hold tight on a wild whitewater rafting trip down the Gauley River. **P.156**

Along the C&O Canal

Cyclists, this one's for you, with many places to pedal on a historic towpath beside the Potomac River.
P.116

Delmarva

Take a boat tour, wander a wildlife refuge and camp near the beach at Assateague Island National Seashore.
P.134

Adirondack Peaks & Valleys

In summer, hold tight on a bobsled or a luge at the Olympic Sports Complex in Lake Placid.
P.46

ZACK FRANK/SHUTTERSTOCK ©

Shenandoah National Park (p150)

Whitewater rafting, Gauley River (p160)

Our Picks

BEST ART & ARCHITECTURE ROUTES

Every taste is satisfied, whether you're a fan of Frank Lloyd Wright or stately pre–Revolutionary Row houses, world-class museums or massive open-air sculpture parks. From Warhol to Winterthur, murals to Monticello, the collision of talent, imagination and form are celebrated across the region. Many homes and museums offer guided tours, which are typically worth the time for their helpful context and history. Art walks typically celebrate with wine.

TOP TIP
Historic homes like Monticello and Fallingwater offer standard tours, but check ahead for specialty visits that may dig into unique perspectives.

 1

Pittsburgh & the Laurel Highlands

Enjoy architectural masterpieces in the country and top-flight museums in the city.

P.94

 2

Eastern Shore Odyssey

The cute red brick of Dover contrasts nicely with the palatial gardens of nearby Brandywine Valley.

P.140

 3

Hudson Valley

This trip includes modern art at Dia Beacon, spectacular mansions and the valley's own school of painting.

P.24

 4

Niagara Falls & Around

Art deco, Frank Lloyd Wright and stellar galleries in Buffalo, plus the show-stopping Niagara Falls.

P.52

 5

Peninsula to the Piedmont

18th-century buildings in Williamsburg, colonial estates by the James River and fine art at Jefferson's Monticello.

P.180

KHAIRIL AZHAR JUNOS/SHUTTERSTOCK ©

Williamsburg (182)

Our Picks

BEST OFFBEAT ROUTES

From kitschy to creepy, America does weird like no other. And New York and the Mid-Atlantic? Can you say Mystery Hole? Offbeat attractions across the region often have ties to important events or famous figures, which adds context to history. But sometimes they are just stand-alone weird. Wacky attractions are often easy to reach because the Mid-Atlantic is fairly compact.

TOP TIP

Typically found in a creaky old house, these collections have quirky hours and even quirkier docents.

Luray Caverns (p152)

The Appalachians & the AT

Everything is tilted at the Mystery Hole, while the John Brown Wax Museum offers animatronic history.

P.156

The Civil War Tour

This trip swings past the burial spot for Stonewall Jackson's arm and the site of the Battle of the Crater.

P.162

Maryland's National Historic Road

Peruse outsider art inside the mismatched confines of the American Visionary Art Museum in Baltimore.

P.110

Skyline Drive

Explore kitschy Dinosaur Land, then listen to the world's largest musical instrument inside Luray Caverns.

P.150

Eastern Shore Odyssey

Delaware loves its scrapple, and scrapple vodka is a thing, as are historic potato houses.

P.140

When to Go

Road trippers will find the best road conditions from late spring through fall. Most attractions are open then too.

Late spring is a gorgeous time to explore by car. This is the time to pull over for cultivated gardens and to drive the Blue Ridge Parkway and Skyline Drive, when green foliage frames lofty views and redbuds brighten the roadsides. Waterfalls are flush from snowmelt and spring rains.

Summer is high season across the region, with families traveling during school breaks, and others enjoying the warm weather. Beaches and big-city attractions alike will be busy. The pluses of summer travel from June through August? Summer is festival season and evenings are alive with outdoor concerts. With foliage changing colors across the Appalachians, fall is another great time for a mountain road trip.

Shenandoah National Park (p150)

Weather Watch (New York City)

JANUARY	FEBRUARY	MARCH	APRIL	MAY	JUNE
Average daytime max: **40°F**	Average daytime max: **42°F**	Average daytime max: **50°F**	Average daytime max: **62°F**	Average daytime max: **71°F**	Average daytime max: **80°F**
Days of rainfall: **3.6**	Days of rainfall: **3.3**	Days of rainfall: **4.3**	Days of rainfall: **4**	Days of rainfall: **4**	Days of rainfall: **4.5**

New River Gorge (p160)

Accommodation

Peak season is generally May to September. Book lodging a few months ahead of your visit, particularly along the Atlantic Coast. Hotel prices in the mountains increase during the fall foliage season. Prices can also be high in college towns during football game weekends.

Camping at a Beach

Who needs white noise when you can sleep steps from the waves? Beach-adjacent campgrounds in the Mid-Atlantic include Assateague Island National Seashore in Maryland, Delaware Seashore State Park in Rehoboth Beach and First Landing State Park in Virginia Beach.

SAFE TRAVEL: HURRICANES

Hurricane season along the Atlantic seaboard extends from June through November, but the peak season is late August through October. The chances of encountering a hurricane are slim, but if you do, take the threat of danger seriously. Pay close attention to any evacuation orders.

TOP TIP

Peak foliage along Skyline Drive and the Blue Ridge Parkway in Virginia is typically in mid-October, but peak color varies annually. Higher-elevation trees will change color first. Check Shenandoah National Park's social media feeds and the Fall Foliage report at virginia.org for updates.

BIG EVENTS FOR EVERYONE

National Cherry Blossom Festival

The brilliant blooms of Japanese cherry blossoms around DC's Tidal Basin are celebrated with concerts, parades, taiko drumming, kite-flying and other events during the three-week festival. More than 1.5 million attend, so book ahead. **March**

Tribeca Film Festival

A major star of the indie movie circuit, with loads of movies, panels and celebs in NYC. **April**

Artscape

Listen to the music, watch the films, admire the sculptures and appreciate the dancers. Art in all its forms grabs the spotlight in Baltimore during America's largest free arts festival. **August**

Bridge Day

Watch BASE jumpers leap from the New River Gorge Bridge in Fayetteville, WV, on the third Saturday of October. It's the only day that the bridge is open for jumps. Live music in town. **October**

JULY	AUGUST	SEPTEMBER	OCTOBER	NOVEMBER	DECEMBER
Average daytime max: **85°F**	Average daytime max: **84°F**	Average daytime max: **76°F**	Average daytime max: **65°F**	Average daytime max: **54°F**	Average daytime max: **45°F**
Days of rainfall: **4.8**	Days of rainfall: **4.6**	Days of rainfall: **4.5**	Days of rainfall: **4.4**	Days of rainfall: **3.6**	Days of rainfall: **4.3**

Get Prepared for New York & the Mid-Atlantic

Useful things to load in your bag, your ears and your brain

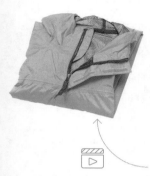

▶

WATCH

The Civil War
(Ken Burns; 1990)
Nine-part documentary
about America's
bloodiest conflict.

A Walk in the Woods
(Ken Kwapis; 2014)
Cinematic take on
author Bill Bryson's
attempt to hike the
Appalachian Trail.

Dirty Dancing
(Emile Ardolino; 1987)
Love story set in the
Catskills and filmed in
southwestern Virginia.

The West Wing
(Aaron Sorkin; 1999–
2006) Fast-talking
political drama with
Josiah Bartlet in the
White House tackling
issues of the day.

The Wire
(David Simon;
2002–2008) HBO
drama exploring the
relationships between
crime, education, the
media and power in
Baltimore

Clothing

Layers Many recreational areas are located in the mountains, where the temperatures can change quickly, particularly in the spring and fall. For that reason, pack several layers of light clothing that you can take on and off while hiking. Even in summer, synthetic layers (which don't absorb moisture) are preferred over cotton for strenuous outdoor activities. Layering is also a good idea for city exploring from fall through spring.

Casual versus chic America is pretty casual when it comes to day-to-day clothing, and road trippers should be fine in jeans and shorts in most places. Dress up for upscale restaurants in larger cities.

Footwear Trail-running shoes with grippy soles are the best all-around footwear for recreational activities. If you'll be hiking through mountain streams, kayaking or canoeing, water shoes or closed-toe sandals (not flip-flops) are also useful. Sandals and sneakers are fine for walking around big cities. But if you're headed out for the evening? Bring a second pair of nicer shoes.

Hat and sunscreen The sun can be brutal, and not just at the beach. Consider a hat with a wide brim to protect your face. And slather on sunscreen regularly.

CHARLES BRUTLAG/SHUTTERSTOCK ©

Words

Submarines Also known as subs, these are meat-and-cheese sandwiches served in a large roll or baguette. They have varied nicknames across New York and the Mid-Atlantic and are often associated with early 20th-century Italian immigrants.

Hero A submarine sandwich in New York City. According to *Bon Appétit* magazine, the term originated in a 1930s food column suggesting you needed to be a 'hero' to eat one.

Hoagie Philly-style sub. May have derived from the term for the packed lunches that shipyard workers took to Hog Island – the sandwich was originally called a Hoggie. According to another story, a local sandwich maker said you had to be a hog to eat one.

Hooch A nickname in Appalachia for moonshine, which is un-aged whiskey. Also known as mountain dew and white lightning.

Pepperoni roll Soft rolls stuffed with cured meats like pepperoni; popular across West Virginia. These low-maintenance snacks trace back to Italian immigrants who ate them in the coal mines.

Pierogies Filled dumplings from eastern Europe are a staple in the western part of Pennsylvania. Common fillings are potatoes and cheese.

Scrapple Pork fillings (snout, livers and hearts) combined with cornmeal and flour to form a loaf, which is sliced, fried and served at breakfast or between two slices of bread. A Delaware specialty.

Shoo-fly pie Basically a molasses pie, it's often topped with brown sugar. Look for it on menus in Pennsylvania Dutch Country.

LISTEN

Birthplace of Country Music Radio (birthplaceofcountry music.org) Listen to old-time, bluegrass and country music live from Bristol, VA.

Illadelph Halflife (The Roots; 1996) Third album from the long-running Philly hip-hop group and *Tonight Show* house band.

Hamilton: The Soundtrack (Lin-Manuel Miranda) Recording of the songs from the Broadway musical about the life of Alexander Hamilton.

The Bowery Boys: New York City History Podcast spotlighting the stories behind various NYC places and people.

READ

All the President's Men (Carl Bernstein & Bob Woodward; 1974) Classic political tale by the reporters who broke Watergate.

Demon Copperhead (Barbara Kingsolver; 2022) The story of the opioid crisis and its devastating effects in Virginia's Appalachian Mountains.

Just Kids (Patti Smith; 2010) Evocative memoir describing Smith's 1960s and '70s NYC adventures.

Narrative of the Life of Frederick Douglass (Frederick Douglass; 1845) Autobiography of the orator and abolitionist born into slavery near Easton, MA.

ROAD TRIPS

Mabry Mill (p170)
SERGEY DEMO SVDPHOTO/SHUTTERSTOCK ©

Contents

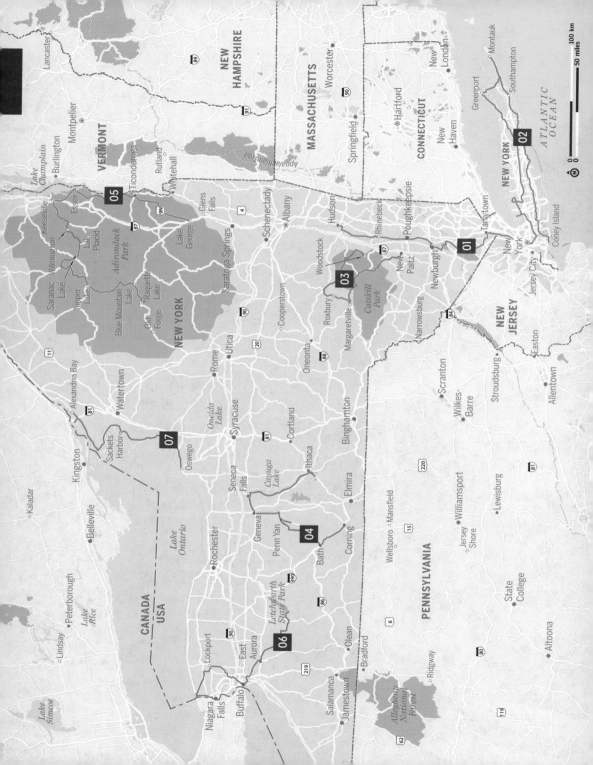

MICHAEL SHAKE/SHUTTERSTOCK ©

Taughannock Falls (p44)

New York

01 Hudson Valley

Urban cares fall away on this drive north from the Big Apple along the Hudson River past pristine forests. **p24**

02 Long Island

Vineyards and beaches await on this boomerang drive from Central Park to the well-moneyed Hamptons. **p30**

03 Tranquil Catskills

Mountains, gorges and forests are a pretty backdrop for a drive linking charming towns west of the Hudson Valley. **p36**

04 Finger Lakes Loop

Waterfalls galore, top-notch vineyards and the town that birthed the women's rights movement. **p42**

05 Adirondack Peaks & Valleys

New York's wild side is visually stunning, with glacial lakes and 4000ft-high peaks providing the backdrop. **p46**

06 Niagara Falls & Around

This trip is all about grade-A sights and thrills: magnificent waterfalls, a dramatic gorge and iconic architecture. **p52**

07 St Lawrence Seaway

Remote drive along Lake Ontario and the St Lawrence River, braking for cute hamlets and maritime museums. **p56**

Explore
New York

New York is most famous for its eponymous city, which is home to a kaleidoscopic array of sights. And thanks to its airports and train stations, the city is a logical launchpad for exploring the rest of the state. New York holds deep mountain ravines, swift rivers and quaint villages. Upstate has lush forests, clear lakes and dark hills, while the Catskills are a haven for artists. Top-notch wines flow in the Finger Lakes, iconic views await at Niagara Falls, big adventures are the draw in the Adirondacks, and tasty 'mudslides' bring end-of-the-road fun at Claudio's beside Greenport Harbor.

New York City

People say they love the 'energy' of New York City. That energy is up close and personal at tourist hotspots like the High Line and the Brooklyn Bridge. But it's the shared day-to-day experiences that really produce the city's unique thrum – the daily interactions that constitute life in a crowded city, linking artists, immigrants and finance kids in one big and bustling tableau. The city is an epicenter of fashion, theater, food, music and publishing and home to a staggering number of museums, parks and neighborhoods. The best way to tackle it on a road trip? Pick a handful of spots, allow room for serendipity and dig in.

Greenport

Greenport has an end-of-the-road joie de vivre that's a fitting cap to a drive east through Long Island. The largest town in the North Fork, it's home to working fishing boats, a vintage carousel and a small downtown. A handful of bars overlook the pier, where sleek cigarette boats, sailing sloops and motorized yachts pause for libations and live music. Downtown holds a mix of inns, motels and bed and breakfasts, plus a couple of restaurants. The LIRR station and the jitney stop are a quick walk from town, and Shelter Island is a short ferry ride away.

WHEN TO GO

The best time for a road trip through the western and northern reaches of the state is May through October. From the lakes to the mountains, this is the best time to enjoy farmers markets, sunny vistas and warm-weather activities like hiking and paddling. Early September is recommended for Long Island, when summer crowds dissipate but water temperatures are still comfortable.

Buffalo

The second-largest city in New York, Buffalo is not a desirable hub in winter, which is long and cold. But in warmer months the Queen City is a compelling place to base-camp during drives through western New York. Buffalo enjoyed a period of heady prosperity in the early 1900s thanks to Niagara Falls, which is 20 miles north and a source of hydroelectric power. The city faltered economically over the decades, but today Buffalo is enjoying a revival. Masterpieces of 19th- and early 20th-century architecture have been restored and its museums are earning kudos. And for the road-weary, Buffalo has more variety in lodging than Niagara Falls.

Lake Placid

The site of the 1932 and 1980 Winter Olympics, Lake Placid has long been associated with winter sports. But its perch in the center of the High Peaks region makes it a convenient and supportive launchpad for hiking in the Adirondacks and paddling on one of the many lakes in the region. Lodges, from simple to swank, and small inns are common in the region. Many of them overlook beautiful lakes.

TRANSPORT

Three major international airports – JFK International, LaGuardia and Newark Liberty International – serve New York City and surrounding areas. Buffalo Niagara International is a major regional airport. Amtrak offers train service across the state and into Canada, crossing the border at Niagara Falls. Moynihan Train Hall, an extension of Penn Station, is Amtrak's new hub in New York City.

WHERE TO STAY

Swanky boutique hotels are a New York City specialty, and the best of them embrace a theme or vibe that is reflected down to the smallest details. Lodges are a top choice in the mountainous Catskills and Adirondacks, and often the less swanky they are the better. Two top picks are Scribner's Catskill Lodge (scribners lodge.com), an updated 1960s motor inn, and the rustic Adirondack Loj (adk.org). Lakeside 'great camps' (for example, Great Camp Sagamore, sagamore.org) are a throwback to an earlier era and provide a fun communal atmosphere, particularly for families. Historic properties like the InnBuffalo off Elmwood (innbuffalo.com) blend the past and present with aplomb.

WHAT'S ON

St Patricks Day Parade

On March 17 the patron saint of Ireland is honored in New York City with the largest parade in the world.

Hudson Valley Shakespeare Festival

Summer theater company near Cold Spring stages impressive productions of the Bard's classics from mid-May through early September.

Summerstage, New York City

This concert series in Central Park features an incredible lineup from June through August.

Resources

NYC: The Official Guide
(nyctourism.com) New York City's official tourism portal.

New York Magazine
(nymag.com) News, culture and the latest happenings.

Long Island Convention & Visitors Bureau
(discoverlongisland.com) Detailed listings for museums, activities and attractions.

State Office of Parks, Recreation and Historic Preservation
(parks.ny.gov) Camping, lodging and general info.

01

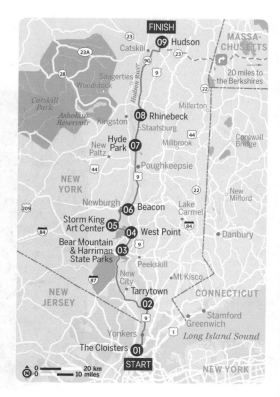

Hudson Valley

DURATION	DISTANCE	GREAT FOR
5 days	115 miles / 185km	History & Culture, Outdoors

BEST TIME TO GO	Grounds of historic estates open mid-May through September.

Immediately north of New York City, green becomes the dominant color and the vistas of the Hudson River and the mountains breathe life into your urban-weary body. The history of the region, home to the Hudson River School of painting in the 19th century and a retreat for Gilded Age industrialists, is preserved in the many grand estates, flowering gardens and picturesque villages.

Link your trip

03 Tranquil Catskills

Head into forested mountain roads from Rte 9W near Kingston or off I-87 at New Paltz.

05 Adirondack Peaks & Valleys

For true wilderness, follow the Hudson River to its source by taking I-87 north to Lake George.

01 THE CLOISTERS

This trip along the Hudson begins at one of New York City's most magnificent riverside locations. Gaze at medieval tapestries, frescoes, carvings and gold treasures, including a St John the Evangelist plaque dating from the 9th century, inside the **Cloisters Museum & Gardens** (metmuseum. org/cloisters). This magnificent Metropolitan Museum annex, built to look like an old castle, is set in Fort Tryon Park overlooking the Hudson River, near the northern tip of Manhattan and not far from the George Washington Bridge. Works such as a 1290 ivory sculpture of the Virgin Mary, ancient stained-

BEST FOR

FOODIES
It's worth making a pilgrimage to Blue Hill at Stone Barns (bluehillfarm. com).

The Cloisters

glass windows, and oil-on-wood religious paintings are displayed in galleries connected by grand archways and topped by Moorish terra-cotta roofs, all facing an airy courtyard. The extensive grounds – with rolling hills blanketed in lush green grass – contain more than 250 varieties of medieval herbs and flowers. In summer months, concerts and perform-ances are held regularly.

 THE DRIVE
Rte 9A north crosses a bridge over the Spuyten Duyvil Creek, mark-ing the boundary between Manhattan and the Bronx with some nice river views. Taking Rte 9 north is a slow option compared to hopping on I-87, the New York Thruway, and you pass

through some run-down parts of Yon-kers, but you do get a feel for several nice residential communities. The whole drive is about 18.5 miles long.

02 TARRYTOWN
Washington Irving's home, **Sunnyside** (hudsonvalley.org), a quaint, cozy Dutch cottage – which Irving said had more nooks and crannies than a cocked hat – has been left pretty much the way it was when the author who dreamed up the Headless Horseman and Ichabod Crane lived there. The wisteria he planted 100 years ago still climbs the walls, and the spindly piano inside still carries a tune.

Not far north on Rte 9 is **Philipsburg Manor** (hudson valley.org), a working farm in 17th-century Dutch style. Wealthy Dutchman Frederick Philips brought his family here around 1680 and meticulously built his new farm. Inside the rough-hewn clapboard barns and three-story, whitewashed fieldstone manor, it's all sighs and clanks as old fireplaces and strained beams do their work.

From Philipsburg Manor, grab a shuttle to the sprawling splendor of **Kykuit** (hudsonvalley.org), the Rockefeller family's old European-style estate perched on a bluff high atop the Hudson River. The exterior is stately neoclassical revival, while inside it's more fine-art gallery than summer home. The carefully sculpted gardens, dotted with modern art installations from the likes of Giacometti and Picasso, are a delight to wander through.

 THE DRIVE
Start this 32-mile drive by crossing over the Hudson River at one of its widest points on the New NY Bridge to South Nyack. This new eight-lane span started to replace the decommissioned Tappan Zee Bridge in late 2017. Take the Palisades Pkwy north from here.

03 BEAR MOUNTAIN & HARRIMAN STATE PARKS

Surprisingly, only 40 miles north of New York City is a pristine forest with miles of hiking trails, along with swimming and wilderness camping. The 72 sq miles of **Harriman State Park** (parks.ny.gov) were donated to the state in 1910 by the widow of railroad magnate Edward Henry Harriman, director of the transcontinental Union Pacific Railroad and frequent target of Teddy Roosevelt's trustbusters. Adjacent **Bear Mountain State Park** (parks.ny.gov) offers great views from its 1305ft peak, with the Manhattan skyline looming beyond the river and surrounding greenery, and there's a restaurant and lodging at the inn on Hessian Lake. In both parks there are several scenic roads snaking their way past mountain-fed streams and secluded lakes with gorgeous vistas; you'll spot shy, white-tailed deer, stately blue herons and – in the remotest regions – even a big cat or two.

Head to **Fort Montgomery State Historic Site** (parks.ny.gov) in Bear Mountain for picture-perfect views from its cliffside perch overlooking the Hudson. The pastoral site was host to a fierce skirmish with the British on October 6, 1777. American soldiers hunkered behind fortresses while they tried to hold off the enemy; the ruins are still visible in the red earth. A museum at the entrance has artifacts and more details on the bloody battle.

 THE DRIVE
It's only 14 miles to West Point – take Rte 9W to the town of Highland Falls and continue on Main St until you reach the parking entrance for West Point Visitors Center on the right.

White-tailed deer, Bear Mountain State Park

04 WEST POINT

Occupying one of the most breathtaking bends in the river is West Point US Military Academy. Prior to 1802, it was a strategic fort with a commanding position over a narrow stretch of the Hudson. **West Point Guided Tours** (westpoint tours.com) offers one- and two-hour combo walking and bus tours of the stately campus; try to go when school is in session since the cadets' presence livens things up. Guides move swiftly through the academy's history, noting illustrious graduates (too many to mention... Robert E Lee, Ulysses S Grant, Buzz Aldrin and Norman Schwarzkopf are on the list) as well as famous dropouts (Edgar Allen Poe for one). Guides will also explain the rigorous admissions criteria for parents hoping to land a spot for their kids. At least as interesting is the highly regimented daily collegiate life they lead.

Next to the visitor center is the fascinating – even for the pacifists among us – **West Point Museum** (usma.edu/museum), which traces the role of war and the military throughout human history. Displays of weapons from Stone Age clubs to artillery pieces highlight technology's role in the evolution of warfare, and elaborate miniature dioramas of important moments such as the siege of Avaricum (52 BC) and the Battle of Austerlitz (1805) will mesmerize anyone who played with toy soldiers as a kid. Give yourself enough time to take in the substantial exhibits and, when you've had enough of fighting, check out the paintings and drawings by Hudson River School artists scattered around the museum.

THE DRIVE

On this 11.5-mile drive, take Rte 218 north leaving Highland Falls and connect to Rte 9W (not Storm King Hwy which Rte 218 becomes). Exit on Quaker Ave, right on Rte 32 and left on Orrs Mills Rd. You can see Storm King from the New York State Thruway (and vice versa) but there's no convenient exit.

05 STORM KING ART CENTER

Near Mountainville, on the west side of the Hudson River, **Storm King Art Center** (storm king.org) is a giant open-air museum on 500 acres, part sculpture garden and part sculpture landscape. The spot was founded in 1960 as a museum for painters, but it soon began to acquire larger installations and monumental works that were placed outside

TOP TIP:

Summertime Theater

Across the river from West Point and Storm King Art Center, near the town of Cold Spring, the **Hudson Valley Shakespeare Festival** (hvshakespeare.org) takes place between mid-May and early September, staging impressive open-air productions at **Boscobel House & Gardens** (boscobel. org), a magnificent property.

in natural 'rooms' created by the land's indigenous breaks and curves. There's a small museum on-site, formerly a 1935 residence designed like a Norman chateau, and plenty of picnic sites.

Across the expanse of meadow is the Storm King Wall, artist Andy Goldsworthy's famously sinuous structure that starts with rocks, crescendos up and across some hills, encompasses a tree, then dips down into a pond, slithering out the other side and eventually disappearing into the woods. Other permanent pieces were created by Alexander Calder, Henry Moore, Richard Serra and Alice Aycock, to name a few.

THE DRIVE

Rte 32 takes you past the run-down riverside town of Newburgh. If you have time, turn right on Washington St; near the river is Washington's Headquarters State Historic Site where the small stone house that served as General George Washington's longest-lasting Revolutionary War base is preserved as a museum. Otherwise, head over the Newburgh-Beacon bridge ($1 toll).

06 BEACON

This formerly scruffy town is now on the map of art world cognoscenti because of the **Dia Beacon** (diaart.org), a former factory and now a major museum. Inside its industrial walls are big names on a big scale, including an entire room of light sculptures by Dan Flavin, and a hangar-sized space to house Richard Serra's mammoth steel Torqued Ellipses. Beacon's Main St offers many small galleries and craft shops, including **Hudson Beach Glass** (hudsonbeachglass.com), a boutique-gallery where you can buy artfully designed, handcrafted pieces and watch glassblowers at work. If you have time, stroll down to the mini-rapids of **Fishkill Creek** or strike out on the trail up to the summit of **Mount Beacon** (scenichudson.org) for spectacular views.

THE DRIVE

Strip-mall-lined Rte 9 north passes through Poughkeepsie (puh-kip-see), the largest city on the east bank and home to Vassar and Marist colleges. During this 22-mile drive, stop (exit on Marist Dr/Rte 9G north and then left on Parker Ave) for a stroll and incomparable river views on a converted railroad bridge, now a state park known as the Walkway Over the Hudson.

07 HYDE PARK

Hyde Park, just north of Poughkeepsie, has long been associated with the Roosevelts, a prominent family since the 19th century. The **Franklin D Roosevelt Home** (nps.gov/hofr), an estate of 1520 acres and

WHY I LOVE THIS TRIP

Simon Richmond, writer

Zigzagging your way up the Hudson River offers magnificent natural scenery, thrilling outdoor pursuits, beautifully designed historic country estates, stunning contemporary art and culinary treats. Make sure you get out of your car, though, to stride across the Walkway Over the Hudson, a former railroad bridge converted into a broad pedestrian promenade connecting Poughkeepsie on the east side with Lloyd on the west – the river views are stunning.

Photo opportunity

Valley view from Olana for classic panorama

formerly a working farm, includes a library, which details important achievements in FDR's presidency; a visit usually includes a guided tour of Springwood, FDR's lifelong home where he delivered his fireside chats.

Two miles to the east is **Val-Kill** (nps.gov/elro). This 181-acre estate includes Val-Kill Cottage, a two-story building that was originally a furniture factory started by Eleanor Roosevelt to teach young men a trade during the Depression; and Stone Cottage, the former first lady's home after the death of her husband.

Just north of here is the 54-room **Vanderbilt Mansion** (nps.gov/vama), a Gilded Age spectacle of lavish beaux-arts design built by the fabulously wealthy Frederick Vanderbilt, grandson of Cornelius, once a Staten Island farmer, who made millions buying up railroads. Nearly all of the original furnishings imported from European castles and villas remain in this country house – the smallest of any of the Vanderbilt family's! Hudson River views are best from the gardens and the Bard Rock trail.

Further north, Staatsburg is a hot spot for antiquing. If you prefer to look rather than buy, duck into the 100-year-old **Staatsburg**

State Historic Site (parks.ny.gov), a beaux-arts mansion boasting 79 luxurious rooms filled with Flemish tapestries, gilded plasterwork, period paintings and Oriental art.

THE DRIVE

It's only 10 miles north on Rte 9 to Rhinebeck; it's a fairly ordinary stretch but at least it's less congested and less heavily trafficked.

08 RHINEBECK

Just 3 miles north of the charming small town of Rhinebeck is the **Old Rhinebeck Aerodrome** (oldrhinebeck.org), with a collection of pre-1930s planes and automobiles. There are air shows on weekends in the summer; the vintage aircraft that take off at 2pm on Saturdays and Sundays are reserved for a highly choreographed period dogfight. If vicarious thrills aren't enough, you can don helmets and goggles and take an open-cockpit 15-minute flight ($75 per person) in a 1929 New Standard D-25 four-passenger biplane.

In a large red barn out the back of Rhinebeck's **Beekman Arms** (beekmandelamaterinn.com), widely considered the longest continually operating hotel in the US, is the **Beekman Arms Antique Market** (beekmandelamaterinn.com/antique-market), where some 30 local antiques dealers offer up their best Americana.

THE DRIVE

Go with Rte 9G north rather than Rte 9 for this 25-mile drive; it's more rural and every once in a while opens up to views of the Catskill Mountains on the other side of the river in the distance.

09 HUDSON

Gentrification has upgraded parts of the historic port of Hudson into a facsimile of tony areas of Brooklyn or Manhattan. Warren St, the main commercial strip, is lined with chic antiques and interior-design stores, classy galleries, and stylish restaurants and cafes, all patronized by a well-heeled crowd.

There are still some rough edges to the town, though, which in the early 19th century prospered as a busy river port, and was later adopted by the LGBTIQ+ community as an affordable bolthole. Stroll the riverfront and side streets to spot fine heritage architecture, including the restored **Hudson Opera House** (hudsonoperahouse.org).

South of town is **Olana** (olana. org), the splendid-looking 'Persian fantasy' home of Frederic Church, one of the primary artists of the Hudson River School of painting. Church designed the 250-acre property, creating a lake and planting trees and orchards, with his idealized version of a landscape in mind, so that the grounds became a complementary part of the natural views across the valley, with the eastern escarpment of the Catskills looming overhead. On a house tour you can appreciate the totality of Church's aesthetic vision, as well as view paintings from his own collection.

↪ DETOUR
The Berkshires
Start: 09 Hudson

Head east to the Berkshire Mountains in Massachusetts, another region of bucolic scenery, quaint towns and

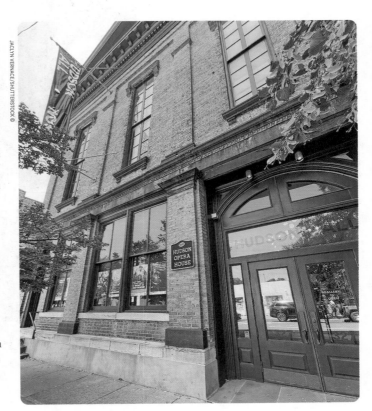

JACLYN VERNACE/SHUTTERSTOCK ©

Hudson Opera House

vibrant arts scenes. Choose one of the following ways to access the area depending on two recommended stops on your way out of New York State. If you head east out of Hudson on Rte 23, you eventually come to Hillsdale and the **Catamount Aerial Adventure Park** (catamountski.com). This is no ordinary zipline or ropes course, but easily the most exciting and challenging one we've ever tried. No matter your strength or agility level or your capacity for tolerating heights, there's a route earmarked for you. From Catamount, it's only an 8-mile drive along Rte 23 to Great Barrington in the Berkshires.

Taking Rte 66 north for 14 miles from Hudson, you come to the small town of Chatham, where in the summer months, Broadway musicals are performed by professional actors at the theater-in-the-round **Mac-Haydn Theatre** (machaydntheatre.org). While productions such as *Brigadoon* tend to border on cheesy, the cast is usually energized and the generally older, pastel-clad crowd appreciative. Definitely stick around for the solo acts in the old-fashioned cafe-cum-cabaret-room, where you can enjoy show tunes while chowing down on a slice of pie.

02

BEST FOR

FAMILIES
Riding the
rickety Cyclone
roller coaster in
Coney Island

Long Island

DURATION	DISTANCE	GREAT FOR
4 days	267 miles / 429km	History & Culture

BEST TIME TO GO	Early September: crowds have dissipated but water temperatures are OK.

Bethesda Fountain, Central Park

Small whaling and fishing ports were here from as early as 1640, but today's Long Island evokes a complicated menagerie of images: cookie-cutter suburbia, nightmare commutes, private-school blazers and moneyed decadence. There's much more to the island than that, as you'll discover with this itinerary that takes you from Central Park to wide ocean and bay beaches, renowned vineyards, mega mansions and important historic sites.

Link your trip

01 Hudson

Head to the Cloisters in upper Manhattan to begin a trip to culturally rich towns along the Hudson.

12 The Jersey Shore

Leave NYC via the Holland Tunnel, take I-95 S to the Garden State Pkwy to explore endless beaches and boardwalks.

01 CENTRAL PARK

Central Park (centralparknyc.org), the rectangular patch of green that occupies Manhattan's heart, began life in the mid-19th century as a swampy piece of land that was carefully bulldozed into the idyllic landscapes you see today, with more than 24,000 trees, 136 acres of woodland, 21 playgrounds and seven bodies of water.

The **Great Lawn** is a massive emerald carpet at the center of the park – between 79th and 86th Sts – and is surrounded by ball fields and London plane trees. Immediately to the southeast is **Delacorte**

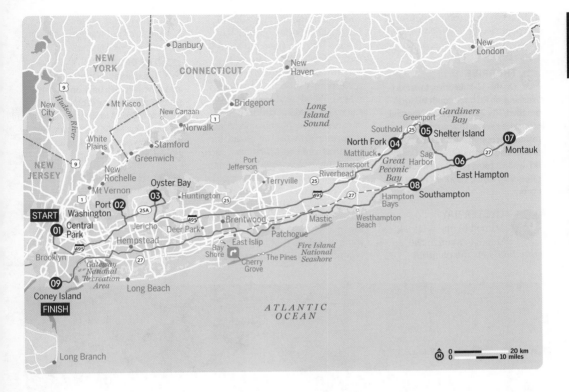

Theater (publictheater.org), home to an annual Shakespeare in the Park festival, as well as **Belvedere Castle**, a lookout. Further south, between 72nd and 79th Sts, is the leafy **Ramble**, a popular birding destination. On the southeastern end is the **Loeb Boathouse**, home to a waterside restaurant that offers rowboat and bicycle rentals.

The arched walkways of **Bethesda Terrace**, crowned by the magnificent Bethesda Fountain (at the level of 72nd St), have long been a gathering area for New Yorkers. To the south is the **Mall**, a promenade shaded by mature North American elms. The southern stretch, known

as Literary Walk, is flanked by statues of famous authors.

 THE DRIVE
Getting out of Manhattan can be a slog. Cross the East River on the Queensboro Bridge (aka the 59th St Bridge) and follow signs for I-495 east, aka the Long Island Expwy or LIE. This too can be a nightmare. Get off at exit 36 to Searingtown Rd, which turns into Port Washington Rd; it's 4.5 miles to Sands Point and Port Washington.

02 PORT WASHINGTON
Long Island's so-called Gold Coast of the roaring twenties, of the Vanderbilts, Chryslers and Guggenheims, not to mention Gatsby, begins outside the suburban town of

Port Washington. Castle Gould, the enormous turreted stable at the entrance to **Sands Point Preserve** (sandspointpreserve conservancy.org) and now a visitor center, was once owned by Howard Gould, the heir to a railroad fortune. And the massive Tudor-style Hempstead House, built by Gould and later sold to a Guggenheim, stands nearby; it's mostly unfurnished and used for events, but you can usually peek in to get a sense of its dimensions and scale. The 1923 Norman-style **Falaise** is intact and furnished and open for guided tours.

Sands Point includes forested nature trails and a beautiful sandy bayfront beach that's worth a stroll; you can even look into the picture windows of several massive modernist beachfront homes.

🚗 THE DRIVE
On this 13-mile drive, take Port Washington Rd back south to Northern Blvd/Rte 25A east, a commercial strip with several tony suburban residential communities and a golf club or two nearby. Go left on Cove Rd; when it turns into Cove Neck Rd it offers very idyllic views of Oyster Bay Harbor.

03 OYSTER BAY
Named by the original Dutch settlers in the early 1600s for the plentiful shellfish found in the waters of Long Island Sound, Oyster Bay is a quaint little town with a nautical feel. It's also home to **Sagamore Hill** (nps.gov/sahi), a 23-room Victorian mansion where Theodore Roosevelt and his wife raised six children and vacationed during his presidency; it's preserved with the books, furnishings and exotic artifacts, such as animal heads, that Roosevelt acquired on his travels. He passed away here and is buried in the nearby Youngs Memorial Cemetery. Spring and summer months mean long waits for guided tours. A nature trail leading from behind the excellent **museum** that's also on the property ends at a picturesque waterfront beach on Cold Spring Harbor.

🚗 THE DRIVE
The quickest way to do this 58-mile drive is to hop back on the I-495 east; 42 miles later, get off at exit 71 and follow Rte 24 to Riverhead, really the beginning of the North Fork. Pass through town and onto Main Rd or Rte 25 where the trip picks up.

04 NORTH FORK
Primarily, the North Fork is known for its unspoiled farmland and wineries – there are more than 40 vineyards, clustered mainly around the towns of Jamesport, Cutchogue and

Sagamore Hill

Southold. The Long Island Wine Council provides details of the local wine trail, which runs along Rte 25 north of Peconic Bay. The quicker way on and off the North Fork, though, is parallel Rte 48, or the coast road.

The main North Fork town and the place for ferries (northferry.com) to Shelter Island, **Greenport** is a charming laid-back place lined with restaurants and cafes, including family-owned **Claudio's** (claudios.com) clam bar, with a wraparound deck perched over the marina. Or grab a sandwich for a picnic at the Harbor Front Park where you can take a spin on the historic carousel.

Photo opportunity

Sunset from Montauk Lighthouse.

THE DRIVE
The Shelter Island ferry (one-way vehicle and driver $11) leaves just a couple of blocks from Main St in Greenport. This could involve something of a wait – open your windows and take the 10 minutes to breathe in the fresh air.

05 SHELTER ISLAND
Between the North and South Forks, Shelter Island is a low-key microcosm of beautiful Hamptons real estate with more of a traditional maritime New England atmosphere. This mellow refuge was once sold by Manhanset Native Americans to a group of prosperous sugar merchants from Barbados who intended to harvest the island's oak trees in order to build barrels to transport their precious cargo. In the 1870s, a group of Methodist clergy and laymen bought property on the heights to establish a religious retreat. Some of these buildings, a variety of colonial revival, Victorian and Queen Anne, make up the island's 'his-

toric district.' The **Mashomack Nature Preserve** (nature.org) covers more than 2000 acres of the southern part of the island and is a great spot for hiking or kayaking.

THE DRIVE
The ferry (one-way vehicle/passenger $15/$1) to North Haven on the South Fork leaves from southern Shelter Island on NY-114. Continue on NY-114 to Sag Harbor. Check out its Whaling & Historical Museum, or simply stroll up and down its narrow, Cape Cod-like streets. NY-114 continues for 7 miles to East Hampton.

06 EAST HAMPTON
Don't be fooled by the oh-so-casual-looking summer attire, heavy on pastels and sweaters tied around the neck – the sunglasses alone are probably equal to a month's rent. Some of the highest-profile celebrities have homes here and a drive down its lanes can evoke nauseatingly intense real-estate envy. However, it's worth swallowing your pride and trying to glimpse what are undoubtedly some of the priciest properties in the country. Examples of fabulous residential architecture (as well as cookie-cutter gaudy McMansions) are concealed behind towering hedgerows and gates. For a chance to rub shoulders with the locals, you

can catch readings, theater and art exhibits at the **Guild Hall** (guildhall.org).

THE DRIVE
Join the parade of cars leaving town on Montauk Hwy (Rte 27), which becomes hilly and more beautiful the further east you go on this 25-mile drive.

07 MONTAUK
Once a sleepy and humble stepsister to the Hamptons – though more working-class Jersey, less Côte d'Azur royalty – these days Montauk, at the far eastern end of Long Island, continues to draw a fashionable, younger crowd, and even a hipster subset, to its beautiful beaches. Longtime residents, fishers and territorial surfers round out a motley mix that makes the dining and bar scene louder and a little more democratic compared to other Hamptons villages.

At the very eastern, wind-whipped tip of the South Fork is Montauk Point State Park, with its impressive, 1796 **Montauk Point Lighthouse** (montauklighthouse.com), the fourth oldest still-active lighthouse in the US. You can camp a few miles west of town at the dune-swept **Hither Hills State Park** (parks.ny.gov), right on the beach; reserve early during summer months. Several miles to the north is the Montauk harbor, with dockside restaurants and hundreds of boats in the marinas.

THE DRIVE
Follow the highway back west until it ends: through rolling sand dunes on either side and past roadside lobster-roll stands, the Montauk Hwy splits off to the Old Montauk Hwy just before town, but both will get you there.

08 SOUTHAMPTON

The village of Southampton appears blemish-free, as if it has been Botoxed. At nighttime, when club-goers dressed in their most glamorous beach chic let their hair down, it can feel as if the plastic-surgery-free are visitors in a foreign land. However, before winemaking and catering to the celebrity crowd became the area's two most dominant industries, it was a whaling and seafaring community. Its colonial roots are evident at Halsey House, the oldest residence in the Hamptons, and the nearby **Southampton History Museum** (southampton history.org), a perfect place to learn more about the region's former seafaring ways. It has a homey collection of local relics displayed in an 1843 sea captain's house, plus Rogers Mansion, an old sea captain's residence full of whaling lore.

Southampton's beaches – only Coopers Beach ($40 per day) and Road D (free) offer parking to nonresidents from May 31 to September 15 – are sweeping and gorgeous, and the **Parrish Art Museum** (parrishart.org) is an impressive regional institution. Its quality exhibitions feature great local artists and there's a cute gift shop stacked with glossy posters of Long Island landscapes.

THE DRIVE

The 95-mile drive back to the city needs to be timed properly – never during rush hour or anytime on a Sunday in the summer. Either take I-495 west back toward the city or Montauk Hwy to the Southern Pkwy and the Belt Pkwy.

DETOUR
Fire Island
Start: 08 Southampton

On a long barrier island running parallel to Long Island, just off the southern shore, are Fire Island's 32 miles of virtually car-free white-sand beaches, shrub-filled forests and hiking trails, as well as 15 hamlets and two villages. The Fire Island Pines and Cherry Grove hamlets (both car-free) comprise a historic, gay bacchanalia that attracts men and women in droves from NYC, while villages on the west end cater to straight singles and families. At the western end of Fire Island, **Robert Moses State Park** (parks.ny.gov) is the only spot accessible by car; check out the lighthouse here, which holds a small museum with a tiny section dedicated to nude sunbathing.

If you just want to get back to nature, enjoy a hike through the 300-year-

SWELLEN AZEVEDO /ISTOCK/GETTY IMAGES ©

Coney Island

old **Sunken Forest** (nps.gov/fiis), where crazily twisted trees have been misshapen by constant salt-spray and sea breezes. It's 'sunken' because its 40 acres are below sea level; it has its own ferry stop (called Sailor's Haven).

There are limited places to stay, and booking in advance is strongly advised (check fireisland.com for accommodation information). **Madison Fire Island Pines** (themadisonfi.com), the first and only boutique hotel here, rivals anything Manhattan has to offer in terms of amenities, and also has killer views from a rooftop deck, and a gorgeous pool. At the eastern end of the island, the 1300-acre preserve of **Otis Pike Fire Island High Dune Wilderness** is a protected oasis of sand dunes that includes beach camping at **Watch Hill** (nps.gov), though mosquitoes can be fierce and reservations far in advance are a must.

Fire Island Ferries (fireislandferries. com) runs services to Fire Island beaches and the national seashore (May to November); the terminals are close to LIRR stations at Bay Shore, Sayville and Patchogue.

To reach Fire Island from Southampton, head west on NY-27 (aka the Sunrise Hwy) for 46 miles until exit 44 for Bay Shore. Take Brentwood Rd a mile south, turn right onto E Main St and after close to another mile make a left onto Maple Ave. The ferry terminal is on your left about a half mile further on.

09 **CONEY ISLAND**
This is about as far from the Hamptons as you can get, not geographically, but, well, in every other way, and still be on

SOUTH FORK VINEYARDS

Most people associate Long Island wineries with the North Fork, but the South Fork has a handful of good ones as well.

You can explore the 30 acres of vine trellises and grape plants of **Channing Daughters Winery** (channingdaughters.com). Step across the wide stone patio dotted with plush chaise lounges that look out onto the property, and keep your eyes peeled for the Alice in Wonderland–like sculptures of owner Walter Channing – his works pop up everywhere, staring down at you from the end posts of vineyard rows and emerging in the shape of towering inverted trees against the horizon.

Further east, past the village of Bridgehampton, is the graceful Tuscan-villa-style tasting room of **Wölffer Estate** (wolffer.com). Massive wooden-beamed ceilings against rough white walls set the scene for sampling the crisp whites and earthy reds Wölffer is renowned for. Experiment with the vineyard's more unusual offerings, including an apple wine, rose wines and sweet dessert drinks.

Long Island. Coney Island became known as 'Sodom by the Sea' by the end of the 19th century, when it was infamous as a den for gamblers, hard drinkers and other cheery sorts you wouldn't want to introduce to mom. In the early 1900s, the family era kicked in as amusement parks were built. The most famous, Luna Park, opened in 1903 – a dreamworld with live camels and elephants and 'rides to the moon.' By the 1960s, Coney Island's pull had slipped and it became a sad, crime-ridden reminder of past glories. A slow, enduring comeback has meant the emergence of the wild Mermaid Parade (third Saturday in June), a newer, more upscale, slightly more generic **Luna Park** (lunaparknyc.com), an aquari-

um, and a minor-league baseball team. The Cyclone is its most legendary ride: a roller coaster that reaches speeds of 60mph and makes near-vertical drops.

The hot dog was invented in Coney Island in 1867, which means that eating a frankfurter at **Nathan's Famous** (nathansfamous.com), which has been around since 1916, is practically obligatory. The hot dogs are the real deal and its clam bar is tops in summer. If you're around in the winter, consider taking a dip in the frigid Atlantic Ocean with the Coney Island Polar Bears Club. It's best known for its New Year's Day Swim, when hundreds of hungover New Yorkers take the plunge.

03

BEST FOR

✓

FAMILIES
A relaxing day
at Belleayre
Beach (p38)
near Phoenicia.

Tranquil Catskills

DURATION	DISTANCE	GREAT FOR
3-4 days	115 miles / 185km	Family

BEST TIME TO GO	April to November for comfortable outdoor temperatures.

New Paltz

Since the mid-19th century, painters have been besotted with this mountainous region rising west of the Hudson Valley. They celebrated its mossy gorges and waterfalls as examples of sublime wilderness rivaling the Alps in Europe. Even though the height and profile of its rounded peaks were exaggerated and romanticized by the artists, the Catskills today remains a beguiling landscape.

Link your trip

01 Hudson Valley

Hop on any east-bound road until you hit the Hudson River to begin touring the valley's mansions and gardens.

05 Adirondack Peaks & Valleys

Get on I-87 N for Lake George, the gateway to a trip through this mountainous wilderness.

01 **NEW PALTZ**
On the western side of the Hudson is New Paltz, home of a campus of the State University of New York (SUNY), natural-food stores and a liberal ecofriendly vibe. A few blocks north of the center are several homes of the original French Huguenot settlers of New Paltz (c 1677) on **Historic Huguenot Street** (huguenotstreet.org), the oldest in the US. This 10-acre National Historic Landmark District includes a visitor center (departure point for guided tours of the area), seven historic stone hous-

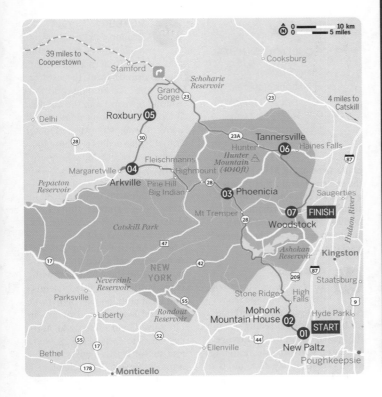

Kaleidoscopic Views

Attached to the Emerson Resort & Spa, and housed in a pitch-black, 60ft silo, is the world's largest kaleidoscope. The gigantic optical instrument spins its bright colors in mesmerizing, hypnotizing patterns, inducing sleep in the road-weary. A boutique sells incredibly designed hand-crafted kaleidoscopes, really pieces of art or sculpture, that range from $20 to thousands of dollars.

es, a reconstructed 1717 Huguenot church and a burial ground.

Water Street Market (water streetmarket.com) on the Wallkill River (access the river walking path here) is an admittedly artificial but pleasant collection of shops, antique stores and cafes with a ski-village vibe.

In the distance behind the town, the ridge of the Shawangunk Mountains (Shon-gum or just the 'Gunks') rises more than 2000ft above sea level. More than two dozen miles of nature trails and some of the best rock climbing in the eastern US is found in the **Mohonk Preserve** (mohonk preserve.org). Contact **Alpine**

Endeavors (alpineendeavors. com) for climbing instruction and equipment. Nearby **Minnewaska State Park Preserve** (parks.ny.gov) has 12,000 acres of wild landscape, the centerpiece of which is two usually ice-cold mountain lakes, Lake Minnewaska and Lake Awosting.

THE DRIVE

Once you cross the small bridge over the Wallkill River at the western edge of town the view is of lush farmland and the 'Gunks' in the distance. Mountain Rest Rd then climbs and winds the 4 miles northwest to Mohonk Mountain House.

02 MOHONK MOUNTAIN HOUSE

The iconic **Mohonk Mountain House** (mohonk.com) looks like it's straight out of a fairy tale: a giant faux 'Victorian castle' perches over a dark lake, offering guests all the luxuries, from lavish meals to golf to spa services, plus a full roster of outdoor excursions, such as hiking and trail rides. Rates include all meals and most activities and you can choose rooms in the main building, cottages or the luxury Grove Lodge.

It's a place to get outdoors or gather with friends and family in rocking chairs set up on a porch and deck overlooking the lake – it feels about as close to the classic mountain lodges in the great parks out west as you can get. Nonstaying guests can visit the grounds by paying admission (adult/child per day $26/21) at the entrance gate – easily worth the price – and you can hike between here and the Minnewaska State Park Preserve. Another recommended hike is the 2-mile one-way scramble up the Lemon Squeeze and Labyrinth (closed in winter) to the Skytop Tower.

THE DRIVE
This pleasant 31-mile leg begins with a scenic drive north on Mohonk Rd to the hamlet of High Falls. Turn left on Rte 213, also signposted 'Scenic Byway S1.' Carry on to the Ashokan Reservoir; pull into the lot for views or a walk. Take Rte 28 to Phoenicia, passing Mt Tremper – home to the Emerson Kaleidoscope – on the way.

03 PHOENICIA
Downtown Phoenicia, all three blocks of it, is the place to go for a day's jaunt – but if you prefer getting back to nature, you can head around 11 miles west on Rte 28 to swim in Pine Hill Lake at **Belleayre Beach** (belleayre.com/summer/belleayre-beach), which has outdoor concerts in the summer; **Belleayre Mountain** (belleayre.com) has skiing in the winter. Kids and train buffs may also enjoy Phoenicia's small **Empire State Railway Museum** (esrm.com), based in the historic Ulster & Delaware Phoenicia Railroad Station.

THE DRIVE
Mountains flank Rte 28 for the 15 miles west to Fleischmanns, once home to the famous yeast company

Photo opportunity
Views from Skytop Tower near Mohonk Mountain House.

of the same name. At weekends in the summer months this otherwise quiet town of handsome old mansions fills up with Orthodox Jewish families who've adopted it as a mountain retreat. Another 5 miles west is Arkville.

04 ARKVILLE
You can get a glimpse of early railroad life from Arkville by hopping aboard one of the vintage sightseeing trains that depart from the **Delaware & Ulster Station** (durr.org), built around 1899. It takes around two hours to travel the 24 miles between Arkville and Roxbury in an open-air carriage on this touristy rail journey; the views are at their best during fall. Alternatively, drop by **Union Grove Distillery** (uniongrovedistillery.com), which specializes in vodka made from apple cider and wheat alcohol. You can take a tour, and there are free tastings of the spirits, which include flavorsome maple-syrup vodka and options infused with black tea, cinnamon and vanilla.

THE DRIVE
Head west to the town of Margaretville, where you then turn north on Rte 30; about 5 miles up is Pakatakan Farmers Market, one of the best in the area, housed in the distinctive-looking red-painted round barn. Roxbury is another 10 miles further along.

05 ROXBURY
Bringing style and panache to this rural region, and a destination in and of itself, the **Roxbury Motel** (theroxbury motel.com) is a fabulous and welcoming retreat. From the outside, it looks like an immaculate, if conventional, whitewashed motel. Initially planned as a tribute to the heyday of the Catskills and mid-century modern style, it soon turned into a project guided by inspiration from 1970s and '80s films and TV shows – think *The Jetsons, The Addams Family, The Wiz, Saturday Night Fever* etc. The decor features items sourced from estate sales and online vendors around the world, and with contributions from artist friends and local craftspeople, owners Greg and Joseph have brought an obsessive attention to detail and aesthetics to each of the 28 rooms and suites. Worth a quick tour if unoccupied is the 'Archeologist's Digs' cottage, which sleeps six, easily the most lavish of Roxbury's offerings. A few details worth mentioning: ibis-shaped bedside lamps in Cleopatra's bedroom; a Murphy bed concealed behind a mural of a Mayan deity; a 'secret' mineshaft cave with a lantern, pictographs and peekaboo hole onto the living room; a bathroom aquarium...

Wintertime means huddling around the fire pit, whereas warm-weather stays involve sunbathing and lounging near the gazebo and small stream that runs along the property; at any time of year it's worth relaxing at the full-service spa split between rooms in the two wings.

Vintage trains, Delaware & Ulster Station, Arkville

THE DRIVE
On this 32-mile route, continue north on Rte 30 to the one-stoplight town of Grand Gorge (the trailhead for the beautiful and highly recommended Mine Kill Falls Overlook is a few miles north) and make a right onto Rte 23, which turns into Rte 23A after the Schoharie Reservoir. You pass Hunter Mountain ski resort a few miles west of Tannersville.

DETOUR
Cooperstown
Start: 05 **Roxbury**

For sports fans, Cooperstown, 50 miles northwest of Roxbury, is instantly recognized as the home of the shrine for the national sport (baseball). But the small-town atmosphere and stun-ning views of the countryside around beautiful Otsego Lake make it worth visiting even for those who don't know the difference between ERA and RBI.

The **National Baseball Hall of Fame & Museum** (baseballhall.org) has exhibits, a theater, a library and an interactive statistical database. The **Fenimore Art Museum** (fenimoreart museum.org) beside the lake has an outstanding collection of Americana and temporary art exhibitions featuring big names.

To reach Cooperstown, leave Roxbury on Rte 30 north and after 6 miles turn onto Rte 23 west. After 28 miles, hook up with Rte 28 north for another 16 miles.

06 TANNERSVILLE
The highest falls in New York (260ft compared to Niagara's 167ft), gorgeous **Kaaterskill Falls** is only a few miles from the small town of Tannersville, which these days primarily services the nearby Hunter Mountain. Popular paintings by Thomas Cole, who settled in nearby Catskill, Asher Durand (check out his painting Kindred Spirits) and other artists in the mid-1800s elevated this two-tier cascade to iconic status. Soon, however, wealthy tourists followed and most artists could no longer afford to stay in the area where the falls are found.

The most traveled trail starts near a horseshoe curve in Rte 23A. You have to park the car in a turnout just up the road, cross to the other side and walk back down behind a guardrail. What you see from here is only Bastion Falls; it's a not very strenuous hike a little more than three-quarters of a mile up to the lower falls. Alternatively head to the **viewing platform** (Laurel House Rd, Palenville) for the best view of the waterfall that you can get without a bit of a hike.

Other delights that are a bit more off the beaten track include hiking to Devil's Kitchen Falls or trekking up the overlooked Kaaterskill High Peak trail. It's lonely, but you'll be rewarded with up-close views of Wildcat, Buttermilk and Santa Cruz waterfalls. Skiers can head to Hunter Mountain in the winter.

THE DRIVE

About seven of the miles south to Woodstock involve white-knuckle driving on Platte Clove Rd/County Hwy 16 (also signposted as 'Plattecove Mountain Rd') through a narrow and steep valley (sometimes no guardrail; no trucks or buses allowed; closed November to April). You're mostly descending 1200ft in this direction (through prime rock-climbing and waterfall-hiking territory). Eventually, make a right onto W Saugerties/Woodstock Rd.

07 WOODSTOCK

Famous for the 1969 concert that didn't actually happen here but in Bethel, Woodstock's two main walkable thoroughfares – Tinker St and Mill Rd – are lined with cafes and shops. The **Woodstock Artists Association & Museum** (WAAM; woodstockart.org) is where you're most likely to bump into a local creative type or a visiting **Byrdcliffe Arts Colony** (woodstockguild.org) resident hanging their latest work. The permanent collection features a wide range of Woodstock artists in all sorts of mediums.

If you feel a frisson upon entering the neighboring **Center for Photography at Woodstock** (cpw.org), that's because it was formerly the Café Espresso, hallowed ground for counter-culture types. Bob Dylan once had a writing studio above the now-defunct Espresso and Janis Joplin was a regular performer. Now the space is hung with contemporary and historical photography exhibits that cover far-flung global events, as well as nature shots of the rugged Catskills.

Get in touch with your spiritual side at **Karma Triyana Dharmachakra** (kagyu.org), a Buddhist monastery in the Catskill Mountains, about 3 miles from Woodstock. Soak up the serenity in the carefully tended grounds or visit the giant golden Buddha statue in the shrine room. In the afternoon drive 5 miles east of Woodstock to explore **Opus 40** (opus40.org), a startling collection of pathways, pools and obelisks spread over 6.5 acres of a former quarry. Creator Harvey Fite, who painstakingly carved and set all the bluestone pieces, thought it would take him 40 years to complete: it took his entire life.

View at Mohonk Mountain House (p37)

04

BEST FOR

☑

WINE
With more than
120 vineyards,
a designated
driver is
needed.

Finger Lakes Loop

DURATION	DISTANCE	GREAT FOR
3 days	144 miles / 231km	Nature

BEST TIME TO GO	May to October for farmers markets and glorious sunny vistas.

Cornell Botanic Gardens, Ithaca

A bird's-eye view of this region of rolling hills and 11 long, narrow lakes – the eponymous fingers – reveals an outdoor paradise stretching all the way from Albany to far-western New York. Of course, there's boating, fishing, cycling, hiking and cross-country skiing, but this is also the state's premier wine-growing region, with enough variety for the most discerning oenophile and palate-cleansing whites and reds available just about every few miles.

Link your trip

07 St Lawrence Seaway

Drive north from any of the eastern lakes to hook up with this trip along a Great Lake – Lake Ontario – and river islands.

14 Through the Wilds Along Route 6

From Corning, it's less than an hour on Rte 15 south to Wellsboro and a trip filled with gorges and wild forests.

01 ITHACA

Ithaca, perched above Cayuga Lake, is an idyllic home for college students and for older generations of hippies who cherish elements of the traditional collegiate lifestyle – laid-back vibes, cafe poetry readings, art-house cinemas, green quads and good eats.

Founded in 1865, Cornell University boasts a lovely campus, mixing traditional and contemporary architecture, and sits high on a hill overlooking the picturesque town below. The modern **Herbert F Johnson Museum of Art** (museum.cornell.edu),

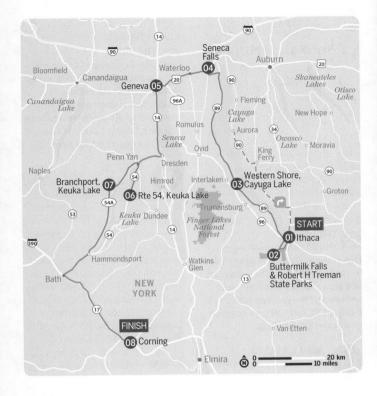

Wine & Dine

Where you find good wine – and the Finger Lakes region produces some of the country's best bottles – it's a sure bet you'll also find great food. Relax, as gourmet isn't stuffy and white-tablecloth here, but friendly and communal, such as at Geneva's FLX Table. Also not to be missed is Hazelnut Kitchen near Ithaca, where you'll also find a stellar farmers market.

in a brutalist building designed by IM Pei, has a major Asian collection, plus pre-Columbian, American and European exhibits. Just east of the center of the campus is **Cornell Botanic Gardens** (cornellbotanicgardens.org), an expertly curated herb and flower garden and arboretum. Kids can go interactive-wild at the extremely hands-on **Sciencenter** (sciencenter.org).

The area around Ithaca is known for its waterfalls, gorges and gorgeous parks.

THE DRIVE

It's only 2 miles south on Rte 13 to Buttermilk Falls State Park.

DETOUR
Aurora
Start: **1** Ithaca

Around 28 miles north of Ithaca on the east side of Cayuga Lake is the picturesque village of Aurora, established in 1795. More than 50 buildings here are on the National Register of Historic Places, including parts of the campus of Wells College, founded in 1868 for the higher education of women (it's now co-ed). The **Inns of Aurora** (innsof aurora.com) is composed of four grand properties – the Aurora Inn (1833), EB Morgan House (1858), Rowland House (1903) and Wallcourt Hall (1909). It is a wonderful place to stay. Stop by the inn's lovely dining room for a meal with lake views and pick up a copy of the self-guided Aurora walking tour.

02 BUTTERMILK FALLS & ROBERT H TREMAN STATE PARKS

A sprawling swath of wilderness, **Buttermilk Falls State Park** (parks.ny.gov) has something for everyone – a beach, cabins, fishing, hiking, recreational fields and camping. The big draw, however, is the waterfalls. There are more than 10, with some sending water tumbling as far as 500ft below into clear pools. Hikers like the raggedy Gorge Trail that brings them up to all the best cliffs. It parallels Buttermilk Creek, winding up about 500ft. On the other side of the falls is the equally popular Rim Trail, a loop of about 1.5 miles around the waterfalls from a different vantage point. Both feed into Bear Trail, which will take you to neighboring Treman Falls.

It's a trek of about 3 miles to Treman, or you can pop back in the car after exploring Buttermilk and drive the 3 miles south to **Robert H Treman State Park** (parks.ny.gov), still on bucolic Rte 13. Also renowned for cascading falls, Treman's gorge trail passes a stunning 12 waterfalls in under 3 miles. The two biggies you don't want to miss are Devil's Kitchen and Lucifer Falls, a multi-tiered wonder that spills Enfield Creek over rocks for about 100ft. At the bottom of yet another watery gorge – Lower Falls – there's a natural swimming hole.

THE DRIVE
Take Rte 13 back into Ithaca to connect with Rte 89 that hugs Cayuga Lake shore for 10 miles. The entrance to Taughannock Falls State Park is just after crossing the river gorge.

03 WESTERN SHORE, CAYUGA LAKE
Trumansburg, a one-street town about 15 miles north of Ithaca, is the gateway to **Taughannock Falls State Park** (parks.ny.gov). At 215ft, the falls of the same name are 30ft higher than Niagara Falls and the highest cascade east of the Rockies. There are five miles of hiking trails, most of which wind their way around the slippery parts to bring you safely to the lookout spots at the top.

A little further along on Rte 89, near the village of Interlaken, is **Lucas Vineyards** (lucasvineyards.com), one of the pioneers of Cayuga wineries. A little further north again, down by the lake

Photo opportunity
The full height of Taughannock Falls.

shore and a small community of modest but charming summer homes, is **Sheldrake Point Winery** (sheldrakepoint.com), which has stunning views and award-winning whites.

THE DRIVE
Rte 89 continues along the lake shore and passes Cayuga Lake State Park, which has beach access and picnic tables. Continue north until you hit the junction with E Bayard St; turn left here to reach downtown Seneca Falls.

04 SENECA FALLS
This small, sleepy town is where the country's organized women's rights movement was born. After being excluded from an anti-slavery meeting, Elizabeth Cady Stanton and her friends drafted an 1848 declaration asserting that 'all men and women are created equal.' The inspirational **Women's Rights National Historical Park** (nps.gov/wori) has a small but impressive museum, with an informative film available for viewing, plus a visitor center offering tours of Cady Stanton's house. The tiny **National Women's Hall of Fame** (womenofthehall.org) honors inspiring American women. Learn about some of the 312 inductees, including first lady Abigail Adams, American Red Cross founder

Clara Barton and civil-rights activist Rosa Parks.

THE DRIVE
The 10 miles on I-20 west to Geneva passes through strip mall-lined Waterloo; Mac's Drive In, a classic 1961-vintage burger joint, is worth a stop. As you drive into town you pass Seneca Lake State Park which is a good spot for a picnic.

05 GENEVA
Geneva, one of the larger towns on this route, has interesting, historic architecture and a lively vibe, with both Hobart and William Smith colleges calling it home. South Main St is lined with an impressive number of turn-of-the-century Italianate, Federal and Greek Revival homes in immaculate condition. The restored 1894 **Smith Opera House** (thesmith.org) is the place to go for theater, concerts and performing arts in the area. Stop by **Microclimate** (facebook.com/microclimatewinebar), a cool little wine bar offering wine flights.

THE DRIVE
On your way south on Rte 14 you pass – what else? – a winery worth visiting. This one is Red Tail Ridge Winery, a certified gold Leadership in Energy & Environmental Design (LEED) little place on Seneca Lake. Then turn right on Rte 54 to Penn Yan

06 ROUTE 54, KEUKA LAKE
Y-shaped Keuka is about 20 miles long and in some parts up to 2 miles wide, its lush vegetation uninterrupted except for neat patches of vineyards. If you have a trail bike you could get a workout on the **Keuka Lake Outlet Trail**, a 7.5-mile route following the old Crooked

Smith Opera House (right), Geneva

latter of which has its tasting room in a restored old barn. Both wineries are family run and edging into their sixth generation. On top of tastings there are tours of the grape-growing facilities and snacks from the vineyards' own kitchens.

THE DRIVE
Rte 54A along the west branch of Keuka passes by several other wineries as well as the Taylor Wine Museum just north of Hammondsport, a quaint town with a charming square. Carry on through to Bath where you connect with I-86 east/Rte 17 east for another 19 miles to Corning.

08 CORNING
The massive **Corning Museum of Glass** (cmog.org) complex is home to fascinating exhibits on glassmaking arts, complete with demonstrations and interactive items. It's possibly the world's finest collection, both in terms of its historic breadth – spanning 35 centuries of craftsmanship – as well as its sculptural pieces. Stop by **Vitrix Hot Glass Studio** (vitrixhotglass.com) in the charming Market Street district to take a gander at museum-quality glass pieces ranging from functional bowls to organic-shaped sculptures.

Housed in the former City Hall, a Romanesque Revival building c 1893, the **Corning Rockwell Museum** (rockwellmuseum.org) has a wide-ranging collection of art of the American West, including great works by Albert Bierstadt, Charles M Russell and Frederic Remington.

Lake Canal between Penn Yan and Dresden on Seneca Lake.

Just south of Penn Yan, the largest village on Keuka Lake's shores, you come to **Keuka Spring Vineyards** (keukaspring winery.com) and then **Rooster Hill Vineyards** (roosterhill.com) – two local favorites that offer tastings and tours in pastoral settings. A few miles further south along Rte 54 brings you to **Barrington Cellars** (barrington cellars.com), 500ft off the lake and flush with Labrusca and Vinifera wines made from local grapes.

On Saturdays in summer everyone flocks to the **Windmill Farm & Craft Market** (thewindmill .com), just outside Penn Yan. Check out Amish and Mennonite

goods, ranging from hand-carved wooden rockers to homegrown veggies and flowers

THE DRIVE
After about 5.5 miles on Rte 54A take a detour south onto Skyline Dr, which runs down the middle of 800ft Bluff Point, for outstanding views. Backtrack to Rte 54A and Branchport is only a few miles further along.

07 BRANCHPORT, KEUKA LAKE
As you pass through the tiny village of Branchport at the tip of Keuka's left fork in its Y, keep an eye out for **Hunt Country Vineyards** (huntwines.com) and **Stever Hill Vineyards** (steverhillvineyards.com), the

05

BEST FOR

☑

SPEED
Bobsled down
an Olympic
track (p49).

Adirondack Peaks & Valleys

DURATION	DISTANCE	GREAT FOR
7 days	237 miles / 381km	History & Culture

BEST TIME TO GO	Backcountry trails and sights open June to September.

Lac du Saint Sacrement steamboat, Lake George

Majestic and wild, the Adirondacks, a mountain range with 42 peaks over 4000ft high, rival any of the nation's wilderness areas for sheer awe-inspiring beauty. The 9375 sq miles of protected parklands and forest preserve, which climb from central New York State to the Canadian border, include towns, mountains, glacial lakes, rivers and more than 2000 miles of hiking trails.

Link your trip

07 St Lawrence Seaway

Head west from Tupper Lake to Alexandria Bay to descend to the waters of the St Lawrence for a bucolic riverside drive.

01 Hudson Valley

Take I-87 south to the town of Catskill for local roads to the small towns and historic sites along the river.

01 LAKE GEORGE

The southern gateway to Adirondack Park is a kitschy little village – think T-shirt shops, a wax museum and a Polynesian-themed hotel – on the shores of the eponymously named 32-mile-long lake. On windy days, the lake froths with whitecaps; on sunny days it shines like the placid blue sky.

Not far from the water is the reconstructed **Fort William Henry Museum** (fwhmuseum.com); the fort was built by the British during the French and Indian War (1754–63) as a staging ground for attacks against the garrison that would later become Fort

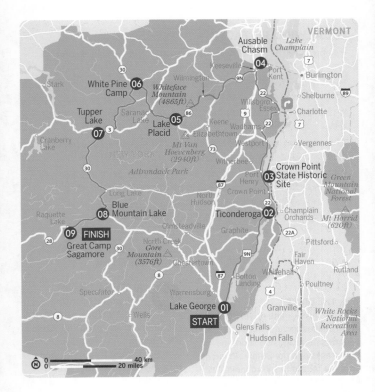

Snowbound in the Deep Woods

The North Creek area of the Adirondacks feels more remote than spots further north and east. For dozens of miles of backwoods hiking and cross-country trails head to **Garnet Hill Lodge** (garnet-hill. com) overlooking Thirteenth Lake. It has the homespun vibe and log-cabin aesthetics of an earlier era and new owners committed to the business. Nearby **Gore Mountain** (gore mountain.com) has some of the best downhill skiing in the area. The easiest way to access North Creek is from Lake George or, for a more scenic route, from Bolton Landing – on Rte NY8 you cross over the Hudson River (yep, the very same that runs down to New York City) and follow it further along on Rte 28. You might spot an eagle or two on the way.

Ticonderoga, and its fall would become the focus of James Fenimore Cooper's epic novel, *The Last of the Mohicans*. Guides dressed in Revolutionary garb muster visitors along, with stops for battle reenactments that include firing period muskets and cannons.

During the summer season you can take to the waters on one of three boats operated by **Lake George Steamboat Cruises** (lakegeorgesteamboat. com): the authentic steamboat *Minnie-Ha-Ha*, the 1907-vintage *Mohican*, and the flagship *Lac du Saint Sacrement*. The cruises last anything from between one hour and a full day.

THE DRIVE

Rte 9N hugs the lake shore on this 40-mile stretch, passing dozens of old-school motels before coming to the prosperous village of Bolton Landing, a good place to stop for a bite to eat. Along the way, peek through the trees to glimpse forested islets and stately waterfront homes once known as 'Millionaires Row.' Rte 9N veers inland and becomes more commercial approaching Ticonderoga.

02 TICONDEROGA

The small town of Ticonderoga secured itself a mention in American history books thanks to events in 1775, when its star-shaped fort was taken from the British by the 'Green Mountain Boys' (a group of independence-loving hotheads from Vermont led by Ethan Allen and Benedict Arnold, a colonel at the time and pre-betrayal). Nowadays **Fort Ticonderoga** (fort ticonderoga.org) has been carefully preserved, and with costumed guides, reenactments, a museum, gardens, a maze and hiking trails, it's easy to spend a full day here. Admission also includes access to **Mt Defiance** (fortticonderoga. org), 3km south and rising 758ft over Lake Champlain, with panoramic views all around.

THE DRIVE
It's a good idea to fuel up on gas before leaving Ticonderoga for this 18-mile drive. Each turn of Rte 22 brings a new view of Lake Champlain's sinuous shores, pushed up against the foothills of the Green Mountains. On the other side, it's all wavy gold meadows and carefully sculpted fields.

03 CROWN POINT STATE HISTORIC SITE
The remains of two major 18th-century forts, the British Crown Point and the French St Frederic, sit on a once-strategic promontory where Lake Champlain narrows between New York and Vermont. The British, after several failed attempts to wrest control of the commanding overlook, finally succeeded in 1759 after it was abandoned by the French. Today, the **Crown Point State Historic Site** (parks. ny.gov) ruins look like they're in the midst of an archaeological dig. Views of the mountains and lake are beautiful and it's interesting to imagine the numerous forks history could have taken when the French first built the

LOCAL WILDLIFE FACTS
» Keep an eye out for rattlesnakes when hiking in the Lake George area.

» Saliva from a water snake bite contains an anticoagulant; though not poisonous, you may bleed profusely.

» The vomit of a turkey vulture – they do this as a defense mechanism – is an assault on your olfactory senses. Don't make them nervous.

»Ravens, considered one of the smartest bird species, can imitate other birds and even human speech.

» Eastern coyotes found in the Adirondacks are larger than other subspecies because they contain added DNA from wolves out west.

» Swarms of black flies and other biting pests typically emerge from streams and rivers from late May through early September.

stone citadel in the 1600s. Check out the exhibits in the small museum to understand the area's role in the quest for empire.

THE DRIVE
On this 50-mile drive, Rte 22 north passes through beautiful countryside, alongside shoreline train tracks and the Boquet River; note the falls in tiny Wadhams. Just before the historic village of Essex (c 1775) and its highly recommended inn (essexinnessex.com), you pass by Essex farm, made famous in Kristin Kimball's book *The Dirty Life: A Memoir of Farming, Food & Love.*

DETOUR
Vermont
Start: 03 **Crown Point State Historic Site**

Neighboring Vermont is within your reach – at Essex just jump onto **Lake Champlain Ferries** (ferries.com) and in 20 minutes you'll be in Charlotte, VT, a quaint hamlet established in 1792 and dedicated to farming and rustic pursuits such as making maple syrup and maple-syrup candy (other ferries are at Port Kent to Burlington and Plattsburgh to Grand Isle further north). Or take the Lake Champlain Bridge at Crown Point State Historic

Site to the college town of Middlebury only a half-hour away.

04 AUSABLE CHASM
One of the country's oldest natural attractions, the dramatically beautiful **Ausable Chasm** (ausablechasm.com) is a 2-mile-long fissure formed by a gushing river that over thousands of years carved its way through deep layers of sandstone, creating 200ft cliffs, waterfalls and rapids. The privately owned site can be explored on foot, by raft or floating in an inner tube – good to do with kids for managed adventure. There's also a rappelling course ($59) and rock climbing (from $50) for those seeking an alternative to the riverside trail. From mid-November to the end of March, it's only open by appointment and you'll need to strap on microspikes to see majestic icicles that complement the unique rock formations.

The visitor center has a large cafe and a small exhibition about the life and work of the naturalist, writer and photographer Seneca Ray Stoddard, whose guidebooks, photos and maps of the region were instrumental in the formation of the Adirondacks Park in 1892 – unregulated logging was threatening to destroy much of the region's forests.

THE DRIVE
Make tracks on 9N, which follows the Ausable River to Rte 86. Views of Whiteface Mountain grow more distinct as you make your way about 30 miles southwest to Lake Placid.

05 LAKE PLACID
While the town of Lake Placid, set on beautiful Mirror Lake, is a fairly typical commercial strip, its Winter Olympic Games legacy (1932 and 1980) remains vital. The official **Olympic Center** (whiteface.com) is a large white building where the inside temperatures are kept bone-chillingly cold, thanks to the four large skating rinks where athletes come to train. Hockey fans will recognize this complex as the location of the 1980 'Miracle on Ice' when the upstart US hockey team managed to defeat the seemingly unstoppable Soviets and go on to win Olympic gold. The **Lake Placid Olympic Museum**, inside the center, has a fairly unexceptional display of memorabilia.

Not far from town on Rte 73 is the **Olympic Jumping Complex** (whiteface.com), an all-weather training facility for ski jump teams; nonacrophobic visitors can take the 20-story elevator ride to the top for impressive views (there's snow tubing on a nearby hill in winter). A 7-mile scenic drive south brings you to **Mt Van Hoevenberg** (mtvanhoevenberg.com), home to Olympic 'sliding sports,' where you can sign up for a bone-rattling, adrenalin-pumping ride as a passenger on a bobsled or go it solo on a luge during certain times of the year.

A multiplicity of backcountry hiking and cross-country trails start from the Adirondack Loj (adk.org) on **Heart Lake**.

THE DRIVE
It's only 9 miles west on Rte 86 to the sleepy town of Saranac Lake; stock up on groceries here. Continue north on Rte 86 past small farms (look for roadside markets in warm months) with mountain views until the turnoff for White Pine Camp.

LEONARD ZHUKOVSKY/SHUTTERSTOCK ©

Ausable Chasm

06 WHITE PINE CAMP

About 14 miles north of the town of Saranac Lake (which was once a center for tuberculosis treatments), you'll find **White Pine Camp** (whitepinecamp.com), one of the few remaining Adirondack 'great camps' where you can spend a night. Great camps were mostly grand lakeside compounds built by the very wealthy, usually all from wood, in the latter half of the 19th century in the Adirondacks. White Pine, however, is far from ostentatious; rather, it's a collection of rustically cozy cabins set amid pine forests, wetlands and scenic Osgood Pond – a boardwalk leads out to an island teahouse and an antique all-wood bowling alley. The fact

Photo opportunity

Heart Lake from the summit of Mt Jo.

that President Calvin Coolidge spent a few summer months here in 1926 is an interesting historical footnote, but the camp's charm comes through in its modest luxuries such as clawfoot tubs and wood-burning fireplaces. Naturalist walking tours are open to nonguests on select days from mid-June to September.

Because White Pine feels so remote, the campus of **Paul Smith's College**, only a few miles away, feels disconcertingly modern. Many students attend the school for degrees in forestry and wildlife-related sciences. The college maintains a system of interpretive and backcountry trails, with cross-country skiing in winter. Check the school's website for trail maps (paulsmiths.edu).

THE DRIVE

From Paul Smith's, Rte 30 winds its way south past several beautiful lakes, ponds and wetland areas, including Lake Clear and Upper Saranac Lake. The final 55-mile stretch on Rte 3 is more mundane.

07 TUPPER LAKE

Only a few miles east of this otherwise nondescript town is the **Wild Center** (wildcenter.org), a jewel of a museum dedicated to the ecology and conservation of the Adiron-

POSNOV/ISTOCK/GETTY IMAGES ©

Heart Lake (p49)

dacks. Interactive exhibits include a digitally rendered spherical Earth that visually displays thousands of science-related issues such as sea-surface temperatures or the history of volcanic activity (there are only about 100 of these in use worldwide). River otters perform acrobatics in an aquarium; walking trails lead to an oxbow overlook and the Raquette River (snowshoes provided gratis in winter months); there are several naturalist films to catch; and don't miss negotiating the Wild Walk, a series of connected platforms and bridges in the treetops with amazing views. Note that ticket prices are lower off-season when the Wild Walk is closed.

Also on offer is a 'back of the house' tour, where you'll see the nuts and bolts of the operation,

such as freezers full of dead mice to feed the center's snakes, owls, skunks and other animals. Give yourself a minimum of a half a day here.

 THE DRIVE
Scenic Rte 30 south takes you past several lakes and ponds on this 33-mile leg. You'll pass through the town of Long Lake, originally settled as a mill town in the 1830s and today a vacation center that swells with visitors in the summer; there's a little public beach on Rte 30 just over the bridge and across from the Adirondack Hotel.

 BLUE MOUNTAIN LAKE
A wonderful pairing with the Wild Center, the **Adirondack Experience** (theadkx.org) tells the other, human-centered story of the mountains (there's a $2 discount if you visit both properties). This large, ambitious and fascinating complex with two-dozen separate buildings occupies a 30-acre compound overlooking Blue Mountain Lake. The history of mining, logging and boat

building is explored, as is the role of 19th-century tourism in the region's development. There are lots of hands-on exhibits and activities for kids, including a bouldering wall and snowshoeing even in summertime.

 THE DRIVE
It's another half-hour southwest on Rte 28 past several beautiful lakes to Great Camp Sagamore.

09 GREAT CAMP SAGAMORE
On the shores of Raquette Lake, **Great Camp Sagamore** (Sagamore Institute; greatcampsagamore.org) is one of the most well known 'great camps,' in part because the Vanderbilt family vacationed here for a half century. You can tour the property between mid-May and mid-October (and other limited times during the rest of the year) and even spend a weekend (from $285 per person for two nights including all meals) in this rustically elaborate retreat originally built in 1895.

06

Niagara Falls & Around

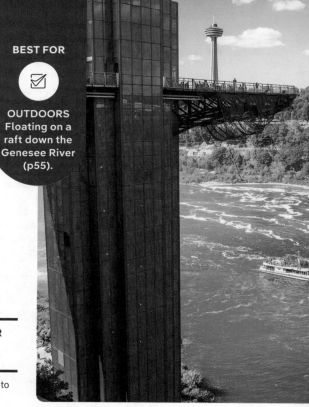

BEST FOR

☑

OUTDOORS
Floating on a
raft down the
Genesee River
(p55).

DURATION	DISTANCE	GREAT FOR
3-4 days	129 miles / 207km	Nature

BEST TIME TO GO	May to early June and September to October to avoid crowds.

Prospect Point Observation Tower

The history of western New York has been determined by the power of water: whether via the Erie Canal that once tethered the Great Lakes and Atlantic seaboard or the massive hydroelectric plants on the Niagara River, or even the long line of daredevils like Nik Wallenda, who tightrope-walked over Niagara Falls. And while industrial boom and bust cycles have come and gone, the canals, rivers, lakes and falls remain eternal attractions.

Link your trip

07 St Lawrence Seaway

Take I-90 E to Rochester and then to Rte 104 to begin a trip along lake shores and to the Thousand Islands.

04 Finger Lakes Loop

From Letchworth, take Rte 436 east and other rural back roads to Keuka Lake for a trip to wineries and beautiful falls.

01 NIAGARA FALLS

These famous falls are in two separate towns: Niagara Falls, New York (USA) and Niagara Falls, Ontario (Canada). The towns face each other across the Niagara River, spanned by the Rainbow Bridge. In contrast to the tourist glitz of the Canadian side, the American town is dominated by the lovely park created in the 1870s by celebrated landscape architect Frederick Law Olmsted, who also designed NYC's Central Park. Further back, the heart of the town is dominated by the purple, glass-covered **Seneca Niagara Resort & Casino** (seneca niagaracasino.com).

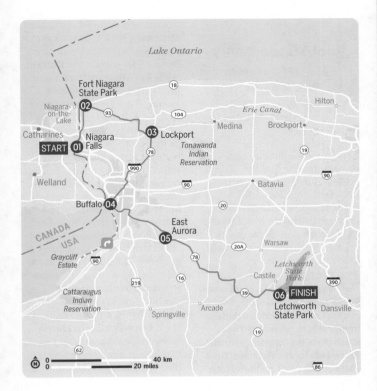

Three waterfalls make up Niagara Falls. You can see views of the **American Falls** and part of the **Bridal Veil Falls**, which drop 180ft, from the **Prospect Point Observation Tower** (niagarafallsstatepark.com). Cross the small bridge to **Goat Island** for close-up viewpoints, including Terrapin Point, which has a fine view of **Horseshoe Falls** and pedestrian bridges to the Three Sisters Islands in the upper rapids. From the north corner of Goat Island, an elevator descends to the **Cave of the Winds** (niagara fallsstatepark.com), where slippery walkways go within 25ft of the cataracts (raincoats provided), the closest viewpoint to the Canadian falls.

The **Maid of the Mist** (maidof themist.com) boat trip around the bottom of the falls has been a major attraction since 1846 and is highly recommended. Boats leave from the base of the Prospect Park Observation Tower on the US side and from the bottom of Clifton Hill on the Canadian side.

🚗 **THE DRIVE**
It's a 15-mile drive north on the Robert Moses Pkwy to the mouth of the Niagara River and Lake Ontario. About 2 miles north of Niagara Falls, NY, pause at Whirlpool State Park – the sharp bend in the river here creates a giant whirlpool easily visible from your vantage point. Steps take you 300ft to the gorge below.

Niagara Falls, Canada

It's easy enough – provided you have your passport – to also head over to the Canadian side of Niagara Falls, which is blessed with superior views. Canada's Horseshoe Falls are wider and especially photogenic from Queen Victoria Park; at night they're illuminated with a colored light show. The city itself, however, especially the Clifton Hill and Lundy's Lane areas, which have grown up around the falls, is the equivalent of a kitschy beach boardwalk, with arcades, a Ripley's Believe It or Not! museum, indoor water parks, T-shirt and souvenir shops, and fast-food and chain restaurants. **Niagara-on-the-Lake**, conversely, 15km to the north, is a small town full of elegant B&Bs, and boasts a famous summertime **theater festival** (shawfest.com).

There are customs and immigration stations at each end of the **Rainbow Bridge** (niagarafallsbridges.com) – US citizens can present either their passport or an enhanced driver's license. Canadian citizens entering the US need one of the following: a passport, a NEXUS card, a Free and Secure Trade (FAST) card or an enhanced driver's license/enhanced identification card. Driving a rental car from the US over the border should not be a problem, but check with your rental company before you depart.

02 FORT NIAGARA STATE PARK

This park, occupying the once very strategic point where the Niagara River flows into Lake Ontario, is home to **Old Fort Niagara** (oldfortniagara. org). The French originally built a garrison here in 1726, which was later used by the British and Americans in Revolutionary War battles. More recently, it was used by the US army in both world wars. It has been stunningly restored and has engaging displays of Native American artifacts, small weapons, furniture and clothing, as well as breathtaking views from its windblown ramparts. In summer months costumed guides conduct tours and demonstrations of what life was like here in the past. Surrounding the fort are well-maintained hiking trails.

🚗 THE DRIVE

Take Rte 93 east for around 19 flat, uneventful miles before turning right onto Stone Rd and then Mill St, which runs down to the Erie Canal

03 LOCKPORT

East of Niagara Falls is the town of Lockport, the western terminus of the Erie Canal, which was once the transportation lifeline connecting the Great Lakes and the Atlantic Ocean. Governor De Witt Clinton broke ground in 1817 on this public works project of unprecedented scale; it was completed eight years later at a cost of $7 million (equivalent to around $4 billion today). The **Erie Canal Discovery Center** (niagarahistory.org/ ECDC) has an excellent museum explaining the canal's complex history.

📷 Photo opportunity

Bridal Veil Falls from the *Maid of the Mist.*

To appreciate another angle on the infrastructure that went into making things hum in the mid-1800s, join the seasonal **Lockport Walking Tour** (lockportcave.com), which takes you through tunnels blasted by engineers to help power regional industry.

🚗 THE DRIVE

It's a straightforward drive on Rte 78 south to I-990 south. The quickest way to downtown Buffalo from here is to get on I-290 west, which skirts the northern 'burb of Tonawanda for about 6 miles. Then connect with I-290 south and take this another 7.5 miles until exit 8 for Rte 266 north, which brings you within a few blocks of the center.

04 BUFFALO

The winters may be long and cold, but Buffalo stays warm with a vibrant creative community and strong local pride. The best place to start exploring the city is at the magnificent art-deco **Buffalo City Hall** (preservationbuffaloniagara.org), where you can take a free tour of the building at noon, which includes a visit to the open-air observation deck on the 32nd floor. Another downtown architectural gem is the terra-cotta-clad **Guaranty Building** (Prudential Building; hodgsonruss.com/ Louis-Sullivans-Guaranty-Building.html).

North of downtown, sprawling **Delaware Park** (bfloparks.org) was designed by Frederick Law Olmsted. Its jewel is the **Buffalo AKG Art Museum** (buffaloakg. org), with a superb collection ranging from Degas and Picasso to Ruscha, Rauschenberg and other abstract expressionists. The gallery, based in a neoclassical building planned for Buffalo's 1905 Pan American Expo, is surrounded by contemporary sculptures and installations. Across the road, the modern **Burchfield Penney Art Center** (burchfield penney.org) is dedicated to artists of western New York, past and present, including Charles Burchfield whose paintings and prints reflect the local landscape.

Frank Lloyd Wright fans shouldn't miss a guided tour of his **Darwin Martin House** (darwinmartinhouse.org). This 15,000-sq-ft home, built between 1903 and 1905, was designed for Wright's friend and patron Darwin D Martin. Representing the architect's Prairie House ideal, it consists of six interconnected buildings, each of which has been meticulously restored inside and out.

🚗 THE DRIVE

Leave the city on I-90 south and then connect to Rte 400 south, which cuts through Buffalo's outlying suburbs.

🏁 DETOUR
Graycliff Estate
Start: 4 Buffalo

It's worth driving 16 miles south of downtown Buffalo along the shores of Lake Erie to visit Graycliff Estate, a 1920s vacation home designed by Frank Lloyd Wright for the wealthy Martin family. For the last 20 years the estate, which had fallen into much disrepair, has been undergoing restoration. There's still some work ongoing, but you can learn a lot about Wright's overall grand plan on interesting tours of the cliff-top property and gardens (book in advance).

05 EAST AURORA

Not exactly a household name today, Elbert Hubbard is considered the 'grandfather of modern marketing' and, at least as importantly, the founder of the Roycroft community in East Aurora. Unfulfilled by his financial success with the Larkin Soap Co in Buffalo, Hubbard took up the pen and became a writer, mostly of the motivational self-help genre. Inspired by William Morris, founder of the England arts-and-crafts movement, Hubbard returned to western New York and established his Roycroft campus here. From 1895 to 1938 it survived as a mostly self-sustaining community of talented artisans and craftspeople. The **Roycroft Campus** (roycroft campuscorporation.com) runs walking tours of six original buildings, and guides provide juicy tidbits and context to Hubbard's fascinating life story as a utopian reformer and entrepreneur.

Along East Aurora's Main St, make time to drop by historic **Vidler's** (vidlers5and10.com), which boasts of being the country's largest 'five and dime' store.

🚗 THE DRIVE
Rte 78 south to Rte 39 east takes you through rural countryside on this 40-mile drive; fill up on gas before heading out this way. The

Portageville entrance, in the southern part of the park, is on Denton Corners Rd.

06 LETCHWORTH STATE PARK

Only 60 miles southeast of Buffalo is the little-visited **Letchworth State Park** (parks. ny.gov), encompassing 14,500 acres including the Genesee River and three magnificent waterfalls, the surrounding gorge and lush forests. There are almost two dozen hiking trails, plus rafting from the end of April to October. Driving the 17 miles through the park from the Mt Morris entrance in the far north to Portageville is a very pretty drive.

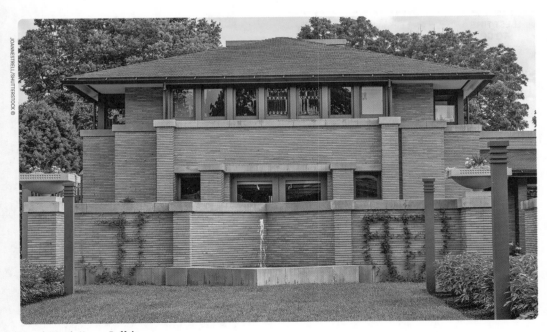

Darwin Martin House, Buffalo

07

St Lawrence Seaway

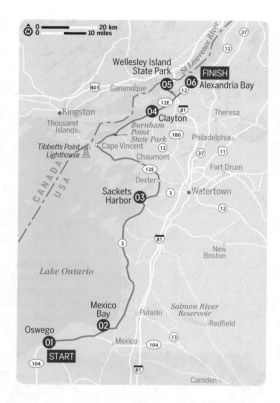

DURATION	DISTANCE	GREAT FOR
2-3 days	118 miles / 189km	Families

BEST TIME TO GO	Get in or out on the water from May to September.

Virtually unknown to downstate New Yorkers, mostly because of its relative inaccessibility, this region of more than 1800 islands – from tiny outcroppings with space for a towel to larger islands with roads and towns – is a scenic wonderland separating the US from Canada. Once a playground for the very rich, who built Gilded Age dream homes, today it's a watery world for boating, camping, swimming and even shipwreck scuba diving.

Link your trip

04 Finger Lakes Loop

From Oswego head west on Rte 104 and then south on Rte 38 for Seneca Falls to begin exploring a region of lakeside wineries.

06 Niagara Falls & Around

Follow the coastal road from Oswego and then I-90 west for a trip to the iconic falls and western New York.

01 OSWEGO

Located where the Oswego River flows into Lake Ontario, Oswego is overlooked by the impressive **Fort Ontario State Historic Site** (parks.ny.gov). This impressive star-shaped fort was built in the 1840s and provides excellent views of the surroundings from its ramparts. Join a tour with costumed interpreters around various sections of the structure, which was built on the ruins of three earlier fortifications dating back to the early 18th century.

From the fort you'll easily spot your next destination, the **H Lee White Maritime Museum** (hlee whitemarinemuseum.com) at the end of the town's

SCOTT CHIMBER PHOTOGRAPHY/SHUTTERSTOCK ©

BEST FOR

FAMILIES
Alex Bay 500
Go-Karts is the
state's longest
outdoor go-
karting track.

Fort Ontario State Historic Site, Oswego

west pier. This small museum offers detailed information about local maritime matters, as well as being the custodian of several interesting naval and commercial vessels (open for tours from mid-May to mid-September), including the tugboat USAT LT-5 *Major Elisha K Henson* that saw action during the Normandy landings of WWII.

The museum has also restored the historic **Oswego West Pierhead Lighthouse** (lighthousefriends.com), which you can see at the end of the breakwater jutting into Lake Ontario. There have been lighthouses at the mouth of the Oswego River since 1822; this is the fourth iteration. In season, boats run to the lighthouse from the museum.

Before leaving town, explore the historic waterfront backed by gorgeous heritage homes, including the **Richardson-Bates House Museum** (rbhousemuseum.org), an Italian villa built by a wealthy family in the late 1800s.

 THE DRIVE
Drive for 16 miles east of Oswego along Rte 104, then Rte 104B through flat countryside to reach Mexico Bay.

02 MEXICO BAY
You'll pass the **Derby Hill Bird Observatory** (onondagaaudubon.com) in the woodsy and rural area north of Oswego, a state park that also contains the famous **Salmon River** – the location fly-fishers dream of when planning their perfect vacation. A walk around

these challenging shores will bring you in close contact with northern New York's fiercely rampant nature – soaring trees, rough marsh grasses and big birds with sharp talons abound. In fact, Derby Hill, one of the premier hawk-watching sites in the eastern US, sees an average of 40,000 of these birds of prey every spring, which use the thermals around the edge of the lake while migrating further north. April is the best month to see them, but summers mean bald eagles, butterflies and local breeding birds.

Beach lovers shouldn't miss a pit stop at **Sandy Pond**, still on your northward route. This barrier beach has walkovers set up so pedestrians can enjoy the

FREDERIC REMINGTON ART MUSEUM

Fewer people travel along the river north of A-Bay, but it's worth a detour to the **Frederic Remington Art Museum** (fredericremington.org) in Ogdensburg. Remington (1861-1909), an artist who romanticized the American West in paintings and sculpture, was born nearby in Canton and his family moved to Ogdensburg when he was 11. He led something of a peripatetic existence as a correspondent and illustrator for high-profile magazines of his day such as *Collier's* and *Harper's Weekly*. The museum not only contains some of his sculptures and paintings, but loads of personal ephemera such as cigars and scrapbooks. A visit here goes well with the Rockwell Museum (p45) in Corning.

From A-Bay, Rte 12 turns into Rte 37 just past Morristown, following the coastline. There are fewer islands in the river the further northeast you drive, but you can pull over at several turnoffs as well as two state parks – King Point and Jaques Cartier.

salty sand without disturbing fragile dunes and adjacent wetlands. There's plenty of wildlife to see, including frogs and turtles, especially if you arrive during the busy sunset hours when the night crawlers start to stir.

THE DRIVE
Rte 3, also known as the 'Seaway Trail,' continues north with a handful of ponds and estuaries on your left between the road and the lake. On this 35-mile trip you'll pass the access road for Southwick Beach, a pretty stretch of sand with good swimming. Further north, turn left on County Hwy 75 for Sackets Harbor.

03 SACKETS HARBOR
An attractive old fishing village perched on a big lakeside bluff, Sackets Harbor was also the site of two important battles in the War of 1812. Swing by the grounds of the **Sackets Harbor Battlefield** (parks.ny.gov); there are many events held here during the summer season, the main one being the **War of 1812 Living History Weekend**,

usually at the end of July, when battle reenactments are staged by locals in uniforms. At other times of year the grounds, with their heritage buildings, make for an attractive stroll along the lake shoreline.

THE DRIVE
Turn left onto Rte 12E from Rte 180 for a longer, more scenic route. You'll pass through the village of Chaumont before coming to the tiny Cape Vincent. Follow signs to the white-stucco and red-roofed Tibbetts Point Lighthouse, now a lakeside hostel. Views are of the headwaters of the St Lawrence and Wolfe Island, Canada. It's another 15 miles northeast to Clayton.

04 CLAYTON
Next up is Clayton, a small, attractive waterside town that is the most appealing of several bases you could use to tour the Thousand Islands region. The town's excellent **Antique Boat Museum** (abm.org) showcases some beautiful examples of small-scale nautical craft; included in the admission is the

chance to try your hand at rowing traditional wooden skiffs. For an additional $3 you can tour the glam 1903 houseboat *La Duchesse*, once owned by George C Boldt, proprietor of Manhattan's Waldorf Astoria Hotel; reserve a tour time in advance. If you get a taste for sailing, **Clayton Island Tours** (claytonislandtours.com) offers boat tours across the St Lawrence River to Canada and back via Boldt Castle (also accessible from Alexandria Bay), as well as a glass-bottom-boat tour to Rock Island lighthouse.

Back on land, the **Thousand Islands Museum** (timuseum. org) has warehoused all kinds of photography and writing about island culture dating from the 1800s. The museum also has a rotating exhibit of local artists, plus examples of the fine carving for which the region is famous.

Arts-and-crafts lovers should drop by the **Thousand Islands Arts Center** (tiartscenter. org), which includes a museum dedicated to handweaving and a pottery studio.

THE DRIVE
It's 7 miles on Rte 12 to the exit for I-81 north. Just over the bridge, take the first exit for County Rd 191; this crosses back under I-81 before turning north to the park.

05 WELLESLEY ISLAND STATE PARK
Take the afternoon to visit **Wellesley Island State Park** (parks.ny.gov), a 2363-acre park at the southern tip of the island, which includes a beautiful swimming beach. To reach it you'll need to cross the Thousand Islands International Bridge (toll $2.75). The park's abundant

wildlife, plus marina, ponds and **Minna Anthony Common Nature Center** (parks.ny.gov) will further pull you into the mysterious allure of these sparsely inhabited islands.

On the other side of Wellesley, at the end of the Thousand Islands International Bridge, is the fantastic **1000 Islands Tower** (1000islandstower.com), a 395ft observation tower that belongs to Canada – but you can enjoy it if you have valid ID on you (a passport is best). The elevator ride to the top gives excellent views of the sprawling Thousand Islands.

🚗 **THE DRIVE**
It's simple – retrace your route back over the bridge to the mainland and exit onto Rte 12 north. From here it's 5 miles north to Alex Bay, passing Alex Bay 500 Go-Karts on the way.

06 **ALEXANDRIA BAY**
Somewhat run-down and tacky Alexandria Bay (A-Bay or Alex Bay), an early 20th-century resort town, is still the center of tourism on the American side of the Thousand Islands area.

Catch ferries from here to Heart Island and **Boldt Castle** (boldtcastle.com), built by George C Boldt. Boldt began building this replica of a 120-room Rhineland, Germany, castle in 1900 for his wife, Louise, who unexpectedly passed away four years later, well before it was finished. Boldt subsequently abandoned the project and it became the provenance of the island's woodland creatures. But since the late 1970s, millions have gone into its restoration, and now the structures are as magnificent as originally intended.

Another not-to-be-missed island experience is a trip to neighboring **Singer Castle** (singercastle.com), perched on Dark Island. Built by the president of the Singer sewing machine company, this 20th-century delight was modeled on a classic Scottish castle, giving it lots of long, spooky hallways and dimly lit passages.

KHAIRIL AZHAR JUNOS/SHUTTERSTOCK ©

Boldt Castle, Alexandria Bay

JOHN AREHART/SHUTTERSTOCK ©

Point Pleasant (p66)

New Jersey & Pennsylvania

Explore

New Jersey & Pennsylvania

Road trips in New Jersey and Pennsylvania embrace the diversity of the American experience. Travelers can visit an Amish family's farm, read the Declaration of Independence and ride a boardwalk roller coaster all in one day. Natural treasures are abundant too, whether enjoying a gentle float down the Delaware River, sunbathing on a pristine beach or gazing into the PA Grand Canyon. Urban centers are strutting their stuff with a newfound enthusiasm. The dining scene in Philadelphia is no longer burgeoning – it's here – and Pittsburgh earns kudos for its vibrant ethnic neighborhoods and top-notch museums.

Philadelphia

Rich history, small-town charm and a red-hot restaurant scene make Philly a compelling place for extended exploring. Must-dos include following in the footsteps of the country's Founding Fathers at Independence Hall and admiring the Liberty Bell, but the city has invigorating contemporary sights too, from buzzy international food markets to high-tech wonders at the Comcast Center. Philadelphia is a city of neighborhoods, all waiting to be discovered, and its museums showcase so much more than just the founding of the country – which they also do quite well, of course. The restaurant scene is generating buzz, but debating the best cheesesteak never goes out of style.

Pittsburgh

Driving into Pittsburgh can be an unexpected thrill, with GPS systems sending you swooping back and forth over the bridges that span the Monongahela and Allegheny rivers as you search for your hotel. Not that we'd known anything about that. Once settled, it's easy to explore the myriad charms of downtown, where old public libraries and brick row houses are tucked between rivers and soaring skyscrapers. Andrew Carnegie modernized steel production in Pittsburgh, and the former industrial buildings now hold an array of of modern homes and businesses. Market Square and the Andy Warhol Museum are highlights on a downtown walk.

WHEN TO GO

High season is June though August, when beaches and tourist destinations fill with families on vacation and lodging prices soar. Late September is a quieter time to hit the Jersey Shore. Fall foliage season is mid-September though October in the Appalachians in northwestern Pennsylvania. In winter, beaches and other tourist-dependent areas may have closures and limited hours.

Princeton

Anchored by Princeton, the nation's fourth-oldest university, this tiny college town with upper-crust inclinations makes a pleasant overnight stop. Settled by an English Quaker missionary, Princeton today is marked by lovely architecture, preppy boutiques, top-notch museums and a slew of college town mainstays, from indie bookstore to arthouse cinema to ice-cream shops. Downtown is a warren of streets and alleys that crisscross Palmer Square. Institute Woods and its 700 acres of green space are a prime spot for walking and birding.

Atlantic City

Charming may not be the first word that comes to mind when thinking of Atlantic City, but with its central location on the Jersey Shore, it works well as a short-term hub. Thanks to the casinos, room rates can be a bargain and the beach itself is lovely – and often empty. The eight-mile boardwalk is lined with blingy distractions, including amusement rides and candy stands at Steel Pier.

TRANSPORT

Key airports for the region include Newark Liberty International Airport in New Jersey and Philadelphia International Airport and Pittsburgh International Airport, both in Pennsylvania. Amtrak's busy Northeast Regional train stops in Philadelphia and Newark and a few smaller cities multiple times per day. The Northeast Regional tends to run more consistently on time compared to other Amtrak routes.

 WHAT'S ON

Mummers Parade

Held every New Year's Day, this wild parade in Philadelphia is a mix of Mardi Gras and a marching band competition.

Battle of Gettysburg Recreation

In early June thousands of costumed soldiers converge on Gettysburg National Military Park for one of the largest reenactments in the world.

AsburyFest

Formerly known as OysterFest, this three-day celebration in June now celebrates a range of cuisines in Asbury Park.

Resources

Visit Philly
(visitphilly.com) Well-organized site run by the city's official tourism bureau.

Visit Pittsburgh
(visitpittsburgh.com) City tourism website shares up-to-the-minute cool tips.

Delaware Water Gap National Recreation Area
(nps.gov/dewa) To get a handle on this 70,000-acre adventure zone, read the *Guide to the Gap*.

 WHERE TO STAY

The campground at Cherry Springs State Park (dcnr.pa.gov) may be primitive, but its view of the cosmos at night is nothing short of cinematic. Cherry Springs is one of a handful of parks east of the Mississippi designated an International Dark Sky Park, and the campground is tucked between two stargazing fields. Revamped grand hotels and historic inns, including the Hotel Fauchere (hotelfauchere.com) in Milford and the Lititz Springs Inn (lititzspringsinn.com) in Lititz, are top picks in Pennsylvania. The Asbury Hotel (theasburyhotel.com) in Asbury Park brings breezy modern cool to the Jersey Shore.

08

The Jersey Shore

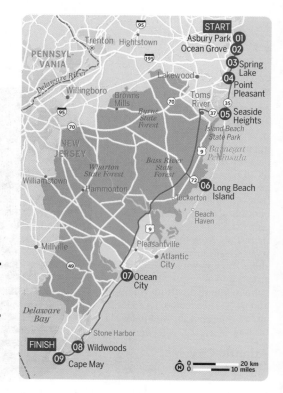

DURATION	DISTANCE	GREAT FOR
3-7 days	129 miles / 207km	Nature

BEST TIME TO GO	Midweek in June – crowds are smaller and rooms cheaper than in the high season. End of September – Indian summer temps and cheaper, too.

The New Jersey coastline is studded with resort towns from classy to tacky that fulfill the Platonic ideal of how a long summer day should be spent. Super-sized raucous boardwalks where singles more than mingle are a short drive from old-fashioned intergenerational family retreats. When the temperature rises, the entire state tips eastward and rushes to the beach to create memories that they'll view later with nostalgia and perhaps some regret.

Link your trip

11 Brandywine Valley to Atlantic City

Atlantic City, the eastern shore's casino capital, and the forested Pine Barrens are easily accessible from the drive between Long Beach Island and Ocean City.

19 Delmarva

Hop on the Cape May–Lewes ferry across Delaware Bay to this peninsula trip for more beach getaways.

01 ASBURY PARK

Let's start with the town that Bruce Springsteen, the most famous of a group of musicians who developed the Asbury Sound in the 1970s, immortalized in song. Several of these musicians – such as Steve Van Zandt, Garry Tallent, and the late Danny Federici and Clarence Clemons – formed Springsteen's supporting E Street Band. The main venues to check out are the still-grungy, seen-it-all clubs **Stone Pony** (stoneponyonline.com) and **Wonder Bar** (wonderbarasburypark.com).

BEST FOR

☑

Polar opposites, the Wildwoods (p68) and Cape May (p68) are both classics.

Carousel building, Asbury Park

Led by wealthy gay men from NYC who snapped up blocks of forgotten Victorian homes and storefronts to refurbish, the **downtown** area includes several blocks of Cookman and Bangs Aves, lined with charming shops, bars, cafes, restaurants and a restored art house cinema.

The **boardwalk** itself is short and unspectacular by Jersey standards: at one end is the gorgeous but empty shell of a 1920s-era carousel and casino building, the Paramount Theatre is near the other end, and there's an attractive, well-cared-for stretch of sand in front. Asbury Park's amusements tend to be more for adults than children: its clubs and bars rock late, it has decent surf, and the shore's liveliest gay scene.

🚗 THE DRIVE

There's no beachfront road to Ocean Grove – the two towns are separated by narrow Wesley Lake. Take the generically commercial Main St/Rte 71 and turn left on Ocean Grove's own Main Ave. It might be worthwhile, however, to first head north on Rte 71 for a few miles to take a gander at the impressively grand homes in the community of Deal.

02 OCEAN GROVE

Next to Asbury Park is Ocean Grove, one of the cutest Victorian seaside towns anywhere, with a boardwalk boasting not a single business to disturb the peace and quiet. Known as 'God's Square Mile at the Jersey Shore,' Ocean Grove is perfectly coiffed, sober, conservative and quaint – it used to shut down entirely on Sundays. Founded by Methodists in the 19th century, the place retains what's left of a post–Civil War **Tent City** revival camp – now a historic site with 114 cottage-like canvas tents clustered together that are used for summer homes.

Towering over the tents, the 1894 mustard-yellow **Great Auditorium** (oceangrove.org) shouldn't be missed: its vaulted interior, amazing acoustics and historic organ recall Utah's Mormon

Tabernacle. Make sure to catch a recital or concert (Wednesday or Saturday during the summer) or one of the open-air services held in the boardwalk pavilion.

THE DRIVE
Follow Rte 71 south through a string of relatively sleepy towns (Bradley Beach, Belmar) for just over 5 miles to reach Spring Lake.

03 SPRING LAKE
The quiet streets of this prosperous community, once known as the 'Irish Riviera,' are lined with grand oceanfront Victorian houses set in meticulously manicured lawns. As a result of Hurricane Sandy, the gorgeous beach is extremely narrow at high tide. If you're interested in a low-key quiet

Photo opportunity
Sunset at Cape May (p68).

base, a stay here is about as far from the typical shore boardwalk experience as you can get. Only 5 miles inland from Spring Lake is the quirky **Historic Village at Allaire** (allairevillage.org), the remains of what was a thriving 19th-century village called Howell Works. You can still visit various 'shops' in this living museum, all run by folks in period costume.

THE DRIVE
For a slow but pleasant drive, take Ocean Ave south – at Wreck Pond turn inland before heading south again. At Crescent Park in the town of Sea Girt, Washington Ave connects back to Union Ave/Rte 71, which leads into Rte 35 and over the Manasquan Inlet.

04 POINT PLEASANT
Point Pleasant is the first of five quintessential bumper-car-and-Skee-Ball boardwalks. On a July weekend, Point Pleasant's long beach is jam-packed: squint, cover up all that nearly naked flesh with striped unitards, and it could be the 1920s, with umbrellas shading every inch of sand and the surf clogged with bodies and bobbing heads.

Seaside Heights

Families with young kids love Point Pleasant, as the boardwalk is big but not overwhelming, and the squeaky-clean amusement rides, fun house and small aquarium – all run by **Jenkinson's** (jenkinsons.com) – are geared to the height and delight of the 10-and-under set. That's not to say Point Pleasant is only for little ones. **Martell's Tiki Bar** (tikibar.com), a place margarita pitchers go to die, makes sure of that: look for the neon-orange palm trees and listen for the live bands.

 THE DRIVE
Head south on Rte 35 past several residential communities laid out on a long barrier island only a block or two wide in parts – Seaside Heights is where it's at its widest on this 11-mile trip.

05 SEASIDE HEIGHTS
Coming from the north, Seaside Heights has the first of the truly overwhelming boardwalks: a sky ride and two rollicking amusement piers with double corridors of arcade

---

---

games and adult-size, adrenaline-pumping rides, roller coasters and various iterations of the vomit-inducing 10-story drop. During the day, it's as family-friendly as Point Pleasant, but once darkness falls Seaside Heights becomes a scene of such hedonistic mating rituals that an evangelical church has felt the need for a permanent booth on the pier. Packs of young men – caps askew, tatts gleaming – check out packs of young women in shimmering spaghetti-strap microdresses as everyone rotates among the string of loud bars, with live bands growling out Eagles tunes. It's pure Jersey.

Detour south on Rte 35 to the 10-mile-long **Island Beach State Park** (islandbeachnj.org), a completely undeveloped barrier island backed by dunes and tall grasses separating the bay from the ocean.

 THE DRIVE
To reach the mainland, take Rte 37 from Seaside Heights; you cross a long bridge over Barnegat Bay before reaching the strip-mall-filled sprawl of Toms River. Hop on the Garden State Pkwy south, then Rte 72 and the bridge over Manahawkin Bay.

06 LONG BEACH ISLAND
Only a very narrow inlet separates this long sliver of an island, with its beautiful beaches and impressive summer homes, from the very southern tip of Island Beach State Park and the northern shore towns. Within throwing distance of the park is the landmark **Barnegat Lighthouse** (nj.gov/dep/parksand forests), which offers panoramic views from the top. Fishers cast off from a jetty extending 2000ft along the Atlantic Ocean, and a short nature trail begins just in front of a visitor center with small history and photography displays.

Nearly every morning practically half the island is jogging, walking, blading or biking on Beach Ave, the 7.5-mile stretch of asphalt that stretches from Ship Bottom to Beach Haven (south of the bridge); it's a great time to exercise, enjoy the sun and people-watch. Tucked down a residential street is **Hudson House** (19 E 13th St, Beach Haven), a nearly locals-only dive bar about as worn and comfortable as an old pair of flip-flops. Don't be intimidated by the fact that it looks like a crumbling biker bar – it is.

THE DRIVE:
Head back over the bridge, then take the Garden State Pkwy south past the marshy pinelands area and Atlantic City. Take exit 30 for Somers Point; Laurel Dr turns into MacArthur Blvd/Rte 52 and then a long causeway crosses Great Egg Harbor Bay. This is a 48-mile drive. When you cross the causeway, turn left for peace and quiet, right for the action

07 OCEAN CITY
An almost heavenly amalgam of Ocean Grove and Point Pleasant, Ocean City is a dry town with a roomy boardwalk packed with genuine family fun and facing an exceedingly pretty beach. There's a small water park, and **Gillian's Wonderland** has a heart-thumpingly tall Ferris wheel, a beautifully restored merry-go-round and kiddie rides galore – and no microphoned teens hawking carnie games. The mood is light and friendly (a lack of alcohol will do that).

Mini-golf aficionados: dingding-dingding! You hit the jackpot. Pint-size duffers can play through on a three-masted schooner, around great white sharks and giant octopuses, under reggae monkeys piloting a helicopter and even in black light. If you haven't already, beat the heat with a delicious Kohr's soft-serve frozen custard, plain or dipped. While saltwater taffy is offered in many places, **Shriver's Taffy** (shrivers. com) is, in our humble opinion, the best: watch machines stretch and wrap it, and then fill a bag with two dozen or more flavors.

THE DRIVE
If time isn't a factor, cruise down local streets and over several small bridges ($1.50 toll on two of the four

in each direction; coins only) through the beachfront communities of Strathmere, Sea Isle City, Avalon and Stone Harbor. Otherwise, head back to the Garden State Pkwy and get off at one of two exits for the Wildwoods on a 30-mile drive.

08 THE WILDWOODS
A party town popular with teens and 20-somethings, Wildwood is the main social focus here. Access to all three beaches is free, and the width of the beach – more than 1000ft in parts, making it the widest in NJ – means there's never a lack of space. Several massive piers are host to water parks and amusement parks – easily the rival of any Six Flags Great Adventure – with roller coasters and rides best suited to aspiring astronauts anchoring the 2-mile-

TOP TIP:
Plan Ahead

We love the shore but let's be honest, in summer months, the traffic's a nightmare, parking's impossible and the beaches are overflowing. Pack the car the night before, leave at dawn and, if at all possible, come midweek. And if you want something besides a run-down, sun-bleached, three-blocks-from-the-water flea box to stay in, make reservations six months to a year in advance.

long Grand Daddy of Jersey Shore boardwalks. Glow-in-the-dark 3D mini-golf is a good example of the Wildwood boardwalk ethos – take it far, then one step further. Maybe the best ride of all is the tram running the length of the boardwalk from Wildwood Crest to North Wildwood. There's always a line for a table at Jersey Shore staple pizzeria Mack & Manco's on the boardwalk (it also has other shore boardwalk locations).

Wildwood Crest is an archaeological find, a kitschy slice of 1950s Americana – whitewashed motels with flashing neon signs. Check out eye-catching motel signs like the Lollipop at 23rd and Atlantic Aves.

THE DRIVE

Take local roads: south on Pacific Ave to Ocean Dr, which passes over a toll bridge over an estuary area separating Jarvis Sound from Cape May Harbor. Then left on Rte 109 over the Cape May harbor. You can turn left anywhere from here, depending on whether you want to head to town or the beach.

09 CAPE MAY
Founded in 1620, Cape May – the only place in New Jersey where the sun both rises and sets over the water – is on the state's southern tip and is the country's oldest seashore resort. Its sweeping beaches get crowded in summer, but the stunning Victorian architecture is attractive year-round. In addition to 600 gingerbread-style houses, the city boasts antique shops and places for dolphin-, whale- (May to December) and bird-watching, and is just outside the **Cape May Point State Park** (nj.gov/dep/

Cape May Lighthouse

parksandforests) and its 157ft **Cape May Lighthouse** (capemay mac.org), with 199 steps to the observation deck at the top; there's an excellent visitor center and museum with exhibits on wildlife in the area, as well as trails to ponds, dunes and marshes. A mile-long loop of the nearby **Cape May Bird Observatory** (birdcapemay.org) is a pleasant stroll through preserved wetlands. The wide sandy beach at the park (free) or the one in town is the main attraction in summer months. **Aqua Trails** (aquatrails. com) offers kayak tours of the coastal wetlands.

09

Bucks County & Around

BEST FOR

FAMILIES
Coloring with
Crayolas (p72)
in Easton.

Princeton University

DURATION	DISTANCE	GREAT FOR
3-4 days	132 miles / 212km	History & Culture, Food & Drink

BEST TIME TO GO	Spring and fall for lush green and gold foliage.

Since the turn of the 20th century, painters have found inspiration in the soothing beauty of the region's tree-lined riverbanks and canals. And despite the fact that Revolutionary War struggles took place amid its picturesque setting, the flowing Delaware has a way of softening not only the afternoon light but one's mood as well. It's no surprise artists and city dwellers seeking to commune with nature continue to flock here.

Link your trip

11 Brandywine Valley to Atlantic City

Start on I-95 south from Philly to access the rural byways and gardens of the Brandywine Valley.

08 The Jersey Shore

It's a straight shot down the Atlantic City Expwy to Atlantic City, from where all of the shore is within reach.

01 PRINCETON

It was here, on January 3, 1777, that George Washington and his untrained, ill-equipped troops won their first victory against British Regulars, then the world's most powerful army. Today's town is home to **Princeton University**, the country's fourth oldest and a bastion of the Ivy League. Its impressive campus with wrought-iron gates, Gothic spires and manicured quads personify the ideals of a classic liberal-arts education. Running along the campus' edge is Nassau St, the town's principal commercial thoroughfare where Albert Einstein

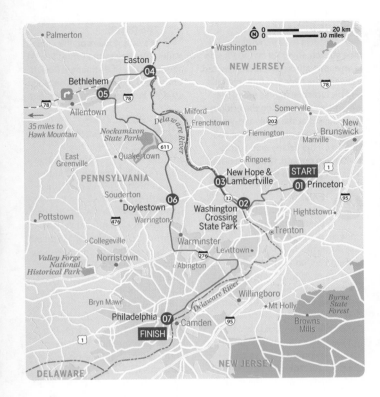

02 WASHINGTON CROSSING STATE PARK

Ten days before the battle at Princeton on Christmas night 1776, George Washington led his army across the ice-packed Delaware River from the Pennsylvania side to the New Jersey side in a raging snowstorm. He took the risk knowing that if he didn't win something before winter closed in, his army might desert him entirely come spring. **Washington Crossing State Park** (nj.gov/dep/parks andforests) offers an overstuffed exhibit in the visitor center, historic buildings and nice trails through pretty woods. Though good for a picnic, the park isn't very evocative. A copy of the painting Washington Crossing the Delaware is on the Pennsylvania side (Washington Crossing Historic Park); the original is in the Metropolitan Museum of Art in NYC. According to historians, the artist, Emanuel Leutze, got almost none of the details right: the boats, the light, the river, Washington himself – all wrong. Rather, the scene is a caricature that captures not the moment itself, but how everyone felt about it afterward.

Just 4 miles south on the Jersey side of the river is the **New Jersey State Police Museum** (njsp.org). Where else can you gawk at confiscated sawn-off shotguns, Colt .45s, or the electric chair that killed Bruno Hauptmann? Yes, the guy who kidnapped Lindbergh's baby – or did he? A fantastic exhibit guides you through the trial, then you can test your detective skills on a fictional crime scene.

once window-shopped – he lived in Princeton from 1933 until his death in 1955.

The **Princeton University Art Museum** (princetonartmuseum.org) is akin to a mini Metropolitan Museum of Art in terms of its variety and quality of works, which range from ancient Greek pottery to pieces by Andy Warhol. At the time of writing, the museum was closed, with a new building under construction. It's expected to open in 2025.

Afterwards, stop by the nearby **Morven Museum & Garden** (morven.org) for fine displays of decorative arts and fully furnished period rooms; other galleries change their exhibitions periodically. The gardens and house, a perfectly coiffed colonial-revival mansion originally built by Richard Stockton, a prominent lawyer in the mid-18th century and signatory of the Declaration of Independence, are worth a visit in and of themselves.

🚙 THE DRIVE

Surrounding Princeton, to the west especially, gorgeous homes line the streets – surely only the most tenured professors could afford to live here. So take local roads – Rosedale Rd, right on Carter, left on Elm Ridge and then left on Pennington Rocky Hill Rd. Take one more left on Rte 31/Pennington Rd and finally a right on Washington Crossing Pennington Rd.

THE DRIVE

The 13-mile drive north is prettier on the PA side, so cross the extremely narrow bridge and turn right on River Rd. You'll pass Washington Crossing Historic Park and, further along, the Delaware Canal State Park. Across the street from the latter is the entrance to Bowman's Hill Wildflower Preserve. The meadows and ponds are worth a stroll.

03 NEW HOPE & LAMBERTVILLE

These two towns, built along the banks of the wide Delaware River separating New Jersey and Pennsylvania, are connected by a pedestrian-friendly bridge. The intersection of Bridge and Main Sts is the center of New Hope's action, which consists mostly of small craft, vintage and antique shops, as well as a number of restaurants with outdoor patios – great spots for drinks when the weather permits.

Smaller and quainter Lambertville has antique shops, art galleries and a few cozy coffee shops and restaurants. The restored 19th-century train station near the foot of the bridge now houses the town's signature restaurant. About a mile south of town on Rte 29 is the **Golden Nugget Antique Flea Market** (gnflea.com), where more than 250 dealers congregate along with food vendors every Wednesday, Saturday and Sunday year-round. Seven miles north is **Bull's Island Recreation Area**, a lovely place to stroll along the canal; a pedestrian bridge crosses the Delaware to the tiny, historic hamlet of Lumberville, PA, which has a general store where you can pick up deli food.

THE DRIVE

Settle in for a picturesque 34-mile stretch; River Rd on the PA side is an especially scenic drive, nestled between the river and forested hills and picturesque homes along the way. It's worth crossing the bridges and pausing at the blink-and-you'll-miss-it villages of Frenchtown and Milford on the Jersey side before continuing onward. Cross the Delaware once more to enter Easton.

04 EASTON

The historic city of Easton, home to Lafayette College, is in the Lehigh Valley, just over the New Jersey border and on the banks of the Delaware River. While there are a few charming cobblestone blocks and bohemian elements, there's also an undeniable air of decay around the fringes of this otherwise picturesque town. Families with kids should head to the **Crayola Factory** (crayola experience.com) – it's decidedly not a factory, rather more an interactive 'museum' where you can watch crayons and markers get made, plus enjoy hands-on exhibits where you're invited to write on the walls.

No longer awkwardly sharing space with the Crayola Factory, the **National Canal Museum** (canals.org) is now housed in a plain two-story brick building that's, appropriately enough, along the canal. With fascinating exhibits on the integral role canals played in fostering the nation's economy, it's less dry than you might imagine. You can also hop aboard the *Josiah White II*, a rebuilt 19th-century boat, or learn about the life of a lock tender from a costumed interpreter.

THE DRIVE

It's only 4 miles on the Lehigh Valley Thruway to the exit at Rte 191 south/Nazareth Bethlehem Pike. It turns into Linden St and takes you straight into downtown Bethlehem.

05 BETHLEHEM

From its initial founding by a small religious community to a heavy industry center to its current incarnation as a gambling destination, the city of Bethlehem on the Lehigh River retains a charming historic quality. On Christmas Eve 1741 the leader of a group of Moravian settlers from Saxony in Germany christened the town 'Bethlehem,' and ever since its Christmas celebrations have drawn visitors from afar. Fourteen acres of the original community in which men, women and children lived in separate housing have been granted national historic landmark status, and you can tour several buildings, including the **Moravian Museum of Bethlehem** (historicbethlehem.org), housed in the oldest still-standing structure in town.

The 10-acre campus of **SteelStacks** (steelstacks.org), an arts and culture organization, is located directly underneath the towering, prehistoric-looking blast furnaces of the former Bethlehem Steel factory, left neglected and decaying for years. This formerly forlorn site has been revitalized and now includes **ArtsQuest Center** (artsquest.org), a state-of-the-art performance space with a cinema, restaurant and the Levitt Pavilion, which hosts free outdoor concerts, and walking tours explaining the history and architecture of this industrial giant.

Bridge between New Hope and Lambertville

Even if you don't intend on throwing down any cash, the massive casino built on the site of the former factory (it takes its design cues from its utilitarian past) is worth a drive-by. You can park and walk around the Hoover Mason Trestle walkway on your own, feeling dwarfed by the giant decaying ruins of what was once the biggest industry in the area.

🎡 THE DRIVE

It's only 30 miles south through the heart of Bucks County to Doylestown. You'll pass by Nockamixon State Park, a large lake with a few miles of hiking trails, shortly before Rte 412 turns into Rte 611.

Photo opportunity

Eerie blast furnaces of Bethlehem Steel.

🧭 DETOUR
Hawk Mountain
Start: 05 Bethlehem

When the East Coast gratefully turns the page on August's heat and humidity, it's time to head for the mountains. Cooler temperatures make hiking more pleasant and as the leaves turn, nature paints the mid-Atlantic's deciduous forests every shade of red and yellow. With so many mountains to choose

from, why pick Hawk Mountain? Because raptors start their annual migration south, and during September, October and November some 18,000 hawks, eagles, osprey, kestrels and vultures pass this particular windy updraft along the Kittatinny Ridge. From Hawk Mountain's North Lookout, you can see more than 17 species fly by, some at eye-level. On a good day, observers count a thousand birds, though broad-winged hawks, the rare raptor that flies in a group, have been known to arrive 7000 at a time. At other times of the year, the soft carpeted hills of the Appalachians are just as beautiful, and those for whom Hawk Mountain's relatively short trails are not enough can pick up the Appalachian Trail from here. The **Hawk Mountain Visitor Center** (hawkmountain.org) has loaner optics and trail guides.

SteelStacks (p72), Bethlehem

To get to Hawk Mountain, leave Bethlehem on Rte 378 north to connect to US 22 west. After 10.5 miles this merges with I-78 west for another 16 miles. Take exit 35 at Lenhartsville and head north on Rte 143 for another 4 miles. Turn left onto Hawk Mountain Rd (there's a blue Hawk Mountain sign here); it's another 7 miles to the parking lot at the top of the mountain.

06 DOYLESTOWN

In 1898–99, painters Edward Redfield and William Langson Lathrop moved to New Hope and cofounded an artists colony that changed American painting. Redfield, in particular, became famous for painting outside (en plein air) in winter storms so bad he had to tie his easel to a tree. He worked

fast, not even sketching first, creating moody, muted landscapes in a day. For the whole story on the New Hope School of painters and other top-flight American artists, head to Doylestown's **Michener Art Museum** (michenermuseum.org). Housed in an impressive-looking stone building, a refurbished prison from the 1880s, the museum is named after the popular Pulitzer Prize–winning author James A Michener (*Tales of the South Pacific* is probably his best-known work) who supported the museum. A small permanent exhibition includes Michener's writing desk and other objects from his Bucks County home, including a collection of this inveterate traveler's personal road maps to cities and countries around the world.

🚗 THE DRIVE

Continue south on Rte 611 to I-276 east; a shortcut to I-95 south, which takes you to Penn's Landing, is to exit onto US 1 toward Philadelphia and then take Rte 63 east. Otherwise, keep going on I-276 east until you can take another exit for I-95 south.

07 PHILADELPHIA

Penn's Landing – Philadelphia's waterfront area along the Delaware River between Market and Lombard Sts, where William Penn landed on a barge

in 1682 – was a very active port area from the early 18th century into the 20th. Today most of the excitement is about boarding booze cruises, or simply strolling along the water's edge. The 1.8-mile Benjamin Franklin Bridge, the world's largest suspension bridge when completed in 1926, spans the Delaware River and dominates the view. Check out the **Independence Seaport Museum** (phillyseaport.org), which highlights Philadelphia's role as an immigration hub; its shipyard closed in 1995 after 200 years.

Old City – the area bounded by Walnut, Vine, Front and 6th Sts – picks up where Independence National Historical Park (p82) leaves off. Along with Society Hill, Old City was early Philadelphia. The 1970s saw revitalization, with many warehouses converted into apartments, galleries and small businesses. Today it's a quaint place for a stroll, especially along tiny, cobblestoned **Elfreth's Alley** (elfrethsalley.org) – its 32 well-preserved brick row houses make up what's believed to be the oldest continuously occupied street in the USA. Stop into Elfreth's Alley Museum, built in 1755 by blacksmith and alley namesake Jeremiah Elfreth; it's been restored and furnished to its 1790 appearance.

10

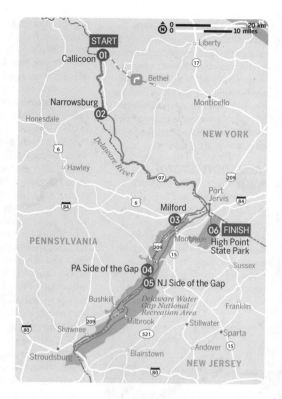

Down the Delaware

DURATION	DISTANCE	GREAT FOR
3-4 days	125 miles / 201km	Families

BEST TIME TO GO	Mid-April through October for boating.

Flowing along the New York and Pennsylvania border and then through New Jersey, the Delaware River is a particularly scenic state boundary. Snaking past riverside towns where locals coexist with downstaters discovering the pleasures of rural living, it makes its most dramatic appearance at an S-shaped curve in a gap in the mountains. Whatever side you're on, beautiful waterfalls – some hidden deep in the forest – can be found down little-known backcountry roads.

Link your trip

03 Tranquil Catskills

Callicoon is already in the southern tier of the Catskills; head northeast to access the heart of this mountainous region.

09 Bucks County & Around

From Stroudsburg at the southern end of the Gap, take Rte 33 to historic Bethlehem and a trip with other perspectives on the Delaware.

01 CALLICOON

Callicoon was settled in the 1760s when lumbering was all the rage; the railroad, which still runs through this postage-stamp-sized town (freight only), linked the Great Lakes to the eastern seaboard a century later. Today Callicoon is a mix of year-round residents and second-homers, rural rhythms and independently minded retirees, artists and farmers. Built in the 1940s, you can see a movie at **Callicoon Theater** (callicoontheater.com) in its single-screen cavernous Quonset-hut-style auditorium. Throw in the sophisticated **Callicoon Wine**

BRAD AARON/SHUTTERSTOCK ©

BEST FOR

☑

OUTDOORS
Paddling your
way down the
Delaware.

Canoes, Delaware River, Callicoon

Merchant (callicoonwine merchant.com), several antiques stores, some good restaurants, plus a farmers market on Sundays (11am to 3pm) in the summer, and you might start window-shopping at the local real-estate office.

Rent a canoe or kayak from **Lander's River Trips** (landers rivertrips.com) which has a branch in the Shell gas station at the foot of the bridge, for a relaxing float down the Delaware. You can take out at the Lander's office at Skinners Falls, where there's a little white water and a **campground**. When the water's low, the rocks around Skinners Falls create small pools and eddies – a great place for sunbathing and swimming.

Between Callicoon and Narrowsburg, the river is wide and slow with a few bends and islets of tall grass and flotillas of family and friends on hot days – hop in and cool off.

THE DRIVE
The quick way is Rte 97 south. A scenic alternative is River Rd on the Pennsylvania side of the Delaware – after crossing the bridge in Callicoon, turn left onto a rough dirt road. Just 5.5 miles later at an intersection with the bridge to Cochecton (cuh-SHEK-ton), make a right and then a quick left back onto the paved portion of River Rd.

DETOUR
Where Woodstock Really Happened: Bethel
Start: 01 **Callicoon**

About 13 miles southeast of Callicoon on Rte 17B is Bethel, the site of the former pig farm that for three rainy summer days in 1969 hosted Woodstock, a concert that came to symbolize the dreams and aspirations of an entire generation. These days, it's a bucolic rolling field of green. The **Bethel Woods Center for the Arts** (bethelwoodscenter.org), a state-of-the-art performance and recital center, is designed to be perfectly in harmony with the terrain. As you walk the stone pathways, you can get a bird's-eye view of the gorgeous Pavilion Stage, which has about 50,000 seats set into a sloping lawn, and the outdoor Terrace Stage, which is like a Greek amphitheater set down in a mossy field. Big acts like Joan Baez, Blake Shelton, John Mayer and Yo-Yo Ma perform in the summer.

The jewel of the complex is the museum at the center's entrance, a groovy look back at the tumultuous, spontaneous concert that's come to define the Summer of Love. The captivating multimedia displays use a combination of stock footage, documentaries, retrospectives, letters, books and – above all else – music to capture the all-embracing spirit of the 1960s. A 21-minute film runs every half-hour. You can pick up very undeniably non-freelove, commercialized souvenirs like tie-dyes and key chains emblazoned with a Woodstock logo in the gift shop.

02 NARROWSBURG

Another small, essentially one-street town, Narrowsburg overlooks the deepest (113ft) and widest spot on the Delaware. There's an overlook with excellent views on Main St where you can spot bald eagles soaring overhead.

As you'll soon surmise from the chic, arty shops along and around Main St, Narrowsburg has been adopted by hipster New Yorkers as a weekend destination. Check out the **River Gallery**, a high-end boutique filled with an eclectic mix of oil paintings, handcrafted glassware and other whimsically designed home accessory items; the charming bookstore **One Grand** (onegrand books.com) with Top 10 lists nominated by celebs, movers and

shakers; and **Maison Bergogne** (maisonbergogne.com), a 1920s ivy-covered garage and attached shop packed with antiques, curios and modern-day craft products handpicked from across the Catskills.

North of the town, past Peck's grocery store, is **Fort Delaware Museum** (thedelawarecompany. org), a reconstructed log fort (not a military outpost) from the 1750s, when English settlers and Lenape Indians coexisted in what was then wilderness territory. Interpreters in period dress demonstrate skills such as candle-making, quilting, weaving and food preparation, and will explain how the ABCs were taught in the late 18th century.

RONALDU/SHUTTERSTOCK ©

Raymondskill Falls

THE DRIVE

Heading south on Rte 97, you'll initially head inland before hugging the river all the way to the city of Port Jervis. Stop in the Zane Grey Museum – famous novelist of the American West – in Lackawaxen on the Pennsylvania side if you have time. Milford is 7 miles to the southwest from here.

03 MILFORD

Gifford Pinchot, the first director of the US Forest Service and two-term governor of Pennsylvania, has left his mark on this small town at the northern end of the Delaware Water Gap. Pinchot, who took the position in 1905 with the support of his friend President Roosevelt and was fired five years later by President Taft, oversaw spectacular growth in the number and size of federally managed forests and is widely considered a pioneer of American conservation. From June to the end of October you can take a guided tour of **Grey Towers** (greytowers.org), the gorgeous French-chateau-style home built by Gifford's parents in the 1880s; otherwise, much of the 1600-acre property is open for wandering.

The gray slate and stone of Grey Towers can be seen in other buildings on Main St in Milford, but there's also been something of a resurgence in recent years with a new library and the refurbishing of the old movie theater that hosts the **Black Bear Film Festival** (blackbearfilm.com) every October, featuring independent films with a local focus.

THE DRIVE

It's a simple drive south on Rte 209 to the entrance of the Delaware Water Gap National Recreation Area on the Pennsylvania side.

04 PA SIDE OF THE GAP

River Rd, the 30-mile stretch of good paved road on the Pennsylvania side of the **Delaware Water Gap National Recreation Area** (nps.gov/dewa), includes several worthwhile stops. **Raymondskill Falls** is a stunningly beautiful multi-level cascade and the highest in Pennsylvania; a steep mile-long trail descends to the creek at the bottom. If you want a nearby shortcut over to the Jersey side, the Dingman's Ferry bridge ($1 toll) is your chance.

Otherwise, the Swiss-chalet-style Dingman's Falls Visitor Center is the place to begin a quarter-mile boardwalk trail to the base of the eponymous falls.

The **Pocono Environmental Education Center** (peec.org) offers workshops on fly-fishing, nature photography, birding and other related outdoor skills; five self-guided hiking trails begin from here as well.

Further south, the privately owned and very developed **Bushkill Falls** (visitbushkillfalls.com) encompasses a miniature golf course, ice-cream parlor, gift shop and paddleboat rentals, so it's far from a wilderness experience. Nevertheless, the series of eight falls surrounded by lush forest is undeniably beautiful.

Finally, the hamlet of Shawnee, toward the southern end of the park, has a general store with sandwiches and burgers, and a large resort with a golf course along the river. Nearby **Adventure Sports** (adventuresport.com) is one of a half-dozen companies that rent canoes and kayaks for trips down the river.

 THE DRIVE
To reach Old Mine Rd/Rte 606 on the Jersey side, get on I-80 east and take the exit to your right signposted as Kittatinny Point Visitor Center (closed indefinitely), through an underpass, past a pullout for the Appalachian Trail and back onto I-80 west. Then take exit 1, again on your right, toward Milbrook/Flatbrookville. Just before the river, veer right onto River Rd.

Photo opportunity

Delaware River and Mt Minsi from Mt Tammany.

05 **NJ SIDE OF THE GAP**
Old Mine Rd, one of the oldest continually operating commercial roads in the US, meanders along the eastern side of the Delaware. A few miles inland, a 25-mile stretch of the Appalachian Trail runs along the Kittatinny Ridge. Day hikers can climb to the top of the 1547ft Mt Tammany in **Worthington State Forest** (nj.gov/dep/parksand forests) for great views (the 1.8-mile Blue Dot trail is the easiest route, though it's still strenuous) or walk to the serene-looking glacial Sunfish Pond. Hawks, bald eagles and ravens soar over the hemlock forest.

The recreated site of **Milbrook Village** (nps.gov/dewa), composed of about two-dozen buildings, some original, others moved or built here since the 1970s, is meant to evoke a late-19th-century farming community. From a peak of 75 inhabitants in 1875, by 1950 only a blacksmith remained. On Saturdays and other select days in summer, as well as the first weekend in October during the Milbrook Days

Festival, costumed interpreters perform period skills. Otherwise, it's a picturesque ghost town. A steep wooden stairway takes you to the top of the spectacular **Buttermilk Falls** (nps.gov/dewa), but it's equally impressive from the bottom. It's accessed down a dirt road after turning right after the cemetery in Walpack Center.

 THE DRIVE
Head toward Port Jervis, then take Rte 23 to High Point State Park.

06 **HIGH POINT STATE PARK**
Southeast of Port Jervis, the aptly named **High Point State Park** (nj.gov/dep/parksand forests) has wonderful panoramas of the surrounding lakes, hills and farmland – the Poconos to the west, the Catskills to the north and the Wallkill River Valley to the southeast. A 220ft monument marks the highest point in the park (and in New Jersey) at 1803ft. Trails in the park snake off into the forests and there's a small beach with a lake to cool off in during the summer. If you only have time for one walk, try the 2.3-mile Dryden Kuser National Area interpretive trail through a white cedar bog with a variety of birdlife. In winter months, contact the information center for snowshoe 'tracking' programs where you learn how to search for the snowy footprints of weasels, bobcats and coyotes.

11

BEST FOR

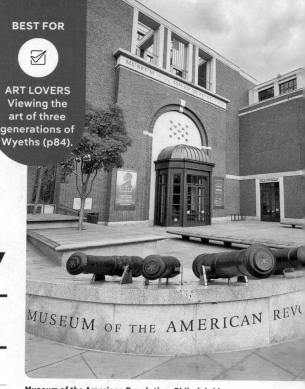

☑

ART LOVERS
Viewing the
art of three
generations of
Wyeths (p84).

Brandywine Valley to Atlantic City

DURATION	DISTANCE	GREAT FOR
4 days	165 miles / 265km	History & Culture, Nature

BEST TIME TO GO	May through October for camping in the Pines.

Museum of the American Revolution, Philadelphia

From the beginnings of American democracy to the height of American aristocracy, from pine forests as far as the eye can see to endless rows of slot machines, this trip covers the gamut. Only a short drive from isolated wilderness, as far from stereotypical Jersey as you get, is Atlantic City, perhaps its epitome. Bone up on the Founding Fathers' principles to grasp these dizzying shifts in culture and landscape.

Link your trip

08 The Jersey Shore

From Atlantic City, you have your pick of shore beaches. Head north or south on the Garden State Pkwy or Rte 9.

09 Bucks County & Around

You're already in Philly, this trip's last stop, so just put it in reverse to explore this scenic stretch of the Delaware.

01 **PHILADELPHIA**
Independence National Historical Park
(nps.gov/inde), along with Old City, has been dubbed 'America's most historic square mile.' Once the backbone of the United States government, it has become the backbone of Philadelphia's tourist trade. Stroll around and you'll see storied buildings in which the seeds for the Revolutionary War were planted and where the US government came into bloom. You'll also find beautiful, shaded urban lawns dotted with plenty of squirrels, pigeons and costumed actors.

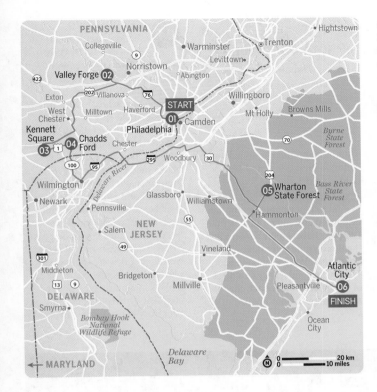

around 12.5 miles until the exit for 202 north toward King of Prussia, then quickly take a right onto US 422 west; the exit for Valley Forge is a few miles further on.

02 VALLEY FORGE

After being defeated at the Battle of Brandywine Creek and the British occupation of Philadelphia in 1777, General Washington and 12,000 continental troops withdrew to Valley Forge. Today, Valley Forge symbolizes Washington's endurance and leadership. The **Valley Forge National Historical Park** (nps.gov/vafo) contains 5.5 sq miles of scenic beauty and open space 20 miles northwest of downtown Philadelphia, a remembrance of where 2000 of George Washington's 12,000 troops perished from freezing temperatures, hunger and disease, while many others returned home. Its wide fields are dotted with soldier's huts and light-blue cannons and, despite the occasional statue of a horse-mounted general, the park has an egalitarian focus.

THE DRIVE

US 202 south/US 322 east passes along the eastern edge of the town of West Chester – the quaint downtown is only a few blocks long and has several good restaurants and cafes. A couple miles further south, make a right on W St Rd/Rte 926 west.

03 KENNETT SQUARE

The small town of Kennett Square, founded in 1705, boasts several art galleries, bistros and cafes, but is generally known for two things: it's the 'mushroom capital' of the US (60% of the nation's mushrooms come from the area); and the

The **Museum of the American Revolution** (amrevmuseum.org) brings the nation's birth to life with a series of stunning exhibits and interactive displays.

Independence Hall (nps.gov/inde) is the 'birthplace of American government,' where delegates from the 13 colonies met to approve the Declaration of Independence on July 4, 1776. An excellent example of Georgian architecture, it sports understated lines that reveal Philadelphia's Quaker heritage.

The **Liberty Bell** (nps.gov/inde) is Philadelphia's top tourist attraction. Made in London and tolled at the first public reading of the Declaration of Independence,

the bell became famous when abolitionists adopted it as a symbol of freedom. The highly recommended **National Constitution Center** (constitutioncenter.org) makes the United States Constitution interesting for a general audience through theater-in-the-round reenactments. There are exhibits including interactive voting booths and Signer's Hall, which contains lifelike bronze statues of the signers in action.

Philly also has a number of elegant squares and attractive streetscapes – perfect for an afternoon stroll.

THE DRIVE

Access I-76 west just over the Schuylkill River and follow it for spectacular **Longwood Gardens** (longwoodgardens.org), only 3 miles to the east. Pierre du Pont, the great-grandson of the DuPont chemical company founder, began designing the property in 1906 with the grand gardens of Europe in mind – especially French and Italian ones. Virtually every inch of the 1050 acres has been carefully sculpted into a display of horticultural magnificence. Whatever your mood, it can't help but be buoyed by the colors of the tulips, which seem too vivid to be real, and the overwhelming variety of species testifying to nature's creativity. With one of the world's largest greenhouses and 11,000 kinds of plants, something is always in bloom. There's also a Children's Garden with a maze, fireworks,

Photo opportunity

Fountain show at Longwood Gardens, Kennett Square.

illuminated fountains, outdoor concerts in summer and festive lights at Christmas.

THE DRIVE

In summer months traffic can be backed up heading east on Rte 1. Midway between the gardens and the Brandywine River Museum is Chaddsford Winery (noon to 6pm Tuesday to Sunday) – grab a glass of vino and an Adirondack chair for a pleasant afternoon break.

04 CHADDS FORD

A showcase of American artwork, the **Brandywine Museum of Art** (brandywine.org/museum), at Chadds Ford, includes the work of the Brandywine School – Howard Pyle, Maxfield Parrish and, of course, three generations of Wyeths (NC, Andrew and Jamie). NC's illustrations for popular books such as *The Last of the Mohicans* and *Treasure Island* are displayed along with rough sketches and finished paintings. One of our favorite paintings by Andrew that's not among his iconic works is Snow Hill, a large canvas that despite the snowy, playful scene somehow manages to evoke menace and a haunted quality. Also check out the backstory behind Jamie's Portrait

Longwood Gardens, Kennett Square

of a Pig and the trompe l'oeil paintings in separate 3rd-floor galleries. The handsome building is a converted mill with pine-wood floors and walls of glass overlooking the slow-moving Brandywine River. **NC's house and studio** are open to the public on guided tours, as are **Andrew's studio** and the **Kuerner Farm**, the noticeable setting for some of Andrew's most famous works. He roamed there every fall and winter for 70 years and found much of his inspiration. Tours of each site cost $8 in addition to museum admission, and can be booked at and leave from the Brandywine River Museum.

THE DRIVE
Only a mile further east on Rte 1 is Brandywine Battlefield State Park; Batsto, in the Wharton State Forest, is about 66 miles further. Take Rte 100 south past lovely rolling hills, then I-95 north to the Commodore Barry Bridge over the Delaware. From here, take I-295 north toward Camden and exit at US 30 east. It's more rural approaching Hammonton, where Rte 206 and Rte 542 lead into the forest.

05 WHARTON STATE FOREST
Your introduction to this region, variously referred to as 'the Pines,' 'the Pinelands,' the 'Pine Barrens' and 'the Pine Belt' (locals are 'Pineys'), is the 12,000-acre Wharton State Forest.

To understand the region's early history, begin at the well-preserved village of **Batsto** (batstovillage.org). Founded in 1766, Batsto forged 'bog iron' for the Revolutionary War and re-mained an important ironworks until the 1850s; a self-guided cell phone audio tour provides

Lake Absegami

BRANCH OUT IN THE PINE BARRENS

The 27,000-acre **Bass River State Forest** (state.nj.us), New Jersey's first state park, typifies the strange character of the Pine Barrens, where it's quite easy to feel as if you're in isolated wilderness, forget-ting there's a major highway within throwing distance. **Lake Absegami**, near the park offices, is packed with swimmers in summer months, but you can escape the crowds on the half-mile interpretive trail on a boardwalk that passes over a section of eerie and mysterious-looking white-cedar bog.

For a short detour when traveling on Rte 539 between Bass River and Brendan T Byrne State Forest, turn onto the ominously named **Bombing Range Rd** – a sign reads '177th FW/DETI Warren Grove Air to Ground Range.' A half-mile on this dirt road provides unobstructed views of the surrounding pygmy forest (mostly dwarf pitch pine trees all the way to the horizon). Oh, and you can't go any further – there's a large gate and fence marking the site where Air National Guard units practice bombing and strafing runs nearby.

New Jersey is one of the largest producers of cultivated blueberries in the US and the world. **Whitesbog** (whitesbog.org), in Brendan T Byrne State Forest – where blueberries were first cultivated – is really nothing more than a ghost town out of blueberry season, but is worth visiting during the annual June festival.

Camping in the Pine Barrens, the most recommended way to experi-ence the true wilderness of the parks, can be 'buggy.' In summer, pre-pare for mosquitoes, strawberry flies, greenheads and other quaintly named biting pests, all of which diminish in spring and fall.

a dry primer on the uses of the various structures. The **visitors center**, also the primary one for Wharton State Forest, has an interesting collection of exhibits dedicated to the economic, cultural and natural history of the Pinelands. Several 1- to 4-mile loop trails start here and pass through scrub oak and pine, swamp maple and Atlantic white cedar, a typical mix found in the forests' woodlands.

The best-known trail is the epic 50-mile **Batona Trail** that cuts through several state parks and forests; look for endangered pitcher plants, which take nutrients they can't get from the soil from hapless insects. Stop and climb the **Apple Pie Hill fire tower** – the Batona Trail passes by it – for magnificent 360-degree views of hundreds of square miles of forests. The climb to the top is completely ex-

posed and the steps and railing feel less than sturdy, so it's not for the acrophobic.

THE DRIVE
From Batsto, it's the AC Expwy all the way for 28 miles.

ATLANTIC CITY
06 It's not exactly Vegas, but for many a trip to Atlantic City conjures *Hangover*-like scenes of debauchery. And inside the casinos that never see the light of day, it's easy to forget there's a sandy beach just outside and boarded-up shop windows a few blocks in the other direction. The AC known throughout the late 19th and early 20th century for its grand boardwalk and oceanside amusement pier, and the glamorously corrupt one of the HBO series *Boardwalk Empire* (set in 1920s Prohibition-era AC), have been thoroughly

overturned. Gray-haired retirees and vacationing families are at least as common as bachelors and bachelorettes.

It's worth noting that AC's famous boardwalk, 8 miles long and still the lifeline of the city, was the first in the world. Built in 1870 by local business owners who wanted to cut down on sand being tracked into hotel lobbies, it was named in honor of Alexander Boardman, who came up with the idea – Boardman's Walk later became 'Boardwalk.'

The **Steel Pier** (steelpier. com), directly in front of the Taj Mahal casino, was the site of the famous high-diving horses that plunged into the Atlantic before crowds of spectators from the 1920s to the '70s. Today it's a collection of amusement rides, games of chance, candy stands and a Go-Kart track.

12

BEST FOR

☑

FOODIES
Almost
everything
here comes in a
buffet.

Pennsylvania Dutch Country

DURATION	DISTANCE	GREAT FOR
3-4 days	102 miles / 164km	Food & Drink, History & Culture

BEST TIME TO GO	Less crowded in early spring or September.

Lancaster

The Amish really do drive buggies and plow their fields by hand. In Dutch Country, the pace is slower, and it's no costumed reenactment. For the most evocative Dutch Country experience, go driving along the winding, narrow lanes between the thruways – past rolling green fields of alfalfa, asparagus and corn, past pungent working barnyards and manicured lawns, waving to Amish families in buggies and straw-hatted teens on scooters.

Link your trip

11 Brandywine Valley to Atlantic City

Take US 30 east to West Chester to begin exploring this trip's gardens and rural byways.

13 Pittsburgh & the Laurel Highlands

I-76 west winds through southern Pennsylvania before beginning a trip with architectural highlights and urban fun.

01 LANCASTER

A good place to start is the walkable, red-brick historic district of Lancaster (LANK-uh-stir), just off Penn Sq. The Romanesque-revival-style **Central Market** (centralmarket lancaster.com), which is like a smaller version of Philadelphia's Reading Terminal Market, has all the regional gastronomic delicacies – fresh horseradish, whoopie pies, soft pretzels, and sub sandwiches stuffed with cured meats and dripping with oil. You'll find surprises, too, such as Spanish and Middle Eastern food. Plus, of course, the market is crowded with handicraft booths staffed by plain-dressed, bonneted Amish women.

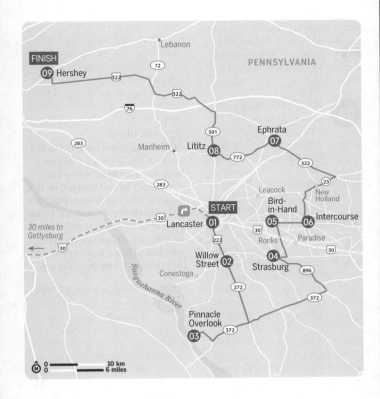

The Amish

The Amish (ah-mish), Mennonite and Brethren religious communities are collectively known as the 'Plain People.' All are Anabaptist sects (only those who choose the faith are baptized) who were persecuted in their native Switzerland, and from the early 1700s settled in tolerant Pennsylvania. Speaking German dialects, they became known as 'Dutch' (from 'Deutsch'). Most Pennsylvania Dutch live on farms and their beliefs vary from sect to sect. Many do not use electricity, and most opt for horse-drawn buggies – a delightful sight, and sound, in the area. The strictest believers, the Old Order Amish who make up nearly 90% of Lancaster County's Amish, wear dark, plain clothing (no zippers, only buttons, snaps and safety pins) and live a simple, Bible-centered life – but have, ironically, become a major tourist attraction, thus bringing busloads of gawkers and the requisite strip malls, chain restaurants and hotels that lend this entire area an oxymoronic quality, to say the least. Because there is so much commercial development continually encroaching on multigenerational family farms, it takes some doing to appreciate the unique nature of the area.

In the 18th century, German immigrants flooded southeastern Pennsylvania, and only some were Amish. Most lived like the costumed docents at the **Landis Valley Museum** (landisvalley museum.org), a recreation of Pennsylvania German village life that includes a working smithy, weavers, stables and more. It's only a few miles north of Lancaster off Rte 272/Oregon Pike.

THE DRIVE

From downtown Lancaster head south on Prince St, which turns into Rte 222 and then Rte 272 all the way to Willow Street.

DETOUR
Gettysburg
Start: 01 Lancaster

Take US 30 west (also referred to as Lincoln Hwy) for 55 miles right into downtown Gettysburg. This tranquil, compact and memorial-laden town saw one of the Civil War's most decisive and bloody battles for three days in July, 1863. It's also where, four months later, Lincoln delivered his Gettysburg Address, consecrating, eulogizing and declaring the mission unfinished. At only 200-plus words, surely it's one of the most defining and effective rhetorical examples in US history. Much of the ground where Robert E Lee's Army of Northern Virginia and Major General Joseph Hooker's Union

Army of the Potomac skirmished and fought can be explored – either on your own, on a bus tour or on a two-hour guide-led tour in your own car. The latter is recommended, but if you're short on time it's still worth driving the narrow lanes past fields with monuments marking significant sites and moments in the battle.

Don't miss the massive **Gettysburg National Military Park Museum & Visitor Center** (nps.gov/gett) several miles south of town, which houses a fairly incredible museum filled with artifacts and displays exploring every nuance of the battle; a film explaining Gettysburg's context and why it's considered a turning point in the war; and Paul Philippoteaux's 377ft cyclorama painting of Pickett's Charge. The aforementioned bus tours and ranger-led tours are booked here. While overwhelming, at the very least, it's a foundation for understanding the Civil War's primacy and lingering impact in the nation's evolution.

The annual Civil War Heritage Days festival, taking place from the last weekend of June through the first weekend of July, features living history encampments, battle reenactments, a lecture series and book fair that draws war reenactment aficionados from near and wide. You can find reenactments at other times throughout the year as well.

 02 WILLOW STREET

Before the arrival of European emigres, Coney, Lenape, Mohawk, Seneca and other Native Americans lived in the area. However, Pennsylvania remains one of the few states with no officially recognized tribal reserves – or, for that matter, tribes. In something of a gesture to rectify their erasure from history, a replica longhouse now stands on the property of the **1719 Hans Herr House** (hansherr.org), generally regarded as the oldest original Mennonite meeting house in the western hemisphere and where the Herr family settled. Today, Hans Herr House displays colonial-era artifacts in period furnished rooms; there's also a blacksmith shop and a barn. 'Living history interpreters' provide an idea of how life was lived in the 18th century.

The interior of the longhouse, a typical narrow, single room multi-family home built only from natural materials, is divided into pre- and post-European contact sides and decorated and furnished with artifacts typical of each era. The primary mission, which is done quite well, is to teach visitors about the history of Native American life in Lancaster County from around 1570 to 1770 when, for all intents and purposes, they ceased to exist as distinctive groups in the area. And this includes the infamous Conestoga Massacre of 1763 when vigilante colonists from Paxton (given the curiously anodyne epithet the 'Paxton Boys') murdered 20 Native American men, women and children from the settlement of Conestoga. A guided tour of both the Hans Herr House and the longhouse makes for an interesting juxtaposition of historical perspectives.

 THE DRIVE

The simplest route is Rte 272 south to Rte 372 west. If you have time, however, head west on W Penn Grant Rd and then left on New Danville Pike, which turns into Main St in Conestoga. From there, follow Main St to a T-junction and turn left on River Rd, a backcountry road with lots of turns, passing Tucquan Glen Nature Preserve on the way.

03 PINNACLE OVERLOOK

High over Lake Aldred, a wide portion of the Susquehanna River just up from a large dam, is this overlook (8am to 9pm) with beautiful views, and eagles and other raptors soaring overhead. This and the adjoining Holtwood Environmental Preserve are parts of a large swath of riverfront property maintained by the Pennsylvania Power & Light Co. But electrical plant infrastructure and accompanying truck traffic is largely kept at bay, making this a popular spot for locals, non-Amish, that is (it's too far to travel by horse and buggy). The 4-mile-long Fire Line Trail to the adjoining Kelly's Run Natural Area is challenging and steep in parts and the rugged Conestoga Trail follows the east side of the lake for 15 miles. It's worth coming out this way if only to see more rough-hewn landscape and the rural byways that reveal another facet to Lancaster County's character, which most visitors bypass.

LEE SNIDER PHOTO IMAGES/SHUTTERSTOCK ©

1719 Hans Herr House, Willow Street

THE DRIVE
You could retrace your route back to Willow Street and then head on to Strasburg, but to make a scenic loop, take Rte 372 east, passing some agrarian scenes as well as suburban housing, to the small hamlet of Georgetown. Make a left onto Rte 896 – vistas open up on either side of the road

04 STRASBURG
The main attraction in Strasburg is trains – the old-fashioned, steam-driven kind. Since 1832 the **Strasburg Railroad** (strasburgrailroad. com) has run the same route (and speed) to Paradise and back that it does today, and wooden train cars are gorgeously restored with stained glass, shiny brass lamps and plush burgundy seats. Several classes of seats are offered, including the private President's Car; there's also a wine-and-cheese option.

The **Railroad Museum of Pennsylvania** (rrmuseumpa. org) has 100 gigantic mechanical marvels to climb around and admire, but even more delightful is the HO-scale **National Toy Train Museum** (tcatrains.org/ museum). The push-button interactive dioramas are so up-to-date and clever (such as a 'drive-in movie' that's a live video of kids working the trains), and the walls are packed with so many gleaming railcars, that you can't help but feel a bit of that childlike Christmas-morning wonder. Stop at the Red Caboose Motel (red caboosemotel.com) next to the museum – you can climb the silo in back for wonderful views (50c), and kids can enjoy a petting zoo.

THE DRIVE
Continue north on S Ronks Rd past Ronks' bucolic farmland scenery, cross busy Rte 30 (Miller's Smorgasbord restaurant is at this intersection) and carry on for another 2 miles to Bird-in-Hand.

05 BIRD-IN-HAND
The primary reason to make your way to this delightfully named Amish town is the **Bird-in-Hand Farmers Market** (birdinhandfarmers market.com), which is pretty much a one-stop shop of Dutch Country highlights. There's fudge, quilts and crafts, and you can

buy scrapple (pork scraps mixed with cornmeal and wheat flour, shaped into a loaf and fried), homemade jam and shoo-fly pie (a pie made of molasses or brown sugar sprinkled with a crumbly mix of brown sugar, flour and butter). Two lunch counters sell sandwiches, pretzels and juices and smoothies: stock up for the onward drive.

THE DRIVE
It's less than 4 miles east on Old Philadelphia Pike/Rte 340, but traffic can back up, in part because it's a popular route for horse-and-buggy rides.

06 INTERCOURSE
Named for the crossroads, not the act, Intercourse is a little more amenable to walking than Bird-in-Hand.

Photo opportunity
A windmill or grain silo with a horse-drawn plow in the foreground.

The **horse-drawn buggy rides** (amishbuggyrides.com) on offer can also be fun. How much fun depends largely on your driver: some Amish are strict, some liberal, and Mennonites are different again. All drivers strive to present Amish culture to the 'English' (the Amish term for non-Amish, whether English or not), but some are more openly personal than others.

Kitchen Kettle Village, essentially an open-air mall for tourists with stores selling smoked meats, jams, pretzels, gifts and tchotchkes, feels like a Disneyfied version of the Bird-in-the-Hand Farmers Market. It's a one-stop shop for the commercialized 'PA Dutch Country experience,' which means your perception of it will depend on your attitude toward a parking lot jammed with tour buses.

THE DRIVE
Head north on Rte 772 and make your first right onto Centerville Rd (which becomes S Shirk Rd), a country lane that takes you to Rte 23. Turn right here and it's a few miles to Blue Ball (try not to giggle that you're so close to Intercourse) – and then left on the busier Rte 322 all the way to Ephrata.

ZACK FRANK/SHUTTERSTOCK ©

Ephrata Cloister, Ephrata

EPHRATA

07 One of the country's earliest religious communities was founded in 1732 by Conrad Beissel, an emigre escaping religious persecution in his native Germany. Beissel, like others throughout human history dissatisfied with worldly ways and distractions (difficult to imagine what these were in his pre-digital age), sought a mystical, personal relationship with God. At its peak there were close to 300 members, including two celibate orders of brothers and sisters, known collectively as 'the Solitary,' who patterned their dress after Roman Catholic monks (the last of these passed away in 1813), as well as married 'households' who were less all-in, if you will.

Today, the collection of austere, almost medieval-style buildings of the **Ephrata Cloister** (ephrata cloister.org) have been preserved and are open to visitors; guided tours are offered or take an audio cell phone tour on your own. There's a small museum and a short film in the visitor center that very earnestly and efficiently tells the story of Ephrata's founding and demise – if the narrator's tone and rather somber mise-en-scène are any indication, not to mention the extremely spartan sleeping quarters, it was a demanding existence. No doubt Beissel would disapprove of today's Ephrata, the commercial Main St of which is anchored by a Walmart.

If you're around on a Friday, be sure to check out the **Green Dragon Farmers Market** (greendragonmarket.com).

🚗 THE DRIVE
This is a simple 8.5-mile drive; for the most part, Rte 772/Rothsville Rd between Ephrata and Lititz is an ordinary commercial strip.

LITITZ

08 Like other towns in Pennsylvania Dutch Country, Lititz was founded by a religious community from Europe, in this case Moravians who settled here in the 1740s. However, unlike Ephrata, Lititz was more outward looking and integrated with the world beyond its historic center. Many of its original handsome stone and wood buildings still line its streets today. Take a stroll down E Main from the **Sturgis Pretzel House** (juliussturgis. com), the first pretzel factory in the country – you can try your hand at rolling and twisting the dough. Across the street is the Moravian Church (c 1787); then head to the intersection with S Broad.

Rather than feeling sealed in amber, the small shops, which do seem to relish their small-town quality, are nonetheless the type that sophisticated urbanites cherish. There's an unusual effortlessness to this vibe, from the Bulls Head Public House, a traditional English-style pub with an expertly curated beer menu, to Greco's

Italian Ices, a little ground-floor hole-in-the-wall where local teenagers and families head on weekend nights for delicious homemade ice cream.

🚗 THE DRIVE
It's an easy 27 miles on Rte 501 to US 322. Both pass through a combination of farmland and suburban areas, though the latter is generally a fast-moving highway.

HERSHEY

09 Hershey is home to a collection of attractions that detail, hype and, of course, hawk the many trappings of Milton Hershey's chocolate empire. The pièce de résistance is **Hershey Park** (hersheypark.com), an amusement park with more than 60 thrill rides, a zoo and a water park. Don a hairnet and apron and punch in a few choices on a computer screen and then voilà, watch your very own chocolate bar roll down a conveyor belt at the Create Your Own Candy Bar attraction, part of Hershey's Chocolate World, a mock factory and massive candy store with overstimulating features such as singing characters and free chocolate galore.

For a more low-key informative visit, try the **Hershey Story, The Museum on Chocolate Avenue**, which explores the life and fascinating legacy of Mr Hershey through interactive history exhibits; try molding your own candy in the hands-on Chocolate Lab.

13

Pittsburgh & the Laurel Highlands

BEST FOR

☑

ARCHITECTURE
Tour two
Frank Lloyd
Wright homes
and sleep in
another in a
single day.

DURATION	DISTANCE	GREAT FOR
3-4 days	104 miles / 167km	Nature, History & Culture

BEST TIME TO GO	April to November for snow-free outdoor activities.

Ohiopyle State Park (p96)

Most people forget that the British, French and their Native American allies once struggled for control of this southwestern corner of Pennsylvania. The fate of empires hung in the balance in the 1750s, when it was primarily a rugged wilderness. The forested landscape remains – less wild, of course, but a scenic backdrop nevertheless. And Pittsburgh, its skyscrapers nestled in a compact downtown, provides a civilizing influence.

Link your trip

14 Through the Wilds Along Route 6

From Pittsburgh, take I-79 north to explore small towns and the forested northern tier.

12 Pennsylvania Dutch Country

Follow the PA Turnpike (I-76) south and east, or the Lincoln Hwy/Rte30 for a slower, more scenic route to a compact patchwork of Amish farms.

01 LIGONIER

Compared to the Revolutionary War and the Civil War, the French and Indian War, oft referred to as the 'first world war' and known as the Seven Years' War in Europe, is less indelibly stamped as a turning point in America's national narrative. The excellent **Fort Ligonier** (fortligonier.org), both a museum and a reconstructed fort with enthusiastic and knowledgeable historical interpreters, helps correct this oversight, providing an overview of this war over territory and its significance, both in America and elsewhere.

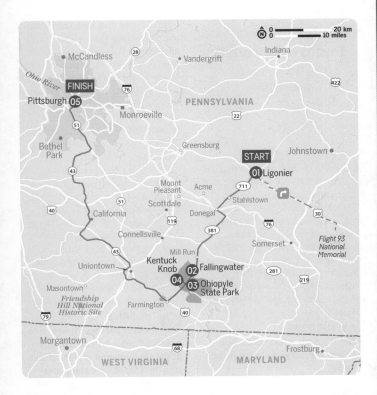

In the fall of 1758, when nearly 5400 soldiers manned the fort, it was the second most populated place in Pennsylvania outside of Philadelphia. It takes a leap of imagination today to picture this otherwise ordinary spot, at a relatively busy intersection surrounded by small homes, as a valuable frontier outpost in a clash of empires.

Brigadier General John Forbes meant for Ligonier to be the final link in a chain of fortifications built across Pennsylvania and the staging post for an attack on the French at Fort Duquesne (today the site of Point State Park in Pittsburgh). Artifacts include one of the few intact British red coat uniforms and George Washing-ton's saddle pistols, once owned by General Andrew Jackson. Battle reenactments are held twice a year.

THE DRIVE
It's a pretty 12.5-mile drive on Rte 711 south to Donegal and the unsightly PA Turnpike. The overpass will take you to Rte 31 east, where you quickly come to the Fire Cafe and Old General Store, two good places to stop for a bite to eat. Take Rte 381 south the rest of the way.

DETOUR
Flight 93
Start: 01 Ligonier

If you're driving between the Laurel Highlands and Gettysburg or PA Dutch Country further east, you might want to pay your respects to the 40 passengers

Wright-eous Accommodation

There's a frisson of excitement when you're sleeping in a house designed by a world-famous architect, in this case Frank Lloyd Wright. Part of Polymath Park, a wooded property with three other homes designed by Wright apprentices, **Duncan House** (franklloydwrightover night.net) was taken apart piece by piece from its original site in Illinois, transported in four trailers 600 miles to Johnstown, PA, and put back together before finally finding its way here and opening to the public in 2007. Don't expect Wright pyrotechnics – the house is a modest Usonia-style design built for just $7000 in 1957. None of the furniture or interior pieces were designed by Wright, but are rather standard mid-century modern furnishings.

If you plan to stay at Duncan House while you're on this road trip, you can access it during the drive from Ligonier to Fallingwater. After heading south from Ligonier for 8.5 miles, make a right onto Rte 130 heading west for 3 miles. Then make a left onto Ridge Rd, which turns into Evergreen Rd a little less than 2 miles later. A half-mile further along you come to Treetops Restaurant where you can check in.

and crew who struggled to retake control of their plane from hijackers on September 11, 2001. The **Flight 93 National Memorial** (nps.gov/flni), about 28 miles southeast of Ligonier on Lincoln Hwy/Rte 30, marks the crash site in a field in rural Somerset Country, only 18 minutes of flying time from the hijackers' intended target, Washington, DC. It's a solemn site with the names of the dead carved on a marble wall aligned in the direction of the flight path leading to a fence, beyond which is their final resting place.

02 FALLINGWATER

A Frank Lloyd Wright masterpiece and a National Historic Landmark, **Fallingwater** (fallingwater. org) looks like an architectural fantasy. Completed in 1938 (when Pittsburgh was called the 'Smoky City') as a weekend retreat for the Kaufmanns, owners of the Pittsburgh department store, the project was extremely over budget at a total of $155,000, though Wright's commission was only $8000 (to give a sense of building costs at the time, master masons working on the home earned around 85¢ an hour). Photos can't do it justice – nor can they transmit the sounds of Fallingwater – and you'll likely need a return visit or two to really appreciate Wright's ingenuity and aesthetic vision.

To see inside you must take one of the hourly guided tours (these began in 1964); during busy times tours leave nearly every six minutes, and reservations several months in advance are highly recommended. The earlier in the morning the better, otherwise it can feel crowded; however, unlike tours of other similar sights, there are no velvet ropes. A two-hour

Photo opportunity

Fallingwater from the waterfall side.

tour with photography permitted is offered. The 2000 acres of attractive forested grounds can also be explored, and the charming cafe serves seasonally inspired salads and sandwiches made from locally sourced ingredients. Pick up Neil Levine's *The Architecture of Frank Lloyd Wright* either in the gift shop or before a visit for an excellent overview of Wright's career.

THE DRIVE

It's a quick and simple hop to Ohiopyle, only 4 miles south on Rte 381.

03 OHIOPYLE STATE PARK

During the off-season no more than 70 people call Ohiopyle, a postage-stamp-sized riverside and falls-side hamlet, home. But from the end of May to the beginning of September, this gateway to the 20,000-acre state park of the same name swells with visitors. Most come looking to run the rapids on the Youghiogheny River (locals simply say 'the Yough,' pronounced 'yawk') with one of four well-equipped operators in town, including the highly recommended **Laurel Highlands River Tours** (laurel highlands.com). Families and beginners run the middle Yough, while the lower Yough has class III and IV whitewater. But for those who find rafting too tame,

kayak clinics and rock climbing are offered. Or take a walk on the nearby Ferncliff Peninsula or the Backman trail, which starts in town and heads up to an overlook. There's a swimming beach at a dam on the Yough 12 miles to the south and an extensive network of cross-country skiing trails for the snowbound winter months.

The town's farmers market, coffee shop, ice-cream parlor, restaurants, bar and handful of guesthouses are even busier in the summer now that the Great Allegheny Passage, a bike path running from Washington, DC, to Pittsburgh has finally reached Ohiopyle, and a new visitors center and viewing spot offers insights into the area attractions.

THE DRIVE

It's only another 3 miles on to Kentuck Knob – cross the bridge at the southern end of Main St and turn right to take the steep and winding Chalk Hill/Ohiopyle Rd to the top. One more left on Kentuck Rd and you're there.

04 KENTUCK KNOB

Less well known than Fallingwater, **Kentuck Knob** (kentuckknob.com), another Frank Lloyd Wright home, is built into the side of a rolling hill with stunning panoramic views. It was completed in 1956 for $82,000 for the Hagan family, friends of the Kaufmanns and owners of an ice-cream manufacturing company, who lived here full time for 28 years. It was purchased by Peter Palumbo (aka Lord Palumbo) in 1986 for $600,000 and opened to the public a decade later – Wright himself never saw the house in its finished state. In general, it's a

cozier, more family-friendly and modest application of Wright's genius than the site at Fallingwater.

Of a comparably small scale and with a fairly plain exterior typical of Wright's Usonian style (which stands for United States of North America), the obsessively designed interior – note the hexagonal design and honey-comb skylights – and creative attention applied to the most trivial detail is singularly Wright. Every nook and cranny of the 22,000 sq ft home balances form and function, especially Wright's signature built-ins, such as the room-length couch and cabinets. While incredibly impressive and inspiring, a visit might lead to a little dispiriting self-reflection upon comparison to one's own living

situation: matching towels to a shower curtain no longer seems like much of an achievement.

House tours last about 45 minutes and you can return to the visitor center, with a small shop and cafe, via a wooded path and a sculpture garden with works by Andy Goldsworthy, Ray Smith and others.

🏎 THE DRIVE

US 40 east, part of the historic National Road, passes by Farmington, Fort Necessity National Battlefield and, soon after, Christian W Klay Winery, the highest mountaintop vineyard east of the Rockies. Carry on down the mountain and around the city of Uniontown to Rte 43 north before merging with Rte 51 north to Pittsburgh to complete this 71-mile leg.

05 PITTSBURGH

Scottish-born immigrant Andrew Carnegie made his fortune here by modernizing steel production, and his legacy is still synonymous with the city and its many cultural and educational institutions. However, the city's industrial buildings are now more likely to house residential lofts and film production studios, and the city's abundant greenery, museums and sports teams have long since supplanted the image of billowing smokestacks.

Pittsburghers are proudly over-the-top obsessive fans of their hometown sports teams – the Steelers (football), Penguins (hockey) and Pirates (baseball). PNC Park is also a good place to start a city walking tour.

Pennsylvania Macaroni Co, Pittsburgh

For a taste of the city's ethnic texture, head to the **Strip District** just east of downtown, stretching from 14th to 30th St between the Allegheny River and Liberty Ave. Stroll along Penn Ave from 17th to 23rd; it's the city's bustling heart, where one-of-a-kind food markets such as **Stamoolis Brothers** (stamoolis.com), **Pennsylvania Macaroni Co** (pennmac.com) and **Wholey** (wholey.com) have been selling goods in bulk as well as retail with a heaping of pride and character for the past 100 years. Between 10am and 3pm is the best time to visit; during the holiday season (when parking is close to impossible), it's especially celebratory and intoxicating, literally, as homemade wine is typically passed out for free.

The historic **funicular railroads** (duquesneincline.org), circa 1877, that run up and down Mt Washington's steep slopes afford great city views, especially at night. At the start of the Monongahela Incline is Station Square, a group of beautiful, renovated railway buildings that now comprise what is essentially a big ol' mall with restaurants and bars.

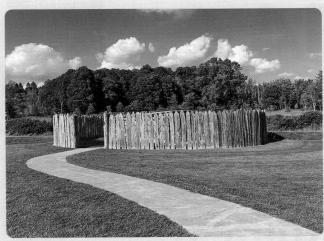

Fort Necessity

WHEN HISTORY TURNED IN THE HIGHLANDS

George Washington surrendered once: on July 3, 1754, at **Fort Necessity** (nps.gov/fone) when he was a 22-year-old colonel. Burned to the ground, the small and rudimentary fort was reconstructed in the 1930s. An excellent visitor center run by the NPS explains the significance of the battle and the war, as does the museum at Fort Ligonier (p94).

A year later and only 2 miles northwest of the fort, Washington officiated at the burial of Major General Edward Braddock, the commander in chief of all British forces in North America and the man responsible for blasting through the forests leading to the major French outpost at Fort Duquesne (now Point State Park in Pittsburgh). Much of Braddock's road eventually became part of the **National Road**, the first federally financed highway and the busiest in America in the early 1800s. A 90-mile corridor of today's Rte 40 follows the general route of the National Road, which originally led from Maryland to Illinois and was the primary thoroughfare for Americans making their way to the western frontier. Alas, new technology brought change and when the first locomotive-powered train reached the Ohio Valley in 1853, the road's demise began in earnest.

In a curious historical coda, Thomas Edison, Henry Ford and Harvey Firestone – friends and business partners – hopped in their Ford motorcars in 1921 to explore the area along **Rte 40** (primarily western Maryland, but they did make it to the Summit Inn in Uniontown, PA). Calling themselves 'vagabonds,' they spent two weeks every summer from 1915 to 1925 exploring the country, preferring dirt roads like Rte 40 to their paved counterparts. Historians point to their trips as the first to famously link camping, cars and the outdoors, and to perhaps popularize and promote the idea of the road trip.

14

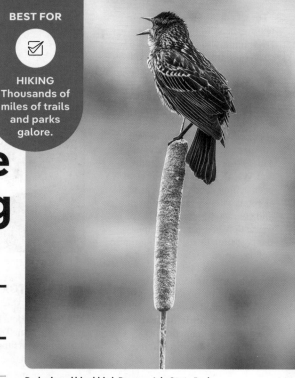

HIKING
Thousands of miles of trails and parks galore.

Through the Wilds Along Route 6

DURATION	DISTANCE	GREAT FOR
4 days	223 miles / 359km	Nature

BEST TIME TO GO	Fall foliage season is mid-September to October.

Red-winged blackbird, Presque Isle State Park

Interspersed throughout this rural region are regal buildings and grand mansions, remnants of a time when lumber, coal and oil brought great wealth and the world's attention to this corner of Pennsylvania. Several museums tell the boom and bust industrial story. But natural resources of another kind remain – known as 'the Wilds,' roads and hundreds of miles of trails snake through vast national forests and state parks.

Link your trip

04 Finger Lakes Loop

It's less than an hour north on Rte 15 from Wellsboro, PA, to Corning, NY, the southern end of a tour to beautiful lakeside wineries.

13 PITTSBURGH & THE LAUREL HIGHLANDS

From Cambridge Springs, it's less than two hours south on I-79 to Pittsburgh and the highlands.

01 PRESQUE ISLE STATE PARK

Jutting out from the city of Erie into the lake of the same name, **Presque Isle State Park** (dcnr.pa.gov) shoots north and then curves back upon itself like Cape Cod in Massachusetts. A slow crawl on the 13-mile loop road that circumnavigates the sandy peninsula takes you to windswept swimming beaches and walking and biking trails that lead past ponds and wooded areas. In warm weather, the picnic areas get crowded and cyclists, runners and inline skaters compete for space. The modern and

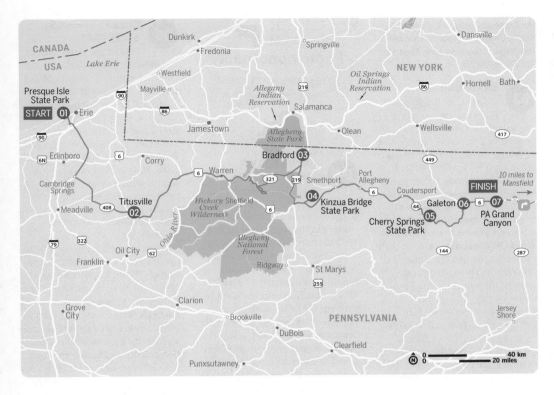

comprehensive **Tom Ridge Environmental Center** (trecf.org), on the mainland side just before the park entrance and across the street from an amusement park, pretty much covers everything you'd want to know about the park, with interactive exhibits for kids. Things pretty much shut down from November to January when snow squalls and cold air blanket the region.

🚗 THE DRIVE
On US 19 it's 27 miles from Erie and the park to the old resort town of Cambridge Springs. Continue another 27 miles to Titusville on the fairly flat and rural Rte 408 east past farms and patches of forest.

02 TITUSVILLE
Before there was oil, coal and timber (with a boost from railroads) fueled Pennsylvania's economy. But even before Edwin Drake's eureka moment in August 1859 (after many failed attempts) when he invented a new method of drilling for oil without collapsing the hole, oil had been seeping from the ground reportedly for centuries. After that first year, wells were producing 4500 barrels. Only three years later the total was three million. And 10 years later kerosene was the nation's fuel. When Edison electrified part of lower Manhattan in 1882, kerosene's relevance was threatened, but along came the automobile and once again gas was king.

To get a sense of this chapter in Pennsylvania's history, head to the **Drake Well Museum** (drakewell.org), which has a replica of Drake's engine house, working antique machinery, a large gallery of exhibits and even an olfactory challenge asking you to smell oil from around the world. Learn about the local boomtowns that drew more migrants than California's gold rush and how Drake never capitalized on his invention and died virtually broke.

🚗 THE DRIVE
Leave Titusville on Rte 27 heading east, then take the junction to the left onto Enterprise-Titusville Rd for 3.5 miles before hooking up again with Rte 27 heading north. Connect with Rte 6 east and then to Rte 59 closer to

the Allegheny Reservoir. Views from Kinzua Creek's high plateau are worth the detour, if you have time. Then it's Rte 770 to Rte 219.

 03 BRADFORD

Evidence of Bradford's glory days when oil barons called the town home can still be seen in a handful of impressive buildings on Main St. Otherwise, downtown feels neglected and vacant, highlighting the disparity between the present and the past, when this small corner of northwestern Pennsylvania was an economic powerhouse. The **Penn Brad Oil Museum** (penn-bradoilmuseum.org), like the Drake Well Museum in Titusville, tells the story of the world's first billion-dollar oil field and includes a 'model home' of an oil field worker and an 80ft-tall working rig typical of the boom time in the late 1800s. Perhaps unsurprisingly, the museum comes off as something of an oil-industry booster, even a promoter, of today's controversial method of fracking, which has unlocked the region's vast natural gas deposits in the Marcellus Shale – at what cost, is the question. If you were to continue driving on Rte 6 all the way east to the Poconos, you'd notice the enormous infrastructure supplying fracking's boom – trucks, equipment suppliers etc – is the most striking new feature of the landscape.

 THE DRIVE

Rte 219 south takes you all the way back to Rte 6 at Lantz Corners, where you head east to Mt Jewett on this 28-mile drive.

Photo opportunity

Gorge views from Leonard Harrison State Park.

 04 KINZUA BRIDGE STATE PARK

The Kinzua railroad viaduct, once the highest and one of the longest railroad suspension bridges in the world, was built in 1882 to transport coal across the valley to customers to the north. In 2003, as it was undergoing repairs to reinforce its deteriorating structure, a tornado swept through the valley destroying a portion of the bridge. After finally being decommissioned, it was re-opened as a 'skywalk' in 2011 and it and the surrounding 329 acres became the **Kinzua Bridge State Park** (visitpaparks.com). The remaining six towers now carry people instead of trains 600ft out to where the viaduct dead-ends in an overlook – a small section here has a glass floor so you can see directly to the valley floor 225ft below.

THE DRIVE

Head through Smethport toward Port Allegheny on this 59-mile drive. After Port Allegheny, Rte 6 follows the Allegheny River, but further east it narrows into a stream. Several miles after Coudersport (that garish gold-colored behemoth on Main St is the former headquarters of cable giant Adelphia Communications Co), make a right onto Rte 44 south.

05 CHERRY SPRINGS STATE PARK

Ponder the immensity of the universe at this dark-sky park, considered one of the best places for stargazing east of the Mississippi. **Cherry Springs** (dcnr.pa.gov) is one of only five parks in the country (the others are in Big Bend, TX; Death Valley, CA; Natural Bridges, UT; and Clayton Lake, NM) to have received the highest rating or certification by the organization in charge of these sorts of things – the International Dark Sky Association (darksky.org).

Essentially two large open fields, one a former runway, at an elevation of 2300ft, Cherry Springs is blessed to be surrounded by the hills of the 410-sq-mile Susquehannock State Forest that tend to block any artificial light. The area also has an extremely low population density. Beginning about an hour after sunset on Friday and Saturday nights from Memorial Day to Labor Day (Saturdays only from mid-April to the end of May and September to the end of October), the park hosts free laser-guided and telescope-assisted tours of the constellations. Crowds of several hundred people are common on clear nights in July and August when the Milky Way is almost directly overhead.

THE DRIVE

Take Rte 44 south to Rte 144 north to Galeton. Both roads twist and turn down the mountain until Rte 144 levels out near Rte 6.

EW/SHUTTERSTOCK ©

Pine Creek Gorge (PA Grand Canyon)

06 **GALETON**
Looking out from any vista in the area, it's difficult to imagine that Galeton was once almost completely denuded of trees, logged until hardly any were left standing. Until the early 1800s only the Seneca and other Native Americans encountered these dense woods, but at the turn of the last century the lumber industry arrived, scraping the land bare but also bringing prosperity and employment. The men who worked in the camps were called 'wood hicks.' Springtime melt meant water was plentiful to float log rafts, white pine and hemlock primarily, to lumber mills along the Susquehanna River.

The **Pennsylvania Lumber Museum** (lumbermuseum.org) includes a recreated lumber camp typical of the late 1800s, two large locomotives housed in a saw mill, and a modernized visitor center with exhibits on the history of our relationship with forests. Logging companies are still active in the northern tier, but are subject to regulations to keep deforestation at bay. Wildlife such as deer, beaver, elk and river otters were slowly reintroduced throughout the 20th century. Consider a visit during the annual **Bark Peeler's Festival** (first week in July), an Olympics for lumberjacks with events such as grease pole fighting, sawing, burling (running on a log in a pond) and the more

tongue-in-cheek tobacco spitting and frog jumping. Coming immediately after Galeton's large 4th of July celebration, accommodation is extremely tight.

THE DRIVE
Head east on Rte 6 and hang a right onto Colton Rd just before the Ansonia cemetery; a sign for Colton Point State Park marks the turn. It's another 5 miles up a narrow and winding paved road until you reach the overlook.

07 **PA GRAND CANYON**
Two state parks on either side of the 47-mile-long **Pine Creek Gorge** make up what's commonly referred to as the 'PA Grand Canyon.' Access to the west rim of the canyon

is from Colton Point State Park (dcnr.pa.gov/stateparks/), which has several viewpoints and camping grounds, and trails into the forest of maple, oak, poplar, aspen and beech trees. The more visited and developed **Leonard Harrison State Park** (dcnr. pa.gov/stateparks) on the east rim has possibly better, fuller views of the 800ft canyon (it's 1450ft at its deepest) and Tioga State Forest beyond. It's a trade-off, however, since it has a paved plaza with steps down to an observation area and there's a gift shop next to the park office.

The way out here is via a turnoff on Rte 6 not far past the one for the Colton Point side. Eventually, you take Rte 660 west past some suburban-style homes and pretty farmland. Both parks have a trail called the Turkey Path that descends to the canyon floor – it's a tough 3-mile round-trip on the Colton Point Side, but you can catch your breath with a stop at a 70ft waterfall.

If you want to explore the east rim of the canyon one day and the west rim the next, consider staying overnight in nearby Wellsboro – it's just 10 miles east from the canyon on Rte 660.

DETOUR
Mansfield
Start: 07 **PA Grand Canyon**

Well worth detouring for, the **Night & Day Coffee Cafe** (facebook.com/nightanddaycoffee) in the small college town of Mansfield proudly claims to be enriching the neighborhood one latte at a time, and it's doing a good job of it. Boutique coffees, great chai, and a wide selection of specialty salads and sandwiches make for a perfect breakfast or a great lunch.

Also a welcome alternative to standard diner food in this area is **Yorkholo Brewing** (yorkholobrewing.com), a brick-walled brewpub with fresh salads, bacon-wrapped scallops, creative pizzas and some excellent Belgian-style beers. Mansfield is roughly a 27-mile drive east from Leonard Harrison State Park along PA-362 then Rte 6.

Calvert Cliffs State Park (p112)

Washington, DC, Maryland & Delaware

Explore

Washington, DC, Maryland & Delaware

A vibrant collision of history, culture and politics, Washington, DC, exudes a unique charisma. Those drawn here tend to be young, engaged and ambitious, but the allure of America's capital extends to neighbors Maryland and Delaware – which look immensely appealing after battling DC traffic. Maryland's unofficial motto for years has been 'America in Miniature,' and with boundaries stretching from the foothills of the Appalachians to the sandy beaches of the Atlantic, the moniker fits. Delaware is the second-smallest state, but it packs a memorable punch with its fun-loving beach towns and cute villages. One regional must-do? Cracking into steamed crabs by the water.

Washington, DC

With world-class museums and superlative monuments lining the National Mall, the nation's capital is an inspirational launchpad well worth exploring for a day or two during a regional road trip. Amtrak trains from across the country stop at Union Station near the Capitol, and two international airports serve the city. Check out the Declaration of Independence at the National Archives, then tour the Capitol. Leafy cobblestone neighborhoods dot the city and welcome visitors with a multicultural array of restaurants.

Baltimore

A waterfront city with working class roots, Baltimore is earning newfound kudos for recent entrepreneurial ventures,
from boutique hotels to older neighborhoods reinvigorated by new food courts. Fells Point and its cobblestone streets are a good base, with an abundance of independent restaurants, lively bars and charismatic lodging options. Tourist hotspots like the National Aquarium bring crowds to the Inner Harbor area, but it's the smaller museums scattered across the city that really shine, from the Walters Art Museum to the American Visionary Art Museum.

Annapolis

Overlooking the Chesapeake Bay, Annapolis has a sunny, waterfront joie de vivre that makes it an attractive overnight stop on any road trip. The city is Maryland's state capital, and its colonial-era downtown is a

WHEN TO GO

Summer (June through August) is high season across the region, with families exploring DC and hitting the beaches. Expect warm, sunny days but higher prices for lodging. Wildflowers in spring and colorful foliage in fall keep the shoulder seasons busy in the mountain foothills of western Maryland. Many attractions, particularly along the coast, keep shorter hours in winter (November through March).

warren of brick row houses, cobblestones and flickering lamps. Annapolis is home to the US Naval Academy, and sailing is a way of life. Numerous inns and good restaurants line the waterfront and surrounding streets.

Frederick

Culture and history convene pleasantly in Frederick, a small city in western Maryland that is a convenient base for exploring Civil War battlefields. It's also close to scenic attractions along the Potomac River, including the C&O Canal towpath and the Appalachian Trail. Red-brick row houses, occupied by indie restaurants and small museums, fill the pedestrian-friendly downtown. Pretty Carroll Creek runs beside it all, flanked by a park filled with art and gardens.

Rehoboth Beach

Rehoboth Ave and the boardwalk are the center of the action in this seaside Delaware town that is family friendly and gay friendly – and a very popular destination in summer. The closest beach to Washington, DC, it's been dubbed 'the nation's summer capital.' Numerous hotels and restaurants line Rehoboth Ave and nearby streets.

TRANSPORT

International airports in the region include Washington Dulles International, Ronald Reagan Washington National Airport and Baltimore/Washington International Thurgood Marshall Airport. Amtrak trains and numerous buses link to Union Station, a huge transportation hub near the capitol. Amtrak's Northeast Regional route connects DC with Baltimore, Wilmington, DE, and numerous cities further north along the eastern seaboard.

WHAT'S ON

Steamed Crab Season

Blue crabs are plentiful in Maryland from summer through early fall, the best time for a waterside crab pickin'.

Firefly Music Festival

Four days of music and camping in Dover, DE, in June with big-name acts and on-the-rise newcomers.

Fourth of July

Huge crowds gather on the Mall to watch marching bands, listen to the National Symphony Orchestra and enjoy spectacular fireworks.

Resources

Washingtonian (washingtonian.com) Covers all elements of DC's cultural scene.

Baltimore Banner (thebaltimorebanner.com) Nonprofit news website created in 2022, with a '7 Things to Do' feature for Baltimore and Annapolis.

C&O Canal Trust (canaltrust.org) Spotlights history and activities along the 184.5-mile towpath.

WHERE TO STAY

Historic inns are an appealing option. There are numerous choices in Annapolis and Frederick (Maryland), as well as in small towns throughout the region. Glossy boutique hotels are prevalent in DC and Baltimore. B&Bs and hostels can be a good choice in western Maryland near the Appalachian Trail and the C&O Canal towpath. For something unique, spend the night in a historic lockhouse (canaltrust.org) beside the towpath and the Potomac River. Campers can pitch their tents close to the beach at Assateague Island National Seashore in Maryland (p136), where a wild horse might gallop by with the sunrise.

15

Maryland's National Historic Road

BEST FOR

OUTDOORS
Hiking along the bottom of Patapsco Valley (p112).

Fort McHenry, Baltimore

DURATION	DISTANCE	GREAT FOR
2 days	92 miles / 150km	Family

BEST TIME TO GO	April to June to soak up late spring's sunniness and warmth.

For such a small state, Maryland has a staggering array of landscapes and citizens, and this trip engages both of these elements of the Old Line State. Move from the Chesapeake Bay and Baltimore, a port that mixes bohemians with blue collar workers, through the picturesque small towns of the Maryland hill country, into the stately cities that mark the lower slopes of the looming Catoctin Mountains.

Link your trip

17 Maritime Maryland

Head south then east from Baltimore into Maryland's rural bayside villages.

23 The Civil War Tour

In Gathland State Park, head 10 miles west to Antietam to begin exploring America's seminal internal conflict.

BALTIMORE

01 Maryland's largest city is one of the most important ports in the country, a center for the arts and culture and melting pot of immigrants from Greece, El Salvador, East Africa, the Caribbean and elsewhere. These streams combine into an idiosyncratic culture that, in many ways, encapsulates Maryland's depth of history and prominent diversity – not just of race, but creed and socioeconomic status.

Baltimore was a notable holdout against the British military during the War of 1812, even after Washington, DC, fell. The morning after an intense

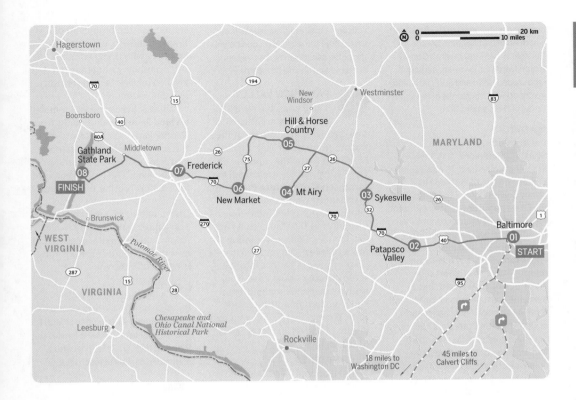

shelling, staring 'through the rockets' red glare,' local lawyer Francis Scott Key saw that 'our flag was still there' and wrote *The Star-Spangled Banner*. The history of that battle and the national anthem are explored at **Fort McHenry** (nps.gov/fomc), located in South Baltimore.

Have a wander through nearby Federal Hill Park, a 70-acre hill that rises above the city, and admire the view out over the harbor.

🚗 **THE DRIVE**
Get on US 40 (Baltimore National Pike – and the basis of the National Historic Road this trip is named for) westbound in Baltimore. The easiest place to access it is at Charles and Franklin St. Franklin becomes US

40/the Pike as you head west out of downtown Baltimore, into the woods that mark the edges of the Patapsco Valley. The whole drive takes about 30 minutes in traffic.

🧭 **DETOUR**
Washington, DC
Start: 01 **Baltimore**
A natural complement to your historical tour is the nation's capital, just 40 miles south of Baltimore on the BWI Pkwy. The **National Mall** has been the site of some of the nation's most iconic protests, from Martin Luther King's March on Washington to rallies for the legalization of gay marriage.

The east end of the mall is filled with the (free!) museums of the **Smithsonian Institution**. All are worth your time. We could easily get lost amid

the silk screens, Japanese prints and sculpture of the often-bypassed **Freer-Sackler Museums of Asian Art** (asia.si.edu).

On the other side of the mall is a cluster of memorials and monuments. The most famous is the back of the penny: the **Lincoln Memorial** (nps. gov/linc). The view over the reflecting pool to the Washington Monument is as spectacular as you've imagined. The **Roosevelt Memorial** (nps.gov/frde) is notable for its layout, which explores the entire term of America's longest-serving president.

On the north flank of the Lincoln Memorial (left if you're facing the pool) is the immensely powerful **Vietnam Veterans Memorial** (nps.gov/vive), a black granite 'V' cut into the soil inscribed with names of the American war dead of that conflict. Search for the nearby but rarely visited **Constitution Gardens**, featuring a tranquil, landscaped pond and artificial island inscribed with the names of the signatories of the Constitution.

DETOUR
Calvert Cliffs
Start: 01 **Baltimore**
In southern Maryland, 75 miles south of Baltimore via US 301 and MD-4, skinny Calvert County scratches at the Chesapeake Bay and the Patuxent River. This is a gentle landscape ('user-friendly' as a local ranger puts it) of low-lying forests, estuarine marshes and placid waters, but there is one rugged feature: the Calvert cliffs. These burnt-umber pillars stretch along the coast for some 24 miles, and form the seminal landscape feature of **Calvert Cliffs State Park** (dnr. maryland.gov/publiclands), where they front the water and a pebbly, honey-sand beach scattered with driftwood and drying beds of kelp.

Back in the day (10 to 20 million years ago), this area sat submerged under a warm sea. Eventually, that sea receded and left the fossilized remains of thousands of prehistoric creatures embedded in the cliffs. Fast forward to the 21st-century, and one of the favorite activities of southern Maryland families is coming to this park, strolling across the sand and plucking out fossils and sharks' teeth from the pebbly debris at the base of the cliffs. Over 600 species of fossils have been identified at the park. In addition, a full 1079 acres and 13 miles of the park are set aside for trails and hiking and biking.

While this spot is pet- and family-friendly, fair warning: it's a 1.8-mile walk from the parking lot to the open beach and the cliffs, so this may not be the best spot to go fossil hunting

with very small children unless they can handle the walk. Also: don't climb the cliffs, as erosion makes this an unstable and unsafe prospect.

02 PATAPSCO VALLEY
The Patapsco river and river valley are the defining geographic features of the region, running through Central Maryland to the Chesapeake Bay. To explore the area, head to **Patapsco Valley State Park** (dnr. maryland.gov/publiclands), an enormous protected area – one of the oldest in the state – that runs for 32 miles along a whopping 170 miles of trails. The main visitor center provides insight into the settled history of the area, from Native Americans to the present, and is housed in a 19th-century stone cottage that looks as though it were plucked from a CS Lewis bedtime story.

THE DRIVE
Get back on US 40/the Pike westbound until you see signs to merge onto I-70W, which is the main connecting road between Baltimore and central and western Maryland. Get on 70, then take exit 80 to get onto MD 32 (Sykesville Rd). Follow for about 5 miles into Sykesville proper.

03 SYKESVILLE
Like many of the towns in the central Maryland hill country between Baltimore and Frederick, Sykesville has a historic center that looks and feels picture perfect. Main St, between Springfield Ave and Sandosky Rd, is filled with structures built between the 1850s and 1930s, and almost looks like an advertisement for small-town America.

The old **Baltimore & Ohio (B&O) train station** was built in 1883 in the Queen Anne style. The

station was the brainchild of E Francis Baldwin, a Baltimore architect who designed many B&O stations, giving that rail line a satisfying aesthetic uniformity along its extent.

Fun fact: Sykesville was founded on land James Sykes bought from George Patterson. Patterson was the son of Elizabeth Patterson and Jerome Bonaparte, brother of Napoleon. The French emperor insisted his brother marry royalty and never let his sister-in-law (the daughter of a merchant) into France; her family estate (which formed the original parcel of land that the town grew from) is the grounds of Sykesville.

THE DRIVE
Although this trip is largely based on US 40 – the actual National Historic Road – detour up to Liberty Rd (MD-26) and take that west 8 miles to Ridge Rd (MD-27). Take Ridge Rd/27 south for 5.5 miles to reach Mt Airy.

04 MT AIRY
Mt Airy is the next major (we use that term with a grain of salt) town along the B&O railroad and US 40/the National Historic Road. Like Sykesville, it's a handsome town, with a stately center that benefited from the commerce the railway brought westward from Baltimore. When the railway was replaced by the highway, Mt Airy, unlike other towns, still retained much of its prosperity thanks to the proximity of jobs in cities like DC and Baltimore.

Today the town centers on a historic district of 19th- and early-20th-century buildings, many of which can be found around Main St. The posher historical homes near 'downtown' Mt Airy were built in the

Second Empire, Queen Anne and Colonial Revival styles, while most 'regular' homes are two-story, center-gable 'I-houses,' once one of the most common housing styles in rural America in the 19th-century, but now largely displaced in this region by modern split-levels.

THE DRIVE

Take Ridge Rd/MD-27 back to Liberty Rd/MD-26. Turn left and proceed for 10 miles to reach Elk Run.

05 HILL & HORSE COUNTRY

Much of Frederick, Carroll, Baltimore and Hartford counties consist of trimmed, rolling hills intersected by copses of pine and broadleaf woods and tangled hedgerows; it's the sort of landscape that could put you in mind of the bocage country of

Photo opportunity

The historic buildings lining New Market, MD.

northern France or rural England. A mix of working farmers and wealthy city folks live out here, and horse breeding and raising is a big industry.

It can be pretty enchanting just driving around and getting lost on some of the local back roads, but if you want a solid destination, it's tough to go wrong with **Elk Run Vineyards** (elkrun. com), almost exactly halfway between Mt Airy and New Market. Free tours are offered at 1pm

and 3pm, and tastings can be arranged without reservations for at least two people.

THE DRIVE

Continue west on Liberty Rd/MD-26 for 6 miles, then turn left (southbound) onto MD-75/Green Valley Rd. After about 7 miles, take a right onto Old New Market Rd to reach New Market's Main St.

06 NEW MARKET

Pretty New Market is the smallest and best preserved of the historical towns that sit between Baltimore and Frederick. Main St, full of antique shops, is lined with Federal and Greek Revival houses. More than 90% of the structures are of brick or frame construction, as opposed to modern vinyl, sheet rock and/ or dry wall; the National Register of Historical Places deems central

Frederick

New Market 'in appearance, the quintessence of the c[irca] 1800 small town in western central Maryland.'

⊙ **THE DRIVE**
Frederick is about 7 miles west of New Market via I-70. Take exit 56 for MD-144 to reach the city center.

07 **FREDERICK**
Frederick boasts a historically preserved center, but unlike the previously listed small towns, this is a mid-sized city, an important commuter base for thousands of federal government employees and a biotechnology hub in its own right.

Central Frederick is, well, perfect. For a city of its size (around 65,000), what more could you want? A pedestrian-friendly center of redbrick row houses with a large, diverse array of restaurants usually found in a larger town; an engaged, cultured arts community anchored by the excellent events calendar at the **Weinberg Center for the Arts** (weinbergcenter.org); and the meandering Carroll Creek running through the center of it all. Walking around downtown is immensely enjoyable.

The creek is crossed by a lovely bit of community art: the mural on **Frederick Bridge**, at S Carroll St between E Patrick & E All Saints. The trompe l'oeil–style art essentially transforms a drab concrete span into an old, ivy-covered stone bridge from Tuscany.

SOME MORE OF BALTIMORE'S BEST

Everyone knows DC is chock-a-block replete with museums, but the capital's scruffier, funkier neighbor to the northeast gives Washington a run for its money in the museum department.

Out by the Baltimore waterfront is a strange building, seemingly half enormous warehouse, half explosion of intense artsy angles, multicolored windmills and rainbow-reflecting murals, like someone had bent the illustrations of a Dr Seuss book through a funky mirror. This is quite possibly the coolest art museum in the country: the **American Visionary Art Museum** (AVAM; avam.org). It's a showcase for self-taught (or 'outsider' art), which is to say art made by people who aren't formally trained artists. It's a celebration of unbridled creativity utterly free of arts-scene pretension. Some of the works come from asylums, others are created by self-inspired visionaries, but it's all rather captivating and well worth a long afternoon.

The Baltimore & Ohio railway was (arguably) the first passenger train in America, and the **B&O Railroad Museum** (borail.org) is a loving testament to both that line and American railroading in general. Train spotters will be in heaven among more than 150 different locomotives. Train rides cost an extra $3; call for the schedule.

If you're traveling with a family, or if you just love science and science education, come by the **Maryland Science Center** (mdsci.org). This awesome center features a three-story atrium, tons of interactive exhibits on dinosaurs, outer space and the human body, and the requisite IMAX theater.

⊙ **THE DRIVE**
Head west on old National Pike (US 40A) and then, after about 6.5 miles, get on MD-17 southbound/Burkittsville Rd. Turn right on Gapland Rd after 6 miles and follow it for 1.5 miles to Gathland.

08 **GATHLAND STATE PARK**
This tiny **park** (dnr.maryland.gov/publiclands) is a fascinating tribute to a profession that doesn't lend itself to many memorials: war correspondents. Civil War correspondent and man of letters George Alfred Townsend fell in love with these mountains and built an impressive arch decorated with classical Greek mythological features and quotes that emphasize the needed qualities of a good war correspondent.

16

BEST FOR

FAMILIES
Pottering
around Harpers
Ferry (p118).

Along the C&O Canal

DURATION	DISTANCE	GREAT FOR
2 days	185 miles / 297km	History & Culture

BEST TIME TO GO	May, June, October and November; pleasant spring weather, gorgeous fall mountain foliage.

C&O Canal towpath, Georgetown

In its day, the Chesapeake and Ohio Canal was both an engineering marvel and a commercial disaster. Today, it's one of the nicest national parks in the mid-Atlantic. Drive along the former canal path from Washington, DC, to West Virginia, now a popular hiking and biking trail (because this was a canal towpath, it's almost completely flat), and experience the lush scenery of the Potomac watershed.

Link your trip

22 The Appalachians & the Appalachian Trail

Head west from Harpers Ferry into the Appalachian wilderness.

15 Maryland's National Historic Road

From Brunswick, head northeast into downtown Frederick.

01 GEORGETOWN

Georgetown is Washington, DC's toniest neighborhood, but it's not all hyper-modern lounges and boutiques. On Thomas Jefferson St, enthusiastic college students dress in scratchy 19th-century costumes, while the adventurous set out on one of the country's great rights-of-way. This is also the beginning of the **C&O Canal Towpath** (nps.gov/choh). Part of a larger national historic park, the towpath shadows a waterway constructed in the mid-1800s to transport goods all the way to West Virginia. In its entirety, the gravel path runs for 185 miles from Georgetown to Cumberland, MD,

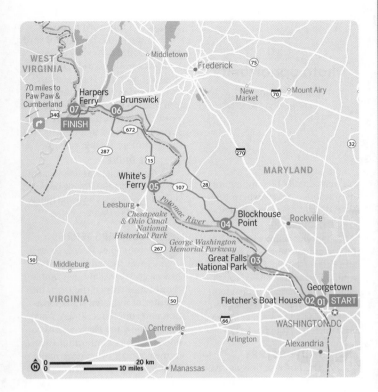

The C&O: Yesterday & today

In case you were wondering: no one uses the C&O Canal today for its original purpose of moving goods. Originally plotted as a transportation line between the eastern seaboard and the industrial heartland west of the Appalachian Mountains, the 'Grand Old Ditch' was completed in 1850, but by the time it opened it was as advanced as a Walkman in a store full of iPhones. The Baltimore & Ohio Railway was already trucking cargo west of the Alleghenies; in a stroke of alphabetical justice, the B&O had supplanted the C&O.

A series of floods, coupled with the canal's own lack of profitability, led to the death of the C&O in 1924, and for some 30 years plans for the land were thrown back and forth: should the canal towpath become a parkway or a park? US Supreme Court Justice William O Douglas firmly believed the latter. The longest-serving justice in history was an environmentalist who argued rivers could be party to litigation, was the lone dissenter on over half of his 300 dissenting opinions, wrote the most speeches and books as a justice, and had the most marriages (four) and divorces (three – his last marriage, to a 23-year-old law student, lasted till his death) on the bench. As part of his commitment to making the C&O a park, he hiked the full length of the path with 58 companions (only nine made it to the end). Public opinion was swayed, and the C&O was saved.

passing through 74 elevation-changing locks.

In Georgetown, the canal runs along a verdant, willow-shaded tunnel of trees. There's a convincing reconstruction of the first leg of the canal path, staffed by the aforementioned costumed interpreters working out of the Georgetown Visitor Center.

THE DRIVE
The drive from Georgetown to Fletcher's Boat House is short but sweet. Head directly west on M St (and be ready to deal with traffic). After 0.5 miles M St becomes Canal Rd, which parallels the towpath. Follow Canal Rd for 1.7 miles; Fletcher will be on your left.

02 FLETCHER'S BOAT HOUSE
The first stop for almost all travelers leaving the towpath from Georgetown is **Fletcher's Boat House** (boatingindc.com/boathouses/fletchers-boathouse), a good spot for a picnic or, if you're looking to boat around, organizing gear rental. Be careful as you go; while the Potomac is beautiful, the currents can be dodgy, despite the calm appearance of the water.

THE DRIVE
Continue northwest along Canal Rd, which becomes the Clara Barton Pkwy when you cross the Maryland border (after 1 mile). Continue along the Clara Barton Pkwy

for about 7 miles, then turn left onto MacArthur Blvd. Follow for 3.5 miles into Great Falls National Park.

03 GREAT FALLS NATIONAL PARK

While you've been driving, the towpath has been twisting and turning for 15 miles to the **Great Falls Tavern Visitor Center** (nps.gov/choh). From here you can book a canal boat ride, a favorite activity among kids. The one-hour trips are a leisurely introduction to the rhythms of the waterway, and are well worth the $8/5 price tag for adults/children. The 4.7-mile Billy Goat Trail, which begins near the visitor center, takes you on an enjoyable scramble over rugged, river-smoothed boulders.

 THE DRIVE
Head back on MacArthur Blvd for 1.2 miles, then turn left onto Falls Rd. Follow it for about 2 miles, then turn left onto River Rd and follow it for 6 miles through some of the poshest suburbs of Montgomery County.

04 BLOCKHOUSE POINT

A little further up the river, Montgomery County has carved the pretty little **Blockhouse Point Conservation Park** (montgomeryparks.org) out of this corner of the Potomac River valley. From Blockhouse Point, you'll see views of the Potomac Valley and ruins of Civil War bunkers. Nearby **Seneca Creek State Park** (dnr.maryland.gov) is a much larger affair, consisting of the woods that hug Seneca Creek, which winds a twisty course to the Potomac. Miles of hiking and biking trails and boating opportunities await in Seneca Creek, though if you're a horror film buff

Photo opportunity
Panorama shot of Harpers Ferry.

you may already be familiar with these woods – this is where 1999's *Blair Witch Project* was filmed.

 THE DRIVE
Stay westbound on River Rd for 3 miles, then turn right to get onto Partnership Rd. Take Partnership for about 4 miles through meadows and farmland, then turn left onto Maryland 107/Fisher Ave. After 5 miles, this becomes White's Ferry Rd; follow it to the ferry.

05 WHITE'S FERRY

The last functioning river service between Maryland and Virginia is **White's Ferry** (whites-ferry.com). Although ferry service was paused in 2024, it is a popular river-crossing option when operating.

 THE DRIVE
Take the ferry to Leesburg, then take VA-15 north for 8 miles. Turn left onto State Route 672 and follow it to VA-287 N to Brunswick. If the ferry is closed, follow River Road from Blockhouse Point to Route 112/Seneca Rd. Take Route 112 to Route 28/Darnestown Rd. Turn left and continue to Point of Rocks and then Brunswick.

06 BRUNSWICK

The C&O Canal's little **Brunswick Visitor Center** (nps.gov/choh) doubles as the Brunswick Rail Museum.

As quiet as this town is, it was once home to the largest rail yard (7 miles long) owned by a single company in the world. Those days are long past, but the museum will appeal to trainspotters, and you have to have a heart of stone not to be charmed by the 1700 sq ft model railroad that depicts the old Baltimore & Ohio railway.

 THE DRIVE
Go west on Knoxville Rd until it becomes MD-180; follow this road and merge onto US 340 and follow it for 5 miles to Harpers Ferry.

07 HARPERS FERRY

In its day, Harpers Ferry was the gateway to the American West. This geographic significance turned the town into a center of industry, transportation and commerce. Today you'd hardly know the Ferry was once one of the most important towns in the country, but it does make for a bucolic, calculatedly cute day trip.

If you'd like to pause here for a break from the towpath, you'll want to first pay admission at the **Harpers Ferry National Historical Park Visitor Center** (nps.gov/hafe), which opens the town's small public museums, located within walking distance of each other, for your perusal. All of these little gems are worth their own small stop; one deals with John Brown's raid (p157) and another with African American history.

⬧ DETOUR
Paw Paw & Cumberland
Start: **07** Harpers Ferry
Northwest of Harpers Ferry, the canal continues into West Virginia and Western, MD.

Paw Paw Tunnel, in Paw Paw, WV, runs directly into the mountains and out of them again; the edifice speaks

Harpers Ferry

to both the will of the canal's builders and the somewhat quixotic nature of their enterprise, as all of this (literal) moving of mountains did nothing to save their investment. Oh well – still makes a nice walk.

Once you hit Cumberland, this is, as the Doors would say, the end – of the C&O Canal. Cumberland, MD, is Mile 184.5, the trail's terminus, marked by the C&O's **Cumberland Visitor Center** (nps.gov/choh), itself an excellent museum on all things related to the canal. Go have a beer, and consider delving into one of our many Appalachian trips.

To get to Paw Paw, take US 340W to VA-7W to hit Winchester. Then take VA-127N to WV-29N and follow signs to Paw Paw. From Paw Paw, take MD-51N to reach Cumberland (two hours from Harpers Ferry).

17

Maritime Maryland

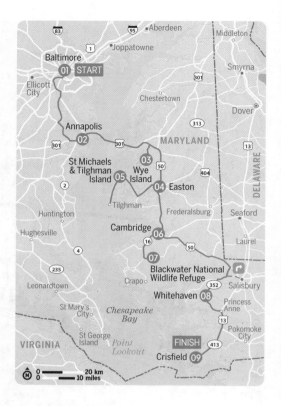

DURATION	DISTANCE	GREAT FOR
4 days	320 miles / 515km	Food & Drink

BEST TIME TO GO	May to September, when it's warm, sunny and sultry.

Inside the marshy, silent spaces of a preserve like Wye Island or Blackwater Wildlife Refuge, you'll realize: this state is utterly tied to the water. You'll know it when you roll past a dozen little towns on the Eastern Shore, each with a small and public pier still used by commercial watermen and local pleasure boaters. This, trippers, is Chesapeake Bay, Maryland's defining geographic and cultural keystone.

Link your trip

15 Maryland's National Historic Road

For more riverside adventures and excellent eating, road trip through Charlevoix. Take the ferry to St Siméon, then turn south.

20 Eastern Shore Odyssey

Drive to Laurel, DE, to begin exploring the back roads and small towns of the Eastern Shore.

01 BALTIMORE

Start in Baltimore, which calls itself the 'Crab Cake' to New York's Big Apple. B'more has always been built around its docks, and is a port city through and through its watery veins. Indeed, the state's most prominent urban renewal project was the **Inner Harbor** overhaul, which turned a rough dock into a waterfront playground for families. The most prominent landmark, and the best way to learn about the state's aquatic fauna (and aquatic wildlife anywhere), is the excellent **National Aquarium** (aqua.org). Standing seven stories high

BEST FOR

FOODIES
Enjoy stupefyingly huge meals at Red Roost.

FHPHOTO/SHUTTERSTOCK ©

Inner Harbor, Baltimore

and capped by a pyramid, it houses 16,500 specimens of 660 species, a rooftop rainforest, a central ray pool and multistory shark tank.

Ship-lovers should consider a visit to **Historic Ships in Baltimore** (historicships.org), which offers access to a coast guard cutter, lightship and submarine. The highlight of the Inner Harbor ships is the **USS *Constellation***, one of the last sail-powered warships built by the US Navy. A joint ticket gets you on board all four ships and the Seven Foot Knoll Lighthouse on Pier 5.

Afterwards, stroll around historic **Fells Point,** a cobblestone district of typical Baltimore rowhouses clustered by the water. Fells is now largely filled with bars and is a fun nightlife area.

THE DRIVE
Get on the Baltimore beltway (I-695) and head south on I-97 for 18 miles. Keep left at the fork, and follow signs for 50 E/301 to Annapolis/the Bay Bridge. There's convenient parking at a garage on the corner of Colonial Ave and West St.

02 ANNAPOLIS
The state's capital is a city of yachts and pleasure boats as opposed to commercial fisheries. The **city docks** off Randall and Dock Sts are where you can see the ships quite literally come in.

WHY I LOVE THIS TRIP

Amy Balfour, writer

Miles and miles of estuaries, wetlands, rivers and oceans border the shores of eastern Maryland. Home to historic sites dating to the earliest days of the country and filled today with maritime distractions, it's a low-key but special place best appreciated on a leisurely drive. You'll also be exposed to small town friendliness and fantastic seafood. Don't miss a trip here.

Nearby is the country's oldest state capitol in continuous legislative use, the stately 1772 **Maryland State House** (msa.maryland.gov/msa/mdstatehouse/html/home.html), which also served as national capital from 1733 to 1734. The Maryland Senate is in action here from January to April. The upside-down giant acorn atop the dome stands for wisdom.

Probably the surest sign of Annapolis' ties to the water is the **Naval Academy**, the officer candidate school of the US Navy. The **Armel-Leftwich visitor center** (usnabsd.com/for-visitors) is the place to book tours and immerse yourself in all things Navy. Come for the formation weekdays at 12:05pm sharp, when the 4000 midshipmen and midshipwomen conduct a 20-minute military

Photo opportunity

The marshes at Blackwater Wildlife Refuge.

marching display in the yard. Photo ID is required for entry.

THE DRIVE

Get on US 50/US 301 and head east over the Chesapeake Bay Bridge (commonly known as the Bay Bridge), which extends 4.3 miles (7km) over the Chesapeake Bay. Once you hit land – Kent Island – travel 12.5 miles eastbound on US 50/US 301, then turn right onto Carmichael Rd. Go about 5 miles on Carmichael and cross the Wye Island Bridge.

03 **WYE ISLAND**

Our introduction to the Eastern Shore is a wild one – specifically the **Wye Island Natural Resource Management Area** (Wye Island NRMA; dnr.maryland.gov).

This small, marshy island encapsulates much of the soft-focus beauty of the Eastern Shore. It's all miles of gently waving sawgrass and marsh prairie, intercut with slow blackwater and red inlets leeching tannins from the thick vegetation. Six miles of easy, flat trails run through the NRMA, weaving under hardwood copses and over rafts of wetland flora. The interlacing tide pools and waterways look like a web, especially in the morning sun. Keep an eye out for bald eagles, osprey, whitetailed deer and red foxes.

JON BILOUS/SHUTTERSTOCK ©

Carmichael Rd, near Wye Island

Kent Narrows

THE DRIVE

Drive back on Carmichael to US 50 and turn right. Take US 50 eastbound (though really, you're going south) for 14 miles and exit onto MD-322 southbound. Follow signs for central Easton.

04 EASTON

Easton, founded in 1710, is both a quintessential Shore town and anything but. The historic center, seemingly lifted from the pages of a children's book, is wedding cake cute; locals are friendly; the antique shops and galleries are well stocked. That's because this isn't what Shore people would call a 'working water town,' which is to say, a town that relies on bay seafood to live.

Rather, Easton relies on the bay for tourism purposes. It has retained the traditional appearance of a working water town by being a weekend retreat for folks from DC, Baltimore and further afield.

The main thing to do here is potter around and feel at peace. The area between Washington St, Dover St, Goldsborough St and East Ave is a good place to start. **First Friday Art Walk** is also a lovely way of engaging with old Easton.

There's a superlative number of good restaurants around for a town of 16,000; be sure to try at least one.

THE DRIVE

Get on MD-33 in Easton and take it westbound for 10 miles to reach St Michaels. Tilghman Island is 14 miles further west of St Michaels via MD-33..

THE EAST COAST COWBOYS

After you drive over the Bay Bridge, the first community you cross into on the Eastern Shore is Kent Island. This is where, in 1631, English trader William Claiborne set up a rival settlement to the Catholic colonists of St Mary's City in southern Maryland. Where those Catholics sought religious freedom from the Church of England, Claiborne sought the American dream: profit, in this case from the beaver fur trade.

In later days Kent became a major seafood processing center. A dozen packing-houses processed the catches of hundreds of watermen. Also known as the 'East Coast cowboys,' watermen usually operate as individuals, piloting their own boats and catching crabs, oysters and fish. Today the industry still exists, but it is fading – independent commercial fisheries yield small profits and have expensive overheads. The cost of a boat can equal a home loan, and the maintenance needed to provide upkeep is prohibitive.

The state enforces environmental regulations on catch size, and the bounty of the bay is declining thanks largely to run-off pollution. In the meantime, many watermen prefer to send their children to college, away from the uncertain income and backbreaking manual labor of independent commercial fishing.

Still, the waterman is an iconic symbol of the Eastern Shore, an embodiment of the area's independent spirit and ties to the land (and water). On Kent Island, drive under the Kent Narrows bridge (the way is signed from US 50) to see the Waterman's Monument. The sculpture depicts two stylized watermen in a skiff laden with their daily catch, and is a small slice of tradition in an area now given over to outlet malls and tourism.

05 ST MICHAELS & TILGHMAN ISLAND

Tiny St Michaels has evolved into a tourism-oriented town, but for centuries this village was known for building some of the best boats in the country. Later, this became a waterman community, and many watermen still set out from the local docks. If you want to learn about these watermen, their community and the local environment, head to the lighthouse and the **Chesapeake Bay Maritime Museum** (cbmm.org), which delves into the deep ties between Shore folk and America's largest estuary.

Tilghman Island is an even smaller, quieter town than St Michaels. Many come here to arrange fishing expeditions.

THE DRIVE
Take MD-33 back to US 50E and go south for 15 miles to reach Cambridge.

BEST. SEASONING. EVER.

You see it everywhere down here: Old Bay seasoning, the deep red, pleasantly hot and unmistakably estuarine spice of Maryland. It's made from celery salt, mustard, black and red pepper, and other secret ingredients, and Marylanders put it on corn, french fries, potato chips and, of course, crabs. A large container of the stuff is the perfect Maryland souvenir, but beware of wiping your face after partaking of the spice: Old Bay in the eyes is incredibly painful.

06 CAMBRIDGE

First settled in 1684, Cambridge is one of the oldest towns in the country. Situated on the Choptank River, it has historically been a farming town.

Cambridge's city center has lots of historic buildings fashioned in Federal style; it may not be as picture perfect as Easton, but the town's populace is less transplant-heavy and more authentically of the Shore, and it's diverse to boot (almost 50-50 split between white and African American).

Wander around the local galleries at the **Dorchester Center for the Arts** (dorchesterarts.org) and check out the **Cambridge Farmers Market** (cambridge mainstreet.com) next to Simmons Center Market, for a colorful and abundant range of fresh produce in the warmer months.

THE DRIVE:
Take Race St to MD-16 W/Church Creek Rd and follow it for 5 miles to MD-335. Follow Route 335 for about 4 miles and turn east on Key Wallace Dr. The visitor center is about 1 mile from the intersection on the right

07 BLACKWATER NATIONAL WILDLIFE REFUGE

The Atlantic Flyway is the main route birds take between northern and southern migratory trips, and in an effort to give our fine feathered friends a bit of a rest stop, the **Blackwater National Wildlife Refuge** (fws.gov/black water) was established.

The Blackwater is technically in the state of Maryland, yet by all appearances it could have fallen from the cutting-room floor of *Jurassic Park*. This enormous expanse of marsh and pine forest contains a third of Maryland's wetland habitat. Thousands upon thousands of birds call the refuge home, or at least stop there on their migratory routes. Driving or cycling around the paved 4-mile **wildlife drive** is perhaps the seminal wildlife experience on the Eastern Shore. A few small walking trails and an observation tour can be accessed via the drive.

Harriet Tubman, 'the Moses of her people', who led thousands of Black enslaved people to freedom, was born on nearby Greenbrier Rd. Don't miss the new **Harriet Tubman Underground Railroad National Historic Park & Visitor Center** (nps.gov/hatu), dedicated to Tubman and the Underground Railroad, the pipeline that sent escaped enslaved people north.

THE DRIVE
Get back on MD-16 and take it 11 miles north to US 50. Get on 50 east and drive 23 miles, then turn right on Rockawalkin Rd and connect to MD-340 southbound (Nanticoke Rd). Take this for 3 miles, then turn left on MD-352W/Whitehaven Rd and follow for 8 miles to Whitehaven.

08 WHITEHAVEN

Nestled in a heart-melting river-and-stream-scape, Whitehaven is a quintessential small Shore town where it feels like the 17th century was yesterday. It boasts one of the finest family restaurants and crab shacks in the state: the low-slung, laughter-packed Red Roost (theredroost.com). When you have devoured your fill of food, enjoy the surrounding countryside and consider taking a short ride in your car across the Wicomico River on the **White-**

Harriet Tubman Underground Railroad National Historic Park & Visitor Center

haven Ferry, which dates to 1685 and is the oldest publicly operated ferry in the country.

The ferry runs from 6am to 7:30pm in summer if there's traffic (there often isn't, so you may need to call the above number; varied hours at other times), and it takes five minutes to cross the river. Check the weather before planning your crossing — the ferry doesn't run if the river is frozen or the wind is over 35 knots, in which case you'll need to go all the way back to Salisbury to cross the river.

🚗 THE DRIVE
Take the ferry across the river and follow Whitehaven Rd to MD-362; take this road for 5 miles to US 13. Take 13 south for 5.5 miles until it becomes 413; follow this for 14 miles to reach Crisfield.

🧭 DETOUR
Salisbury

Start: 08 **Whitehaven**
About 30 minutes east of Whitehaven (take Whitehaven Rd to MD-349 and head east for 7 miles) is Salisbury, the main commercial and population hub of the Eastern Shore.

If you're around in the fall, drop by for the **Maryland Autumn Wine Festival** (marylandwine.org/mwf/), held around the third weekend of October. You can get an enjoyable sousing courtesy of more than 20 state vineyards and wineries, many of which are located on the Eastern Shore.

One potentially interesting destination, which was set to open in the fall of 2024, is the **Museum of Eastern Shore Culture at Salisbury University** (museumofeasternshorecultureatsu. org), formerly known as the Ward Museum of Wildfowl Art. In downtown Salisbury, it will showcase duck decoys, a fascinating art form that was largely perfected by two brothers, Stephen and LT Ward, who rarely left the town of Crisfield, MD. The Eastern Shore's flat marshes and tidal pools have always attracted a plethora of waterfowl, along with dedicated hunters. In the early 20th century, the Ward brothers spent a lifetime carving and painting waterfowl decoys that are wonderful in their realism and attention to detail.

MARYLAND CRAB FESTS

Maryland goes gaga for blue crabs – they even appear on driver's licenses. Here, the most hallowed of state social halls is the crab house, where crabs are steamed in water, beer and Old Bay seasoning to produce sweet, juicy white flesh cut by cayenne, onion and salt. Crab houses also offer these favorites: crab cakes (crabmeat mixed with breadcrumbs and secret spice combinations, then fried); crab balls (as above, but smaller); soft crabs (crabs that have molted their shells and are fried, looking like giant breaded spiders – they're delicious); red crab or cream of crab soup; and fish stuffed with crab imperial (crab sautéed in butter, mayonnaise and mustard, occasionally topped with cheese). Join the locals in a crab fest – eating together in messy camaraderie can't be beat.

On the campus of Salisbury University, the **Nabb Research Center** (salisbury.edu/libraries/nabb) contains what is likely the world's most comprehensive archive of artifacts related to the Delmarva peninsula (Delaware and the Maryland and Virginia Eastern Shore). Stop by for the small rotating exhibits about local history.

 CRISFIELD

Crisfield is a true working water town, where the livelihood of residents is tied to harvesting the Chesapeake Bay. Catch the local watermen at their favorite hangout, having 4am coffee at **Gordon's Confection-ery** before shipping off to check and set traps. Or just drop in to Gordon's for some scrapple (a local specialty – it's pig...bits) before sunset. There will usually be a waterman hanging around willing to bend your ear with a story.

For a more formal education on watermen, head to the **J Millard Tawes Historical Museum** (crisfieldheritage.org/museum), which gives an insight into the ecology of the bay and the life of working watermen. Local docents also lead walking tours of Crisfield. End your trip on the Crisfield docks, by the old crab-shelling and packing plants, and let the salt breeze move you while you're in a most maritime spot, in the most maritime of states.

18

Southern Maryland Triangle

BEST FOR

FOODIES Steamed hard crabs at Courtney's (courtneysseafoodrestaurant.com).

Piscataway Park

DURATION	DISTANCE	GREAT FOR
2 days	170 miles / 273km	History & Culture

BEST TIME TO GO	April to June, when it's warm but not sultry.

The little-known slice of the Old Line State known as Southern Maryland is a patchwork of marsh, fields and forests, the state's oldest European settlements and stunning riverscape vistas – all an hour or so from Washington, DC. On this trip you'll shift from down-home crab shacks to upscale wine bars, all while probing back roads that are often quite removed from the tourist radar.

Link your trip

17 Maritime Maryland

Take MD 2-4 to Annapolis, then cross the Bay Bridge to explore Maryland's watery edges.

15 Maryland's National Historic Road

Head north to Frederick along I-270 to see the small, historical towns of Central Maryland.

01 ACCOKEEK

About 23 miles south of Washington, DC, via the Indian Head Hwy (MD-210), Accokeek is the first community that feels more Southern Maryland than DC suburb.

This quilt of farms, fields and forests was (and to a degree remains) a popular retreat for scientists and intellectuals who wanted to live in a rural community within DC's orbit. The aesthetic they were attracted to is exemplified by **Piscataway Park** (nps.gov/pisc), a small satellite of the National Park System (NPS) that consists of nature trails, boardwalks over freshwater wetlands, views of

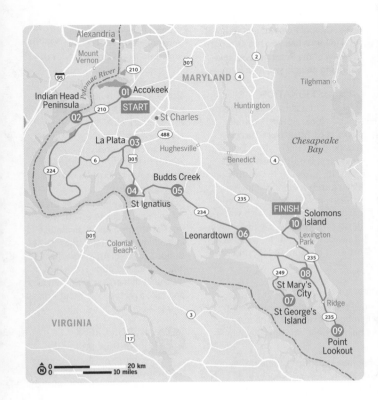

Tobacco Barns

The Bridges of Madison County just sounds like a great novel, right? How about 'The Tobacco Barns of Southern Maryland?' No? Well, those barns are in a similar vein to those flashy covered bridges: a piece of hyper-regional American architectural heritage. Tobacco was once the cash crop of Southern Maryland. It was the crop that made the original Maryland colony economically viable, and the area's stubborn loyalty to tobacco, coupled with Southern Maryland's geographic position under the I-95 corridor, was largely what kept the region rural for so many centuries. But declining profits, and a 2001 state-sponsored buyout of tobacco farms, largely ended the industry in the past decade.

Tobacco was stored in frame-built barns with gabled roofs and adjustable ventilation slats. The frames provided space for 'sticks' (poles) that were hung with tobacco leaf, which was cured and air-dried through a combination of the elements and charcoal or (later) propane fires.

Preservation Maryland (preservationmaryland.org) and similar organizations have made tobacco barn preservation a cause celebre, and as such, hundreds of rickety tobacco barns dot the Southern Maryland triangle. They have a creaky, spidery aesthethic, like they were drawn by children's book illustrator Stephen Gammell, and they're as integral to the local landscape as the water and the woods.

the Potomac River and **National Colonial Farm**, a living history museum that recreates a middle-class Maryland family farm circa the Revolutionary War period.

THE DRIVE
Get back on MD-210 and head south for 8 miles to reach the entrance to Indian Head.

02 INDIAN HEAD PENINSULA
There's not a lot to see in little Indian Head, but it's a logical jumping-off point for exploring the Indian Head peninsula, which is hugged by the Potomac River.

Smallwood State Park (dnr.maryland.gov/publiclands) sits between the Potomac and Mattawoman Creek. There are a few very easy nature trails that run through local hardwood forests, and the **Retreat House**, a restored tidewater plantation and tobacco barn; these historic properties are open on Sundays from 1pm to 5pm.

THE DRIVE
You can drive around the entire peninsula on MD-224. When you're ready to move on, hop on MD-425N and take it to MD-6; take 6 eastbound for 11 miles through bucolic countryside to reach La Plata.

03 LA PLATA

Named for a river in Argentina, La Plata is the seat of Charles County. It's a prosperous little country town, but for all that, it's subject to the sprawl that creeps south from DC. The **Port Tobacco Players** (ptplayers.com) are a local theater company that puts on Broadway and off-Broadway standards, plus a few lesser-known pieces. Catch a show – not for the production values, but for the chance to peek into a hyper-local arts scene.

THE DRIVE
Get back on MD-6 and backtrack west for around 2 miles. Turn left at Chapel Point Rd and follow it for 4 miles. When you see an amazing view of the Potomac next to a charming church, you're in business.

04 ST IGNATIUS

On a gentle slope overlooking the Potomac River is **St Ignatius Church** (chapelpoint.org), which hosts the oldest continuously active Catholic parish in the country. The church itself has a lovely exterior profile. If you visit, you can content yourself with wandering the cemetery, which offers great views out to the water. The forested bottomlands visible from Ignatius' backslope constitute 600 acres of state-owned land; you're welcome to stomp around, but there are no trails.

If you continue on Chapel Point Rd, you'll hit US 301; take this for 1.5 miles, then turn right onto Popes Creek Rd. This 2-mile country lane is quite pretty, and was also the escape route John Wilkes Booth took to Virginia after assassinating Abraham Lincoln.

THE DRIVE
Turn around on Popes Creek Rd and head back to US 301. Turn left (north) onto 301, then almost immediately turn right onto MD-234, Budds Creek Rd. After barely a mile you'll pass Allen Fresh Run, a magnificent marshscape – pull over and take a picture. It's about 7 miles to the speedway.

05 BUDDS CREEK

Before you properly explore St Mary's County, the first county in the state and one of the oldest counties in the country, consider this: you have been driving (hopefully) responsibly for perhaps thousands of miles on our trips. Maybe it's time to see some people drive like maniacs. Enter **Budds Creek** (buddscreek.com), one of the premier motocross racetracks on the eastern seaboard. It's always a blast here – a blast of hot exhaust and speed across your face, but a blast nonetheless.

THE DRIVE
Continue on MD-234 for 12 miles (you'll pass through a traffic circle). When 234 hits MD-5, turn right and continue through Leonardtown for about 2 miles. Turn right on Washington St and look for the Bank of America building; this small square is 'downtown' Leonardtown.

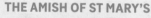

THE AMISH OF ST MARY'S

St Mary's County has always had a rural feel to it, but horse and buggy carriages? Straw hats? One-room schoolhouses? In the 21st century? Yes, thanks to a sizable presence of Amish settlers, who have been in the county since 1940.

The Amish are a Christian sect that embraces simplicity, humility, manual labor and the countryside; conversely, they are reluctant to adopt modern technology, although they do not, as stereotypes would have it, reject it wholesale. Men usually wear their beards long and women wear head coverings, and internally, Amish communities speak a dialect of German known as Pennsylvania German.

The local Amish live in northern St Mary's County, near the town of Mechanicsville. Their farms are sprinkled along Rte 236 South and Rte 247, and their homes can be found on quiet country lanes like Parsons Mill Rd, Friendship School Rd and the perhaps ironically dubbed Busy Corner Rd. You'll know you're in Amish country when you see horse-drawn buggies clop-clop by on the roadside, or when you see German surnames like Kurtz, Hertzler and Zimmerman on mailboxes.

It is important to remember the Amish aren't frozen in amber. Farmers sometimes carry cell phones for emergencies. And local markets now often feature bilingual signage, a testament to the growing Latino population of the area, particularly within the agricultural sector.

If you'd like to interact with the Mechanicsville Amish, the easiest way is at the **North St Mary's County Farmers Market**, where local Amish farming families sell produce and crafts. To really see the Pennsylvania Dutch in their element, check out the **produce auction** held during spring and summer harvest seasons on Mondays, Wednesdays and Fridays at 40454 Bishop Rd, in the town of Loveville.

St Ignatius Church

06 LEONARDTOWN

The seat of St Mary's County has worked hard to maintain its small-town atmosphere. The central square (Fenwick and Washington Sts) is the closest thing this community has to a town green. Maryland is a border state between the North and South, a legacy evident in the square's on-site **World War I memorial**, divided into 'white' and 'colored' sections.

Look for a rock in front of the nearby **circuit courthouse** (Courthouse Dr and Washington); legend has it that Moll Dwyer, a local 'witch', froze to death while kneeling on it and cursed the town with her dying breath. Her faint knee imprints are supposedly still visible in the stone.

Nearby **Fenwick St Used Books & Music** (fenwickbooks. com) is a good spot for learning about local history and current events. On the first Friday of each month, music fills the town square and businesses throw open their doors.

THE DRIVE

Continue south on MD-5 for 7.5 miles. Turn right onto Piney Point Rd (MD-249) and follow that route for 10 miles, which includes crossing a small bridge at the end, to get to St George's Island.

07 ST GEORGE'S ISLAND

This beautiful little island shifts between woods of skeletal loblolly pines and acres of waving marsh grass and cattails. The pines were once so prevalent that the British used the island as a base during the

War of 1812; the trees were used to repair their ships during raids up the Potomac and Chesapeake. It takes maybe 20 minutes to drive around the island; while here, you'll pass by the Paul Hall Center, one of the largest merchant marine training academies in the country.

THE DRIVE

Head back up Piney Point Rd. Turn right onto MD-5 and follow it south for 8 miles. When you enter the campus of St Mary's College you'll see the 'Freedom of Conscience' statue (a man emerging from a rock wall); take a slight right onto Trinity Church Rd and follow to the Historic St Mary's City parking lot.

Photo opportunity

The river flowing past Historic St Mary's City.

08 **ST MARY'S CITY**

The Potomac and its tributary, St Mary's River, along with the Chesapeake Bay, cut a lush triangle of land out of the southern edge of Southern Maryland. This is where, in 1634, on high green bluffs overlooking the water, Catholic settlers began the state of Maryland.

The settlement has been recreated into **Historic St Mary's City** (HSMC; stmaryscity.org), a living history museum romantically positioned among the surrounding forests, fields and farmlands. Given its distance from anything resembling a crowd, HSMC feels more colonial than similar places like Williamsburg.

A recreation of the *Maryland Dove*, the supply ship that accompanied the original British colonists, sits docked on the St Mary's River. Next door Trinity Church and St Mary's College of Maryland are both lovely – they're easy to walk around and get satisfyingly lazy in.

St Mary's City

THE DRIVE
Getting to Point Lookout is straightforward: roll south for 10 miles on MD-5, and there you are.

09 POINT LOOKOUT
The western shore of Maryland – that is, the western peninsula created by the Chesapeake Bay – terminates here, in a preserved space of lagoons, pine-woods and marshes managed by **Point Lookout State Park** (dnr.maryland.gov/publiclands). There's a playground for kids and a sandy beach that's OK for swimming, but watch out for jellyfish in summer; they're not deadly, but their stings hurt.

During the Civil War, the Union Army imprisoned thousands of Confederate POWs here, overseen by Black soldiers. Swampy conditions and harsh treatment by guards led to the death of some 4000 Confederates. A controversial shrine to their memory has been built, and legends persist of Confederate ghosts haunting local swamps at night.

THE DRIVE
Take MD-5 north for 6 miles and bear right onto MD-235 when it splits. (For a little detour, turn left just after MD-5 splits instead; you'll get to Ridge, an unincorporated community with popular seafood restaurants.) Take MD-235 north through the town of Lexington Park; after 16.5 miles, turn right onto MD-4. Follow for 4 miles over the dramatic Thomas Johnson Bridge and immediately bear right as the bridge terminates to reach Solomons Island.

10 SOLOMONS ISLAND
Solomons is a seaside (but not a beachy) town of antique shops, cafes, diners and one of the most famous bars in the state: the **Tiki Bar**, on 85 Charles St. We're not entirely sure *why* the bar is so famous; it's got a sandy beach, some Easter Island heads and tiki torches (and very strong drinks), and that's about it. Nonetheless people come from as far away as DC and Baltimore to drink here on weekends, and the bar's grand opening for the summer season literally attracts thousands of tourists to Solomons Island.

ST MARY'S FIRSTS

Massachusetts and Virginia are usually in a tight race to prove whoever has the most 'historical' state (whatever that means), but Maryland gives them a run for their money, especially when it comes to historic firsts. All of the following are specific to St Mary's City:

» Maryland was the first Catholic colony in British North America. The first Catholic mass in the British colonies was held here.

» The Maryland Toleration Act (1649), also known as the Act Concerning Religion, created the first legal limitations on hate speech in the world, and was the second law requiring religious tolerance in British North American colonies.

» Mathias de Sousa, who served in the colony's 1642 assembly of freemen, may have been the first man of African descent to participate in a legislative assembly in British America. Contemporary accounts describe him as a person of mixed African descent.

» Margaret Brent was the first woman in British North America to appear before a court of the Common Law. She was also appointed executor of the estate of Governor Leonard Calvert upon his death (1647), and publicly demanded a vote within the colonial assembly.

» In 1685 William Nuthead owned the first printer in Maryland. Upon his death, his wife, Dinah, inherited the business and became the first woman licensed as a printer in America.

WASHINGTON, DC, MARYLAND & DELAWARE **18** SOUTHERN MARYLAND TRIANGLE

19

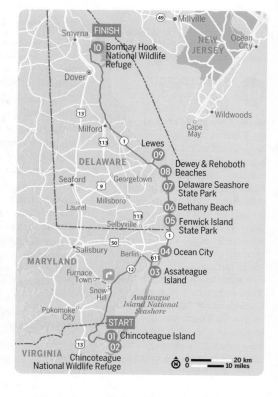

Delmarva

DURATION	DISTANCE	GREAT FOR
3 days	150 miles / 241km	Families

BEST TIME TO GO	Visit from June to September to get the most out of summer.

Yes: the Delmarva peninsula, named for its constituent three states (Delaware, Maryland and Virginia) offers sun, surf and sand. But also: wild horses, salt marshes, estuarine deltas and surprisingly isolated oceanfront scenery, considering we're mere miles from the most densely populated urban corridor in the country. Find neon lights and greasy boardwalk fries, or a lonely patch of sea oats and a view of the ocean – either option exists here.

Link your trip

20 Eastern Shore Odyssey

Head west from Ocean City to reach Berlin, MD, and the small towns of the interior Eastern Shore.

27 Bracketing the Bay

From Chincoteague, head down the Virginia Eastern Shore and cross into the tidewater historic triangle.

01 **CHINCOTEAGUE ISLAND**

Way, way out at the edge of anywhere – a uniform three hours and 20 minutes from Washington, DC, Baltimore, Philadelphia and Richmond – we begin this trip at the isolated end of the road.

That said, Chincoteague (Shink-oh-teeg) hardly feels lonely. Rather, this is a cheerful resort island, populated by fisher and folks seeking an escape in the coastal salt marshes of an Atlantic barrier island.

The best activity around is exploring the unique environment; we recommend boarding a boat with

BEST FOR

☑

FAMILIES
The charms and nostalgia of Bethany Beach (p137).

Chincoteague National Wildlife Refuge

Captain Dan (captaindanstours.com). His personable Around the Island Tours take two to 2½ hours and are excellent value.

🚙 **THE DRIVE**

In the town of Chincoteague, follow Maddox Blvd south to the traffic circle at the Chamber of Commerce. Take the exit into Beach Access Rd, which leads to the national wildlife refuge.

↱ **Detour**
Furnace Town

Start: 01 **Chincoteague Island**
As you drive to Assateague from Chincoteague, you'll have the option, at the MD-12/US 113 split, of detouring northwest on MD-12. Follow this road for 4 miles and you'll

enter a woolly patch of pinewoods and soggy bottomlands.

For years, children who grew up in the far-eastern reaches of the Eastern Shore whispered about a ghost town by these bogs, an abandoned settlement known as 'Furnace Town' named for an old smelting furnace. The ghost of an old African American man, the town's last inhabitant, supposedly stalked the site.

Good story, right? Well, it's true, except for the ghost bit (as far as we know). And whereas in the past this was a cautionary tale about the wild woods, today **Furnace Town** (furnacetown.com) is a living history museum in the same vein as Colonial Williamsburg (p182). Seven artisans, including a blacksmith, a

weaver and a printer, bring the town to life. The actors are pretty scrupulous about doing everything the way it was done back in the day, and they're quite willing to teach, especially if you've got children along. If you need to combine a historical trip with the trappings of a nature walk, Furnace Town is a perfect detour.

02 **CHINCOTEAGUE NATIONAL WILDLIFE REFUGE**

Within the 14,000-acre **Chincoteague National Wildlife Refuge** (fws.gov/refuge/chincoteague) you'll encounter breeze-kissed beaches with no crowds, dunes, maritime forest and freshwater and saltwater marshes. Also keep an eye out for snapping turtles, Virginia opossum, river otters, great blue herons and, of course, a herd of Chincoteague ponies.

Six trails web across the wetlands and woodlands, ranging from a quarter mile to 3¼ miles in length; none offer any serious elevation gain. To make sense of it all drop by the **Herbert H Bateman Educational & Administrative Center**, a marvel of green architecture that, set against the marshes, seems to resemble a futuristic, solar-powered duck blind.

Photo opportunity

Wild horses pounding the beach at Assateague Island National Seashore.

Assateague is another barrier island, a low, sandy sweep of land peppered with the feral horses this region is so famous for. Kayaking, canoeing and particularly cycling are all popular on the island. There are some 37 miles of beach here, all considerably quieter than nearby Ocean City. Plus: you can **camp** (recreation. gov) on the Maryland side of the island. The facilities are basic but decently comfortable. We recommend just bringing your tent and waking up to the wind – who can object to a morning with an Atlantic sunrise and wild horses cantering by the waves?

THE DRIVE
Head back into town, then west on Chincoteague Rd until it hits State Rte 679/Fleming Rd, then turn right. Rte 679 will cross into Maryland and become MD-12. Follow it north for 11 miles, then turn onto US 113. Take 113 north for 16 miles, then right (east) onto MD-376. Drive 4 miles, then turn right (south) onto MD-611; follow it for 4 miles to Assateague Island.

03 **ASSATEAGUE ISLAND**
While there are two entrances to **Assateague Island National Seashore** (nps. gov/asis), we are directing you to the one in Maryland, 8 miles south of Ocean City.

THE DRIVE
Get back on Rte 611 and take it north to reach the southern outskirts of Ocean City. After a little over 8 miles you'll hit Ocean Gateway Rd; turn right here and it's 1.5 miles to the OC.

Camping at Assateague Island National Seashore

04 OCEAN CITY

Ocean City – the 'OC', as some call it – is like the Platonic ideal of an Atlantic seaside resort. You see it from afar as you cross Assawoman Bay, a name that's provoked giggles for generations of Maryland school-kids: a skyline of silver condos, neon, all-you-can-eat buffets and the boardwalk.

Ah, the boardwalk: built in 1902, it extends from Ocean City Inlet at the southern end of the island to 27th St, a distance of some 2.3 miles. Along the way there's a sandy beach on one side and endless T-shirt shops and purveyors of fast food on the other. The most visible landmark is **Ocean Gallery** (facebook. com/oceangalleryworldcenter), an enormous art gallery stuffed with prints of varying quality, but there are a few gems, with an exterior papered in vibrant folk art.

If you really want to engage in tacky seaside fun to the fullest extent possible, hit up **Trimpers Rides** (trimpersrides.com), one of the oldest of old-school amusement parks. For local history, visit the **Ocean City Life-Saving Station Museum** (ocmuseum. org) on the southern tip of the boardwalk.

THE DRIVE
Allow about 30 minutes, depending on traffic, for this trip. Drive north on the Coastal Hwy – also known as Philadelphia Ave and MD-258 – until you hit the Delaware border, where the road becomes DE-1. Fenwick Island State Park is across the border.

05 FENWICK ISLAND STATE PARK

Cross into Delaware and Ocean City's neon gives way to peaceful groves and miles – three, to be exact – of quiet beach and wooded trails. Welcome to **Fenwick Island State Park** (destateparks.com).

Within the park you'll find **Coastal Kayak** (coastalkayak. com), a well-regarded outdoor adventure outfit that can take you on paddling tours of the nearby wetlands and sea islands, and arrange rentals of kayaks, stand-up paddleboards (SUP) and sailing craft (small Hobies).

THE DRIVE
Bethany Beach is 5 miles north of Fenwick Island State Park on DE-1. Along the way you'll pass a few private beach communities; be warned that there are children at play and speed limits in these parts are enforced pretty mercilessly.

06 BETHANY BEACH

You'll know you've reached Bethany when you see **Chief Little Owl**, a 24ft stylized totem pole meant to represent the indigenous Nanticoke Indians, sculpted by Hungarian artist Peter Wolf Toth. The area's most family-friendly beach, Bethany also boasts something like a real town center. Kids and the science-inclined will enjoy the exhibits and nature trail at the **Bethany Beach Nature Center** (inlandbays.org). A bandstand in the middle of town features live performances on weekends.

THE DRIVE
Pretty straightforward: head north on DE-1 for about 8 miles, and you're at Delaware Seashore State Park.

07 DELAWARE SEASHORE STATE PARK

In between Bethany and Dewey Beach, you'll find 6 miles of dramatically wind-whipped dunes, sea oats and crashing Atlantic waves. When skies are gray and the sea is rough, **Delaware Seashore State Park** (destateparks.com) looks remarkably rugged considering the generally placid nature of Delmarva's, well, nature.

There are several miles of hiking trails, some of the prettiest beaches in the region, and during the summer rangers lead daily cultural and wilderness activities.

THE DRIVE
Dewey Beach is 4 miles north of here via DE-1; Rehoboth is 2.5 miles north of Dewey Beach.

08 DEWEY & REHOBOTH BEACHES

Dewey is the wild child of the Delaware beach towns. This is the spot for spring breakers and teenagers and 20-somethings from further north looking to party.

Rehoboth isn't quite as hedonistic, but that's a relative distinction. People still come

TOP TIP:

Off-Season Info

Note that we cover seasonal summer towns on this trip that are busy from Memorial Day (last weekend in May) to Labor Day (first Monday in September). While hotel rates plunge in winter, many tours, activities and museums are closed then as well.

here to let loose, but the crowd is more slanted toward older professionals from DC, Baltimore and Philadelphia. Rehoboth has also been a popular artist colony and, by extension, LGBTIQ+ destination for decades; as such, a small but vibrant gallery scene is manifest. The main public beach for both communities is in Rehoboth, and the intermixing of frat boys in Eagles caps and older gay couples coming from their bohemian summer houses is a sight in and of itself. If you're partying in Dewey and need to get back to Rehoboth, or vice versa, don't stress. During the summer the two towns are connected by the Jolly Trolley, which runs late into the night for you party people.

THE DRIVE
Take DE-1 north out of Rehoboth for 3.5 miles, then turn right onto Rd 268 (you'll see signs for Lewes). You'll drive a little over a mile on 268 to reach Lewes.

09 LEWES

For the brief period of time that this was a Dutch colony (about 300 years ago), Lewes was known as Zwaanendael (Valley of the Swans). Then the Dutch, after a clumsy overture of friendship to the local Leni Lenape tribe, were massacred by the Native Americans. The Dutch were eventually replaced by British colonists and now we all eat cheddar instead of gouda.

This history and other stories of this small, gingerbread-pretty town is explained at the **Zwaanendael Museum** (history. delaware.gov/museums). If you want some beach time away from the crowds of Rehoboth's boardwalk, head to adjacent **Cape Henlopen State Park** (destateparks.com). And if you want to leave Delaware altogether, the **Cape May–Lewes Ferry** (cmlf.com) runs services across Delaware Bay to New Jersey.

THE DRIVE
Take DE-1 north for about 30 miles, then take the exit for DE-9N. Follow it for 13 miles, past miles of marsh and sedge, then turn right at Whitehall Neck Rd and follow it into the refuge.

10 BOMBAY HOOK NATIONAL WILDLIFE REFUGE

You're not the only creature making a trip to **Bombay Hook National Wildlife Refuge** (fws. gov/refuge/Bombay_Hook). Hundreds of thousands of waterfowl use this protected wetland as a stopping point along their migration routes.

A 12-mile wildlife driving trail through 16,251 acres of sweet-smelling saltwater marsh, cordgrass and tidal mud flats is the highlight of this stop, which manages to encapsulate all of the soft beauty of the Delmarva peninsula in one perfectly preserved ecosystem.

There are also five walking trails, two of which are handicapped accessible, as well as observation towers overlooking the entire affair. Across the water you may see the lights and factories of New Jersey, an industrial yin to this area's wilderness yang.

Cormorant, Bombay Hook National Wildlife Refuge

20

Eastern Shore Odyssey

DURATION	DISTANCE	GREAT FOR
3 days	165 miles / 254 km	Families

BEST TIME TO GO	April to September for sunny weather and blue skies.

The Eastern Shore of Maryland and the state of Delaware are made up of bucolic farming villages and postcard-perfect small towns, but there's an urban edge further north, including Wilmington, one of the eastern seaboard's undiscovered major cities. Cross this green slice of America that sits in the shadow of the concrete superhighways but still feels romantically removed from them.

Link your trip

19 Delmarva

From Georgetown, head east to Rehoboth Beach along Rte 9 to get some sun, sand and surf.

17 Maritime Maryland

In Snow Hill, go west to Crisfield via US 113 and US 13 for culinary culture and cracking crabs.

01 SNOW HILL

Attractive Snow Hill, a village of a little more than 2000 people, sits on the banks of the Pocomoke River. It's a postcard-perfect slice of Americana, with its antique shops, cafes and brick buildings, all arrayed in a loose grid around a town hall and a church.

Located in a little house that itself resembles a set piece from a historical movie, the **Julia A Purnell Museum** (visitmaryland.org) is a veritable attic of all things Snow Hill. The attraction isn't so much the exhibits as the town's obvious pride in them.

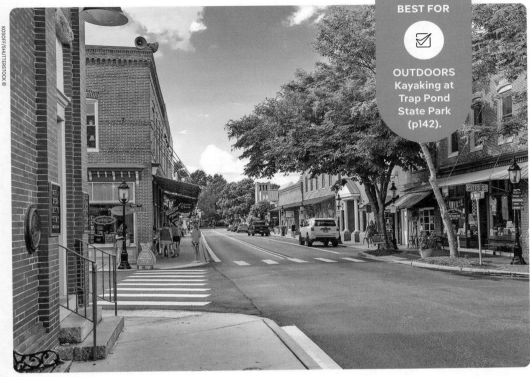

KOSOFF/SHUTTERSTOCK ©

BEST FOR

✅

OUTDOORS
Kayaking at
Trap Pond
State Park
(p142).

Berlin

About 3.5 miles outside of town, **Pocomoke River State Park** (dnr.maryland.gov/publiclands), part of the 15,000-acre Pocomoke State Forest, is an exquisite state park, especially for kids. There are trails, paddling opportunities, wetlands, woods, a nature center and a pool ($6 for day use).

Snow Hill is almost equidistant (two hours and 45 minutes) from Washington, DC, and Baltimore.

🚗 **THE DRIVE**
Drive north on US 113, through a patchwork of corn fields, woodsy groves and flower banks, for 20 miles until you see signs for Berlin.

02 **BERLIN**
There's a red-brick stateliness to Berlin's town center that is quite compelling to travelers, and we're not the first people to notice. The films *Runaway Bride* and *Tuck Everlasting* both used Berlin as their stand-in for a quintessential American small town.

So, what is there to do? Potter about, browse the ubiquitous antique shops, or hit the local **farmers market** (berlinmain street.com/farmersmarket) on Sundays. Or check out a show at the local **Globe Theater** (globeberlin.com), a dinner theater-cum-bar with excellent nosh and a packed performance

schedule that's always good for a date night.

🚗 **THE DRIVE**
Take US 50 westbound from Berlin for about 20 miles until you hit the outskirts of Salisbury, MD. Merge onto the ramp toward US 13 north and follow that for about 8 miles, then turn left onto Bi State Rd. Follow Bi State for 8 miles until you hit Laurel.

03 **LAUREL**
Laurel, the first town you'll come to in Delaware, is...well, it's *nice*. There's not a lot to do besides walk around and soak up the vibe.

If you want to feel transported, head six miles east of Laurel

to **Trap Pond State Park**
(destateparks.com/trappond). The
park is the site of the northern-
most bald cypress habitat – a
flooded forest that looks like it
lurched out of the Louisiana
bayou – in the USA.

 THE DRIVE
Take Rte 9 northeast from
Laurel for about 10.5 miles, cutting
through farmland, fields, forests,
no-name unincorporated areas and
the fantastically named Hardscrabble Rd to reach Georgetown.

04 **GEORGETOWN**
The most attractive buildings in the seat of Sussex
County are arranged around
Georgetown Circle, an atypical
round town green (in these parts,
town centers are usually square)

Photo opportunity

Grab a shot of downtown
Berlin's twee city center in
the early evening.

anchored by a handsome courthouse on its northeast side.

Georgetown's economy is largely
linked to a nearby chicken-
processing plant. The facility is
staffed by many workers from
Central America, giving this small
town a surprisingly large Latin
enclave.

Five miles northwest is the **Redden State Forest**, the largest state
forest (9500 acres) in Delaware.

You can access some 44 miles of
trails, primarily from E Redden
Rd, which leads past the **Redden
State Forest & Education
Center** (agriculture.delaware.gov).

 THE DRIVE
You could get to your next
destination via DE-1, but it's not
the most attractive road. Instead,
head west on DE-404 for 11 miles,
then turn right (north) on US 13 and
follow it for 30 miles until you reach
Dover.

05 **DOVER**
Dover's city center is
quite attractive; the
rowhouse-lined streets are peppered with restaurants and shops,
and, on prettier lanes, broadleaf
trees spread their branches and
provide good shade.

LISA RAPKO/SHUTTERSTOCK ©

Dover Air Force Base

Learn about the first official state – Delaware – at **First State Heritage Park** (destateparks.com). This complex of buildings serves as a welcome center for the city of Dover, the state of Delaware and the adjacent statehouse. Access the latter via the **Georgian Old State House** (history.delaware.gov/museums), built in 1791 and since restored, which contains art galleries and in-depth exhibits on the First State's history and politics.

THE DRIVE
It's a quick 7-mile drive southeast on DE-1 to Dover AFB. Take exit 91 for Delaware 9 toward Little Creek/Kitts Hummock, and keep an eye out for signs leading to the Air Mobility Command Museum.

06 DOVER AIR FORCE BASE
Dover Air Force Base is a visible symbol of American military muscle and a poignant reminder of the cost of war. This is the location of the Department of Defense's largest mortuary, and traditionally the first stop on native soil for the remains of American service members killed overseas.

The base is the site of the **Air Mobility Command Museum** (amcmuseum.org). If you're into aviation, you'll enjoy it; the nearby airfield is filled with restored vintage cargo and freight planes, including C-130s, a Vietnam War–era C-7 and WWII-era 'Flying Boxcar.'

Two miles from the base is the **John Dickinson Plantation** (history.delaware.gov/museums), the restored 18th-century home of the founding father of the same name, also known as the Penman of the Revolution for his eloquent written arguments for independence.

THE DRIVE
The longest drive on this trip is also the simplest and prettiest. Follow DE-9 north for 50 miles, passing several protected wetlands along the way, all the way to New Castle.

07 NEW CASTLE
Like a colonial playset frozen in amber, downtown New Castle is all gray cobbles and beige stonework, with wrought iron details throughout. In fact, the entire four- by five-block area

has been designated a National Historic Landmark. The local **Old Court House** (history.delaware. gov) dates back to the 17th century and is now operated as a museum by the state.

The New Castle Historical Society owns and operates **Amstel House** (newcastlehistory.org) and **Dutch House** (newcastlehistory. org), which are usually visited as part of a joint tour. Amstel House is a surviving remnant of 1730s colonial opulence; Dutch House is a smaller example of a working residence.

THE DRIVE
Follow DE-9 northeast for 7 miles into downtown Wilmington.

08 WILMINGTON
Delaware's biggest city is full of muscular art-deco architecture and a vibrant arts scene, plus a diverse populace that blends Baltimore charm with Philly saltiness.

The **Delaware Art Museum** (delart.org) anchors the local creative community, and exhibits the work of the local Brandywine School, including Edward Hopper, John Sloan and three generations of Wyeths.

The **Wilmington Riverfront** (riverfrontwilm.com) is made up of several blocks of redeveloped waterfront shops, restaurants and cafes; the most striking building is the **Delaware Contemporary** (decontemporary.org), which consistently displays innovative exhibitions.

In the art-deco Woolworth's building, the **Delaware History Museum** (dehistory.org) proves the First State's past includes

---

THE POTATO HOUSE RULES

The most hyper-regional architectural oddity we encountered on our road trips – besides southern Maryland's tobacco barns – were the potato houses of Sussex County, Delaware. These tall and narrow two-story wooden-frame structures were storage facilities for sweet potatoes (yams), once a cash crop of this region. Potato houses can be spotted throughout southern Delaware, often on lonely back roads.

The skinny potato houses held crops from October to February; their proportions allowed them to be heated easily, but also facilitated air circulation. High windows provided a ventilation counterpoint to the heat – sweet potatoes require a uniform, constant temperature of 50°F (10°C).

Eleven potato houses are concentrated near Laurel. They can be a bit tough to find, though, and most reside on private property. Contact the **Laurel Historical Society** (laureldehistoricalsociety.org) for directions. If you're driving around, the rather appropriately dubbed Chipman Potato House is at the intersection of Chipmans Pond Rd & Christ Church Rd (GPS: 38.561004,-75.537342), 2.5 miles east of Laurel.

---

loads more than being head of the line to sign the Constitution.

Detour
Winterthur &
the Brandywine Valley
Start: 08 Wilmington
Head out of Wilmington on the Kennett Pike and then turn north onto Montchanin Rd. Head north for about 6 miles and you're in the intersection of some of the wealthiest suburbs of Wilmington, West Chester, PA, and Philadelphia, a green and lush region also known as the Brandywine Valley.

The grandest of the grand homes that pepper the valley is **Winterthur** (winterthur.org), the palatial mansion of the du Pont family, whose wealth built much of Delaware. Today, the residence and its magnificent gardens are open to the public. Curators maintain the home as both a testament to Henry Francis du Pont's love of early American

architectural styles and American decorative arts and antiques.

Friendly docents lead tours around the grounds, pointing out design and architectural oddities and generally sharing an infectious enthusiasm. The nearby gardens include flower beds that bloom in alternating seasons, which means the grounds are always swathed in some floral fireworks display. Kids will love the Enchanted Forest, built to resemble a children's book come to life.

Just minutes away is **Brandywine Creek State Park** (destateparks. com/brandywinecreek). This green space would be impressive anywhere, but is doubly so considering how close it is to prodigious urban development. Nature trails and shallow streams wend through the park; check the website for information on paddling or tubing down the dark green Brandywine Creek.

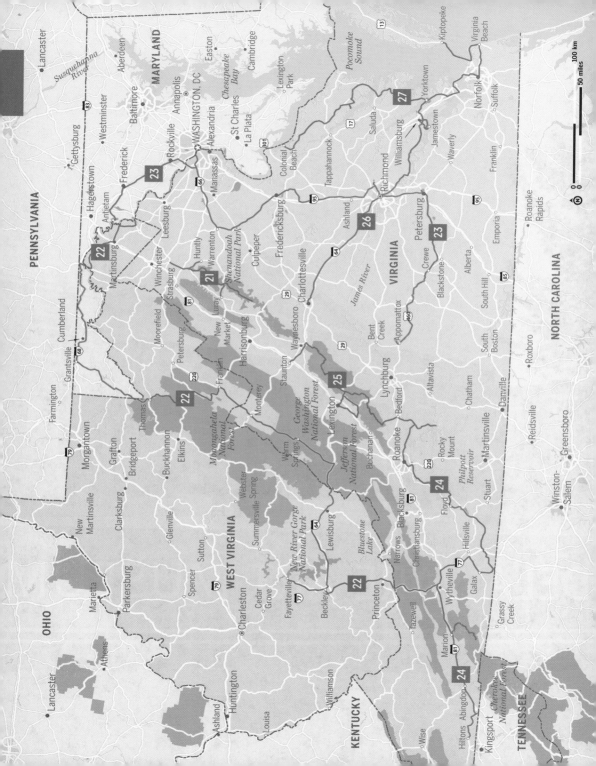

Appomattox Court House National Historical Park (p167)

Virginia & West Virginia

Explore
Virginia & West Virginia

With the Blue Ridge Mountains to the west, the Atlantic Ocean to the east and a slew of historic destinations between them, it's easy to see why Virginians are so proud of their state. Or as they call it here: 'The Commonwealth.' Byways and backroads ribbon past sandy beaches, rolling farmlands and gentle mountains. Small towns and large cities are inviting enclaves at the end of the daily drive, sharing art, food and shelter with welcoming aplomb. Best part? You can get anywhere you want in a day, and the drive will surely be pretty.

Richmond

Civil War history shares space with a thriving downtown riverfront and walkable communities like the Fan and Church Hill, where residents contemplate public art and attend neighborhood events that fill sidewalks and parks. Overlooking the James River, where locals paddle Class IV rapids and catch live music, the city is a convenient base for day trips to colonial-era plantations, Civil War battlefields and scenic hikes in the Blue Ridge Mountains.

Charlottesville

Home to the architecturally resplendent University of Virginia (UVA), this small city in the foothills of the Blue Ridge Mountains is regularly ranked as one of the best places to live in the United States. The grounds of the campus, the adjacent Main Street and the pedestrian Downtown Mall stay busy with students, professors and tourists, keeping the vibe energetic and diverse. Many visitors make the drive to Monticello, the grand home of Thomas Jefferson, who founded the school. More than 100 wineries are located in the countryside just beyond the city.

Shepherdstown

Federal-style brick buildings line tidy streets in historic downtown Shepherdstown, an artsy enclave in West Virginia just a short drive from Harpers Ferry and Antietam National Battlefield. The Appalachian Trail, the Potomac River and the C&O Canal towpath are also nearby. The region is dotted with charming

WHEN TO GO

Virginia is pleasant year round, with fairly mild winters, but the best time for a road trip is spring through mid-fall. Wild flowers and botanical gardens do their best work in May while summer sees festivals across the state. Fall foliage along Skyline Drive and the Blue Ridge Parkway typically peaks in October.

small towns, but Shepherdstown is especially attractive thanks to its robust dining scene and pretty location by the Potomac River. Shepherd University and its student body add an appealing bohemian energy.

Roanoke

This former railroad town was once considered sleepy, but no more. An expanding greenway system, a burgeoning arts scene, mountain biking bona fides and a growing portfolio of farm-to-table restaurants have boosted the city's profile. In some circles, it's considered the next Asheville. Dubbed the Star City thanks to the neon lights of the soaring Mill Mountain Star, which overlooks downtown, Roanoke is a short drive from the Blue Ridge Parkway and the Appalachian Trail.

Norfolk

The James, Nansemond and Elizabeth rivers meet at the Chesapeake Bay, comprising a sprawling region in eastern Virginia known as Hampton Roads. Norfolk is a busy port

TRANSPORT

Washington, DC, is a convenient starting point for numerous trips in this chapter. Airports near the nation's capital include Dulles International and Ronald Reagan Washington National. Union Station is a busy hub for Amtrak trains in DC. There is an international airport in Richmond and regional airports in Charlottesville and Roanoke.

city in the center of it all – as the many bridges and tunnels here confirm. The impressive Chrysler Museum of Art spearheads the rapidly growing arts scene and the downtown Ghent District hosts most of the city's cultural and entertainment events. Lively Virginia Beach and the gorgeous Eastern Shore are a short drive away.

 WHAT'S ON

Fourth of July

From big cities to small towns, everyone pauses to celebrate Independence Day, typically with live music followed by fireworks.

Fall Foliage

Leaves typically change color in the Blue Ridge Mountains in October, drawing road trippers to Skyline Drive and the Blue Ridge Parkway.

Bridge Day

BASE jumpers leap from the New River Gorge Bridge in Fayetteville, WV, the third Saturday of October.

Resources

Appalachian Trail Conservancy (appalachiantrail.org) Manages and preserves the AT, with helpful info and updates for hikers on its website.

Crooked Road (thecrookedroadva.com) Shares information about live shows and venues for mountain music in southwest Virginia.

 WHERE TO STAY

Historic inns are a regional highlight, and they often have a good restaurant or pub on site. B&Bs can be a charming option and typically include good Southern breakfasts. Hotels and motels in Virginia Beach are typically just a short walk from the ocean. Well-managed public campgrounds border Skyline Drive and the Blue Ridge Parkway in the Blue Ridge Mountains, and there are numerous private campgrounds in the mountain foothills. For evening stargazing talks and proximity to waterfalls, pitch a tent at Big Meadows Campground on Skyline Drive in Shenandoah National Park.

21

Skyline Drive

BEST FOR

CULTURE
Byrd Visitor Center (p154) offers an illuminating peek into Appalachian folkways.

DURATION	DISTANCE	GREAT FOR
3 days	150 miles / 240km	Nature

BEST TIME TO GO	From May to Nov for great weather, open facilities and views.

Dinosaur Land

The centerpiece of the ribbon-thin Shenandoah National Park is the jaw-dropping beauty of Skyline Dr, which runs for just over 100 miles atop the Blue Ridge Mountains. Unlike the massive acreage of western parks like Yellowstone or Yosemite, Shenandoah is at times only a mile wide. That may seem to narrow the park's scope, yet it makes it a perfect space for traversing and road-tripping goodness.

Link your trip

26 Peninsula to the Piedmont

At the end of this trip, continue on to the park exit, then turn east to Charlottesville to explore the Piedmont's breweries and wineries.

25 Blue Ridge Parkway

You can also head from the park exit to Staunton, VA, about 20 minutes away, to start America's favorite drive.

FRONT ROYAL

01 Straddling the northern entrance to the park is the tiny city of Front Royal. Although it's not among Virginia's fanciest ports of call, this lush riverside town offers all the urban amenities one might need before a camping or hiking trip up in the mountains.

If you need to gather your bearings, an obvious place to start is the **Front Royal Visitor Center** (frontroyalva.com). Friendly staff are on hand to overwhelm you with information about what to do in the area.

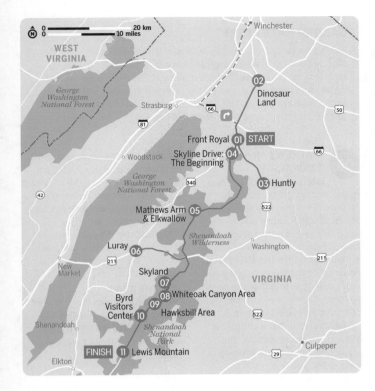

WHY I LOVE THIS TRIP

Amy C Balfour, writer

A drive on Skyline Dr – one of the USA's original scenic byways – is good for the soul. Lined with overlooks and trailheads, the road twists above the Shenandoah Valley through Shenandoah National Park, sharing a beautiful combination of two distinct ecosystems: the rocky, forested mountains of the Appalachians on one side, and the manicured hills of the Virginia Piedmont on the other. This trip includes hearty fare and unique accommodations along the way.

THE DRIVE
Dinosaur Land is 10 miles north of Front Royal, toward Winchester, via US 340 (Stonewall Jackson Hwy).

DETOUR
Museum of the Shenandoah Valley
Start: 01 **Front Royal**

Of all the places where you can begin your journey into Shenandoah National Park, none seem to make quite as much sense as the **Museum of the Shenandoah Valley** (themsv. org), an institution dedicated to its namesake. Located in the town of Winchester, some 25 miles north of Front Royal, the museum is an exhaustive repository of information on the valley, Appalachian culture and its associated folkways, some of the most unique

in the USA. Exhibits are divided into four galleries, accompanied by the restored Glen Burnie historical home and 6 acres of gardens.

To get here, take I-66 west from Front Royal to I-81 and head north for 25 miles. In Winchester, follow signs to the museum, which is located on the outskirts of town.

02 DINOSAUR LAND
Before you head into the national park and its stunning natural beauty, visit **Dinosaur Land** (dinosaurland.com) for some fantastic human-made tackiness. This spectacularly low-brow shrine to concrete sculpture is not to be missed. Although it's an 'educational prehistoric forest,' with more than 50 life-size

dinosaurs (and a King Kong for good measure), you'd probably learn more about the tenants by fast-forwarding through *Jurassic Park 3*. But that's not why you've stopped here, so grab your camera and sidle up to the triceratops for memories that will last a millennium.

THE DRIVE
Head back to Front Royal, then go south on US 522 (Remount Rd) for about 9 miles to reach Huntly.

03 HUNTLY
Huntly is a small-ish town nestled in the green foothills of the Shenandoahs, lying just in the southern shadows of Front Royal. It's a good spot to refuel on some cosmopolitan culture and foodie deliciousness in the form of **Rappahannock Cellars** (rappa hannockcellars.com), one of the nicer wineries of north-central Virginia, where vineyard-covered hills shadow the horizon, like

some slice of northern Italian pastoral prettiness that got lost somewhere in the upcountry of the Old Dominion. Give the port a whirl (well, maybe not if you're driving).

 THE DRIVE
Head back to Front Royal, as you'll enter Skyline Dr from there. From the beginning of Skyline Dr, it's 5.5 miles to Dickey Ridge.

04 **SKYLINE DRIVE: THE BEGINNING**
Skyline Dr is the scenic drive to end all scenic drives. The 75 overlooks, with views into the Shenandoah Valley and the Piedmont, are all breathtaking. In spring and summer, endless variations on the color green are sure to enchant, just as the vibrant reds and yellows will amaze you in autumn. This might be your chance to finally hike a section of the Appalachian Trail, which crosses Skyline Dr at 32 places.

The logical first stop on an exploration of Skyline and Shenandoah National Park is the **Dickey Ridge Visitors Center** (nps.gov/shen). It's not just an informative leaping-off point; it's a building with a fascinating history all of its own. This spot originally operated as a 'wild' dining hall in 1908 (back then, that simply meant it had a terrace for dancing). However, it closed during WWII and didn't reopen until 1958, when it became a visitor center. Now it's one of the park's two main information centers and contains a little bit of everything you'll need to get started on your trip along Skyline Dr.

 THE DRIVE
It's a twisty 19 more miles along Skyline Dr to Mathews Arm.

GARDEN MAZE ALERT

Next to the Luray Caverns is an excellent opportunity to let your inner Shelley Duvall or Scatman Crothers run wild. Go screaming *Shining*-style through the **Garden Maze**, but beware! This maze is harder than it looks and some could spend longer inside it than they anticipated. Paranormal and psychic abilities are permitted, but frowned upon, when solving the hedge maze. Redrum! Redrum!

---

05 **MATHEWS ARM & ELKWALLOW**
Mathews Arm is the first major section of Shenandoah National Park you encounter after leaving Dickey Ridge. Before you get there, you can stop at a pull-over at Mile 19.4 and embark on a 4.8 mile loop hike to **Little Devils Stairs**. Getting through this narrow gorge is as tough as the name suggests; expect hand-over-hand climbing for some portions.

Mathews Arm has a campground, an amphitheater, and some nice breezes; early on in your drive, you're already at 2750ft altitude.

From the amphitheater, it's a 6½-mile moderately taxing hike to lovely **Overall Run Falls**, the

TOP TIP:

Mileposts

Handy stone mileposts (MP) are still the best means of figuring out just where you are on Skyline Dr. They begin at Mile 0 near Front Royal, and end at Mile 105 at the national park's southern entrance near Rockfish Gap.

---

tallest in the national park (93ft). There are plenty of rock ledges where you can enjoy the view and snap a picture, but be warned that the falls sometimes dry out in the summer.

Elkwallow Wayside, which includes a nice picnic area and lookout, is at Mile 24, just past Mathews Arm.

 THE DRIVE
From Mathews Arm, proceed south along Skyline for about 10 miles, then take the US 211 ramp westbound for about 7 miles to reach Luray.

06 **LURAY**
Luray is a good spot to grab some grub and potentially rest your head if you're not into camping. It's also where you'll find the wonderful **Luray Caverns** (luraycaverns.com), one of the most extensive cavern systems on the East Coast.

Here you can take a one-hour, roughly 1-mile guided tour of the caves, opened to the public more than 100 years ago. The rock formations throughout are quite stunning, and Luray boasts what is surely a one-of-a-kind attraction – the Stalacpipe Organ – in the pit of its belly. This crazy contraption has been banging out melodies on the rock formations for decades. As the guide says, the caves are 400 million years old 'if you believe in geological dating' (if the subtext is lost on you, understand this is a conservative part of the country where creationism is widely accepted, if hotly debated). No matter what you believe in, you'll be impressed by the fantastic underground expanses.

THE DRIVE
Take US 211 east for 10 miles to get back on Skyline Dr. Then proceed 10 miles south along Skyline to get to Skyland. Along the way you'll drive over the highest point of Skyline Dr (3680ft). At Mile 40.5, just before reaching Skyland, you can enjoy amazing views from the parking overlook at Thorofare Mountain (3595ft).

07 SKYLAND
Horse-fanciers will want to book a trail ride through Shenandoah at **Skyland Stables** (goshenandoah.com).

Rides last up to 2½ hours and are a great way to see the wildlife and epic vistas. Pony rides are also available for the wee members of your party. This is a good spot to break up your trip if you're into hiking (and if you're on this trip, we're assuming you are).

There's great access to local trailheads around here, and the sunsets are fabulous. The accommodations are a little rustic, but in a charming way (the Trout Cabin was built in 1911, and it feels like it, but we mean this in the most complimentary way possible). The place positively oozes nostalgia, but if you're into amenities, you may find it a little disappointing

THE DRIVE
It's only 1.5 miles south on Skyline Dr to get to the Whiteoak parking area.

08 WHITEOAK CANYON AREA
At Mile 42.6, Whiteoak Canyon is another area of Skyline Dr that offers unmatched hiking and exploration opportunities. There are several parking areas that all provide different entry points to the various trails that snake through this ridge- and stream-scape.

Most hikers are attracted to Whiteoak Canyon for its **waterfalls** – there are six in total, with the tallest topping out at 86ft high. At the Whiteoak parking area, you can make a 4.6-mile round-trip hike to these cascades, but beware – it's a steep climb up and back to your car. To reach the next set of waterfalls, you'll have to add 2.7 miles to the round-trip and prepare yourself for a steep (1100ft) elevation shift.

BIG BLINK CREATIVE/SHUTTERSTOCK ©

Stalacpipe Organ, Luray Caverns

The **Limberlost Trail** and parking area is just south of Whiteoak Canyon. This is a moderately difficult 1.3-mile trek into spruce upcountry thick with hawks, owls and other birds; the boggy ground is home to many salamanders.

THE DRIVE
It's about 3 miles south of Whiteoak Canyon to the Hawksbill area via Skyline Dr.

09 HAWKSBILL AREA
Once you reach Mile 45.6, you've reached **Hawksbill**, the name of both this part of Skyline Dr and the tallest peak in Shenandoah National Park. Numerous trails in this area skirt the summits of the mountain.

Pull into the parking area at Hawksbill Gap (Mile 45.6). You've

Photo opportunity
The fabulous 360-degree horizon at the top of Bearfence Rock Scramble.

got a few hiking options to pick from. The **Lower Hawksbill Trail** is a steep 1.7-mile round-trip that circles Hawksbill Mountain's lower slopes; that huff-inducing ascent yields a pretty great view over the park. Another great lookout lies at the end of the **Upper Hawksbill Trail**, a moderately difficult 2.1-mile trip. You can

link up with the Appalachian Trail here via a spur called the Salamander Trail.

If you continue south for about 5 miles, you'll reach **Fishers Gap Overlook**. The attraction here is the **Rose River Loop**, a 4-mile, moderately strenuous trail that is positively Edenic. Along the way you'll pass by waterfalls, under thick forest canopy and over swift-running streams.

THE DRIVE
From Fishers Gap, head about a mile south to the Byrd Visitor Center, technically located at Mile 51.

10 BYRD VISITORS CENTER
The **Harry F Byrd Visitors Center** (nps. gov/shen) is the central visitor

Dark Hollow Falls

center of Shenandoah National Park, marking (roughly) a halfway point between the two ends of Skyline Dr. It's devoted to explaining the settlement and development of the Shenandoah Valley via a series of small but well-curated exhibitions; as such, it's a good place to stop and learn about the surrounding culture (and pick up backcountry camping permits). There's camping and ranger activities in the **Big Meadows** area, located across the road from the visitors center.

The **Story of the Forest** trail is an easy, paved, 1.8-mile loop that's quite pretty; the trailhead connects to the visitors center.

You can also explore two nearby waterfalls. **Dark Hollow Falls**, which sounds (and looks) like something out of a Tolkien novel, is a 70ft high cascade located at the end of a quite steep 1.4-mile trail. **Lewis Falls**, accessed via Big Meadows, is on a moderately difficult 3.3-mile trail that intersects the Appalachian Trail; at one point you'll be scrabbling up a rocky slope.

THE DRIVE
The Lewis Mountain area is about 5 miles south of the Byrd Visitors Center via Skyline Dr. Stop for good overlooks at Milam Gap and Naked Creek (both clearly signposted from the road).

11 LEWIS MOUNTAIN
Lewis Mountain is both the name of one of the major camping areas of Shenandoah National Park and a nearby 3570ft mountain. The trail to the mountain is only about a mile long with a small elevation gain, and leads to a nice overlook. But the best view here is at the Bearfence Rock Scramble. That name is no joke; this 1.2-mile hike gets steep and rocky, and you don't want to attempt it during or after rainfall. The reward is one of the best panoramas of the Shenandoahs. After you leave, remember there's still about 50 miles of Skyline Dr between you and the park exit at Rockfish Gap.

22

BEST FOR

☑

CULTURE
Live music
at the Purple
Fiddle (p158).

The Appalachians & the AT

DURATION	DISTANCE	GREAT FOR
5 days	495 miles / 796km	Nature

BEST TIME TO GO	From September to November; brisk fall air is good for hikes.

Appalachian Trail, Harpers Ferry

The Appalachian Trail (AT) runs 2175 miles from Maine to Georgia, across the original American frontier and some of the oldest mountains on the continent. This journey fleshes out the unique ecological-cultural sphere of the greater Appalachians, particularly in Maryland, West Virginia and Virginia. Get your hiking boots on and be ready for sun-dappled national forests, quaint tree-shaded towns and many a wild, unfettered mountain range.

Link your trip

16 Along the C&O Canal

In Harpers Ferry, you can embark onto the Potomac towpath for lush scenery and a slice of engineering history.

24 The Crooked Road

From Mt Rogers, head east to Galax for a musical adventure.

01 **HARPERS FERRY**
While the Appalachian Trail isn't integral to this trip, we do honor it where we can. Harpers Ferry, a postcard-perfect little town nestled between the Shenandoah and Potomac Rivers, is home to some of the most beautiful scenery along the trail. Conveniently, this is also the headquarters for the **Appalachian Trail Conservancy** (appalachiantrail. org). The visitor center is located in the heart of town on Washington St and is a great place to ask for advice about how best to explore this region.

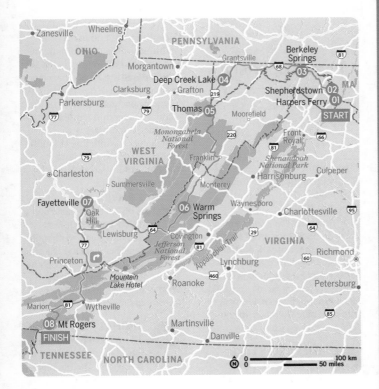

John Brown

A white abolitionist, Brown led an ill-conceived rebellion by enslaved people in Harpers Ferry that helped spark the Civil War. The uprising went wrong from the start. The first casualty was a free Black man, and the raiders were soon surrounded by angry local militia in the Harpers Ferry armory. Local enslaved people did not rise up as Brown hoped, and the next day two of his sons were killed by the militia. Eventually, a contingent of Marines commanded by Robert E Lee captured the armory and arrested Brown. The Albany Patriot, a Georgia newspaper, editorialized on Brown's proposed punishment: 'An undivided South says let him hang.' In the end, that execution was Brown's fate. Northern abolitionists were convinced slavery could only be ended by war, and Southerners were convinced war was required to protect it.

Brown was described as eccentric at best, and perhaps mad at worst, by contemporaries, but Frederick Douglass – a leader of the abolitionist movement – held him up as a hero, and wrote: 'Had some other men made such a display of rigid virtue, I should have rejected it, as affected, false, or hypocritical, but in John Brown, I felt it to be as real as iron or granite.'

For all that West Virginia is associated with the Appalachian Trail, it's only home to a scant 4 miles of it. However, the scenery is so awe-inspiring that it would be a shame to miss it. Take a hike framed by the wild rushing rapids of the Potomac River below, and the craggy, tree-covered mountain peaks above. If you're hiking from Maryland, you'll cross the Potomac River on a footbridge and then the Shenandoah River to pass into Virginia. While in West Virginia proper, stop at the famed **Jefferson Rock**, an ideal place for a picnic.

THE DRIVE

Head west from Harpers Ferry on US 340 for about 3 miles, then turn right onto WV-230N. It's about 9 miles from here to Shepherdstown. Parking downtown is heavily regulated because of the nearby college, so either park a few blocks away and hoof it, or bring coins for the meters.

02 SHEPHERDSTOWN

Shepherdstown is one of many settlements in the mountains cut from a similar cloth – artsy college towns that balance a significant amount of natural beauty with a quirky, bohemian culture. This is the oldest town in West Virginia, founded in 1762, and its **historic district** is packed with Federal-style brick buildings that are heartrendingly cute.

The bulk of the best preservation can be found along German St; all of the cutest historical twee-ness is within walking distance of here. The historic center is also close to Shepherd University; the student presence can be felt pretty strongly in town, but it's balanced out by plenty of pickup-driving West Virginia locals.

THE DRIVE
Head west on WV-45 (the Martinsburg Pike) for around 8 miles. Then turn right onto US 11 N/WV-9 W (which quickly becomes just WV-9) and follow it to the northwest, through the mountains, for 24 miles. Follow the signs for Berkeley Springs.

03 BERKELEY SPRINGS
Welcome to one of America's original spa towns, a mountainside retreat that's been a holiday destination since colonial times (did George Washington sleep here? You bet). The draw has always been the warm mineral springs, long rumored to have healing properties; such rumors have attracted a mix of people, from country folk with pickup trucks and gun racks to hippie refugees from the '60s.

Although this town is still best known for its spas, one of the more enjoyable activities here is strolling around and soaking up the odd New-Age-crystal-therapy-meets-the-Hatfields-and-the-McCoys vibe. If you do need a pamper, immerse yourself in the relaxation that is **Berkeley Springs State Park** (berkeley springssp.com), home to its Roman Bath House and enchanting, spring-fed pools.

Also: keep an eye out for the Samuel Taylor Suit Cottage, more popularly known as **Berkeley Castle**. Perched on a hill above town, it looks like a European

Photo opportunity
The cascades at Muddy Creek Falls, Deep Creek Lake.

fortress and was built in 1885 for Colonel Samuel Taylor Suit of Washington, DC.

THE DRIVE
Head into Maryland by going north on US 522 for about 6 miles; take the exit toward US 40/I-68 westbound. Follow this road west for around 62 miles through Maryland's western mountain spine. Take MD-495 south for 35 miles, then turn right onto Glendale Rd and follow it to Deep Creek Lake.

04 DEEP CREEK LAKE
Deep in western Maryland, plunked into a blue valley at the end of a series of tree-ridged mountains, is Maryland's largest lake: Deep Creek. With some 69 miles of shoreline stretching through the hills, there are a lot of outdoor activities here, as well as a small town for lodging and food. Try to arrive in October, when the **Autumn Glory Festival** (visitdeepcreek. com) celebrates the shocking fire hues of crimson and orange that paint a swath across the local foliage. The **Garrett County Visitor Center** (visitdeepcreek. com) is a good launching point for exploring the region.

The lake is most easily accessed via **Deep Creek Lake State Park** (maryland.gov/publiclands), which sits on a large plateau known as the Tablelands. The

area is carpeted in oak and hickory forest, and black bear sightings, while uncommon, are not unheard of. Nearby is **Swallow Falls State Park** (maryland. gov/publiclands), one of the most rugged, spectacular parks in the state. Hickory and hemlock trees hug the Youghiogheny River, which cuts a white line through wet slate gorges. Also here is the 53ft Muddy Creek Falls, the largest in the state.

THE DRIVE
Take US 219 southbound out of Garrett County and into West Virginia. You'll be climbing through some dramatic mountain scenery on the way. Once you cross the George Washington Hwy, you're almost in West Virginia. It's about 30 miles from Deep Creek Lake to Thomas.

05 THOMAS
Thomas isn't more than a blip on the...where'd it go? Oh, there it is. The big business of note for travelers here is the **Purple Fiddle** (purplefiddle. com), one of those great mountain stores where bluegrass culture and artsy daytrippers from the urban South and Northeast mash up into a stomping good time. There's live music every night and you may want to purchase tickets for weekend shows in advance. The artsy Fiddle is an unexpected surprise out here, and a fun one at that.

About 5 miles south of Thomas is **Blackwater Falls State Park** (blackwaterfalls.com). The falls tumble into an 8-mile gorge lined by red spruce, hickory and hemlock trees. There are loads of hiking options; look for the **Pendleton Point Overlook**, which perches over the deepest, widest point of the Canaan Valley.

THE DRIVE
From Thomas, you'll be taking the Appalachian Hwy south. The numerical and name designation of the road will switch a few times, from US 33 to WV-28 and back. After about 50 miles turn right onto US 220 and follow it for 31 miles to Warm Springs. This entire drive is particularly beautiful, all green mountains and small towns, so take your time and enjoy.

06 WARM SPRINGS
There's barely a gas station in sight out here, let alone a mall. You've crossed back into Virginia, and are now in the middle of the 1.8 million-acre **George Washington & Jefferson National Forests** (fs. usda.gov/gwj). The Warm Springs Ranger District is one of eight districts managing this enormous protected area, which stretches from Virginia to Kentucky.

There are far too many trails in this area alone to list here. Note that most trails are not actually in the town of Warm Springs; there is a ranger office here, and staff can direct you to the best places to explore. Some favorites include the 1-mile **Brushy Ridge Trail**, which wends past abundant blueberry and huckleberry bushes, and the 2.3-mile **Gilliam Run Trail**, which ascends to the top of Beard Mountain.

Post-hike, soak your weary bones in the historic **Warm Springs Pools**, which are managed by the **Omni Resort** (omnihotels.com). Reopened in 2022 after extensive renovations, the bathhouses surrounding the springs look much as they did a century ago. Numerous presidents have enjoyed relaxing in the pools.

THE DRIVE
Take US 220 southbound over more mountain peaks, by more hamlets all the way to I-64. Then take the highway west for around 40 miles. Exit onto US 60 westbound and drive for 35 miles, then merge onto US 19. Follow it for 7 miles over the New River Gorge to Fayetteville.

07 FAYETTEVILLE
You've crossed state lines yet again, and are back in West Virginia. Little Fayetteville serves as the gateway to the **New River Gorge**, a canyon

Warm Springs Pools

cut by a river that is, ironically, one of the oldest rivers in North America. Some 70,000 acres of the gorge is gazetted as national park land. **Canyon Rim Visitor Center** (nps.gov/neri), just north of the impressive gorge bridge, is one of four National Park Service visitor centers along the river and offers information about river outfitters, gorge climbing, hiking and mountain biking, as well as white-water rafting to the north on the Gauley River. A short trail behind the visitor center leads to great views of the bridge.

If you're interested in white-water rafting, also consider contacting the professionals at **Cantrell Ultimate Rafting** (cantrellultimaterafting.com), which runs several varieties of expeditions onto the water.

 THE DRIVE

Take US 19 south for 15 miles until you can merge with I-64/77 (it eventually becomes just I-77) southbound. Take this road south for 75 miles, then get on I-81 south and follow it for 27 miles to Marion.

DETOUR
Mountain Lake Hotel
Start: **07** **Fayetteville**

If you're looking to have the time of your life, head two hours south of Fayetteville into the far southwestern corner of Virginia. The **Mountain Lake Hotel** (mountainlakehotel.com) is an old stalwart of Appalachian tourism plunked on the shores of (imagine that) Mountain Lake. It also doubled as the Catskills resort 'Kellerman's' in a little old movie called *Dirty Dancing*. If you're tired of hiking, you might be interested in taking part in one of the theme weekends, where you can take dance lessons and finally learn to nail

that impossible lift. Sadly, Jennifer Grey, Patrick Swayze and Jerry Orbach are not included. There is a variety of accommodations at the resort: some will prefer the massive, historic flagstone main building with traditional hotel rooms; others seeking the full *Dirty Dancing* experience might enjoy the rustic lakeside cabins (comfortably modern inside) where Baby and her family stayed. Appalachian Trail purists who just can't wait to hit the trail again will find it just north of this 2600-acre resort. The Mountain Lake Hotel offers all sorts of other entertainments as well. Got a talent for the talent show? Nobody puts Baby in a corner!

If you've succeeded in meeting your new partner through a series of impromptu, yet still intricately choreographed dirty dances, you can return home. But, if for some reason you didn't connect, set off on the trail again and maybe find that mountain man or woman of your dreams.

08 **MT ROGERS**

You'll end this trip at the highest mountain in Virginia (and yes, you've crossed state lines again!). There are plenty of trekking opportunities in the **Mt Rogers National Recreation Area** (fs.usda.gov/gwj), which is part of the Washington & Jefferson National Forests (p159). Contact the ranger office for information on summiting the peak of Mt Rogers, and pat yourself on the back for getting here after so many state border hops! The local **Elk Garden Trailhead** is one of the best access points for tackling the local wilderness, and intersects the actual Appalachian Trail, making for an appropriate finish to the trip.

MYSTERY HOLE!

Oh man. We like roadside kitsch. And as such, we want to marry the **Mystery Hole** (mysteryhole.com) and have its Mysterious Hole-y kitschy babies.

So just what is the Mystery Hole? Well, we feel like giving away the secret sort of ruins the nature of this attraction, located about 10 miles northwest of Fayetteville, but on the other hand, we know you can't bear the suspense.

So here's the skinny: the Mystery Hole is a house where everything tilts at an angle! And there's a great gift shop. And the laws of gravity are defied because everything tilts at an angle!

OK: there's not actually a whole (pun intended) lot at the Hole. And that's fine. It's still a hell of a lot fun, if you come without taking things too seriously. What ultimately makes the Mystery Hole successful kitsch is not the Hole itself, but its promise of weirdness, as tantalizingly suggested by the billboards that precede it and the fantastically odd art that surrounds it.

23

The Civil War Tour

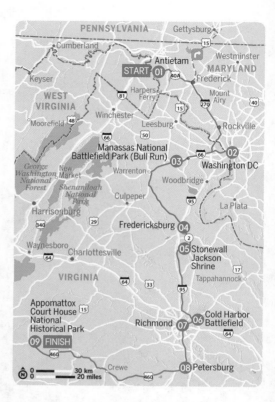

DURATION	DISTANCE	GREAT FOR
3 days	320 miles / 515km	History & Culture

BEST TIME TO GO	September to November; the brisk air still comes with sunny skies and autumnal color shows at preserved battlefields.

The Civil War was fought from 1861–65 in the nation's backyards, and many of those backyards are between Washington, DC and Richmond. On this trip you will cross battlefields where more than 100,000 Americans perished and are buried, foe next to foe. Amid rolling farmlands, sunny hills and deep forests, you'll discover a jarring juxtaposition of bloody legacy and bucolic scenery, and along the way, the places where America forged its identity.

Link your trip

15 Maryland's National Historic Road

For another look into the past, go east from Antietam to the picturesque and historic Frederick.

16 Along the C&O Canal

Enjoy the scenery as you head 10 miles southwest of Antietam to the bucolic Harpers Ferry.

01 ANTIETAM

While the majority of this trip takes place in Virginia, there is Civil War ground to be covered in neighboring Maryland, a border state officially allied with the Union yet close enough to the South to possess Southern sympathies. Confederate General Robert E Lee, hoping to capitalize on a friendly populace, tried to invade Maryland early in the conflict.

The subsequent Battle of Antietam, fought in Sharpsburg, MD, on September 17, 1862, has the dubious distinction of marking the bloodiest day in US history. The battle site is preserved at **Antietam**

BEST FOR

FOODIES
Lamb burgers at Richmond's Burger Bach (theburgerbach.com).

Bloody Lane, Antietam

National Battlefield (nps.gov/anti) in the corn-and-hill country of north-central Maryland.

As befits an engagement that claimed 22,000 casualties in the course of a single, nightmarish day, even the local geographic nomenclature became violent. An area known as the Sunken Rd turned into 'Bloody Lane' after bodies were stacked there. In the park's cemetery, many of the Union gravestones bear the names of Irish and German immigrants who died in a country they had only recently adopted.

THE DRIVE
Take MD-65 south out of Antietam to the town of Sharpsburg. From here, take MD-34 east for 6 miles, then turn right onto US 40A (eastbound).

Take US 40A for 11 miles, then merge onto US 70 south, followed 3 miles later by US 270 (bypassing Frederick). Take 270 south to the Beltway (I-495); access exit 45B to get to I-66 east, which will eventually lead you to the National Mall, where the next stops are located.

DETOUR
Gettysburg National Military Park
Start: 01 **Antietam**

The Battle of Gettysburg, fought in Gettysburg, PA, in July of 1863, marked the turning point of the war and the high water mark of the Confederacy's attempted rebellion. Lee never made a gambit as bold as this invasion of the North, and his army (arguably) never recovered from the defeat it suffered.

WHY I LOVE THIS TRIP

Amy C Balfour, writer

Some of the prettiest countryside on the Eastern seaboard remains hallowed ground, where whispers of brutal battles and unfinished stories drift between the remote farmhouses, dark forests, grassy earthworks and rolling fields, where thousands lost their lives. This tour explores the formative spaces of the nation, much of it unchanged since those deadly clashes of the 1860s.

Gettysburg National Military Park (nps.gov/gett), one hour and 40 minutes north of DC, does an excellent job of explaining the course and context of the combat. Look for Little Round Top hill, where a Union unit checked a Southern flanking maneuver, and the field of Pickett's Charge, where the Confederacy suffered its most crushing defeat up to that point. Following the battle, Abraham Lincoln gave his Gettysburg Address here to mark the victory and the 'new birth of the nation' on the country's birthday: July 4.

You can easily lose a day here just soaking up the scenery – a gorgeous swath of rolling hills and lush forest. On your way from Antietam to Washington, DC, jump on US 15 northbound in Frederick, MD. Follow US 15 north for about 35 miles to Gettysburg.

Photo opportunity

The fences and fields of Antietam at sunset.

 WASHINGTON, DC

Washington, DC, was the capital of the Union during the Civil War, just as it is the capital of the country today. While the city was never invaded by the Confederacy, thousands of Union soldiers passed through, trained and drilled inside of the city; indeed, the official name of the North's main fighting force was the Army of the Potomac.

The **National Museum of American History** (american history.si.edu), located directly on the National Mall, has good permanent exhibitions on the Civil War. Perhaps more importantly, it provides visitors with the context for understanding why the war happened.

Following the war, a grateful nation erected many monuments to Union generals. A statue worth visiting is the **African American Civil War Memorial Museum** (afroamcivilwar.org), next to the eastern exit of the U St metro, inscribed with the names of soldiers of color who served in the Union army.

THE DRIVE

From Washington, DC, it takes about an hour along I-66W through the tangled knots of suburban sprawl that blanket Northern Virginia to reach Manassas.

National Museum of American History, Washington, DC

03 MANASSAS NATIONAL BATTLEFIELD PARK (BULL RUN)

The site of the first major pitched battle of the Civil War is mere minutes from the strip malls of northern Virginia. NPS-run **Manassas National Battlefield Park** (nps.gov/mana) occupies the site where, in 1861, 35,000 Union soldiers and 32,500 Confederates saw the view you have today: a stretch of gorgeous countryside that has miraculously survived the predations of the Army of Northern Virginia real-estate developers. This is as close as many will come to 19th-century rural America; distant hills, dark, brooding tree-lines, low curving fields and the soft hump of overgrown trench works.

Following the battle, both sides realized a long war was at hand. Europe watched nervously; in a matter of weeks, the largest army in the world was the Union Army of the Potomac. The second biggest was the Confederate States of America Army. A year later, at the Battle of Shiloh, 24,000 men were listed as casualties – more than all the accumulated casualties of every previous American war combined.

THE DRIVE
In Manassas, take US 29N for 13 miles and then turn left onto US 17S (Marsh Rd). Follow 17/Marsh Rd south for about 35 miles to get to downtown Fredericksburg.

04 FREDERICKSBURG

If battlefields preserve rural, agricultural America, Fredericksburg is an example of what the nation's main streets once looked like: orderly grids, touches of green and friendly storefronts. But for all its

CIVIL WAR BATTLEFIELDS

What is the appeal of Civil War battlefields?

Civil War battlefields are the touchstone of the not-too-distant past. They are the physical manifestation of the great eruptive moments in American history that defined America for the last 150 years. Large events on a large landscape compel us to think in big terms about big issues.

The Civil War battlefields appeal to visitors because they allow us to walk in the virtual footsteps of great men and women who lived and died fighting for their convictions. Their actions transformed nondescript places into hallmarks of history. The Civil War converted sleepy towns and villages into national shrines based on a moment of intense belief and action. The battlefields literally focus our understanding of the American character. I linger longest on the battlefields that are best preserved, like Antietam and Gettysburg, because they paint the best context for revealing why things happened the way they did, where they did. Walking where they walked, and seeing the ground they saw, makes these battlefields the ultimate outdoor classrooms in the world!

Why is Virginia such a hotbed for Civil War tourism?

Virginia paid a terrible price during the Civil War. Hosting the capital of the Confederacy only 100 miles from the capital of the United States made sure that the ground between and around the two opposing capitals would be a relentless nightmare of fighting and bloodshed. People can visit individual, isolated battlefields all across America – but people come to Virginia to visit several, many, if not all of them. Unlike anywhere else, Virginia offers a Civil War immersion. It gives visitors a sense of how pervasive the Civil War was – it touched every place and everyone. Around the country, people may seek out the Civil War; but in Virginia, it finds you.

– Frank O'Reilly, Historian and Interpretive Ranger with the National Park Service

cuteness, this is the site of one of the worst blunders in American military history. In 1862, when the Northern Army attempted a massed charge against an entrenched Confederate position, a Southern artilleryman looked at the bare slope Union forces had to cross and told a commanding officer, 'A chicken could not live on that field when we open on it.' Sixteen charges resulted in an estimated 6000 to 8000 Union casualties.

Fredericksburg & Spotsylvania National Military Park (nps.gov/frsp) is not as immediately compelling as Manassas because of the thick forest that still covers the battlefields, but the woods themselves are a sylvan wonder. Again, the pretty nature of...well, nature, grows over graves; the nearby Battle of the Wilderness was named for these thick woods, which caught fire and killed hundreds of wounded soldiers after the shooting was finished.

THE DRIVE

THE DRIVE
From Fredericksburg, take US 17 south for 5 miles, after which 7 becomes VA-2 (also known as Sandy Lane Dr and Fredericksburg Turnpike). Follow this road for 5 more miles, then turn right onto Stonewall Jackson Rd (State Rd 606).

05 STONEWALL JACKSON SHRINE
In Chancellorsville, Robert E Lee, outnumbered two to one, split his forces and attacked both flanks of the Union army. The audacity of the move caused the Northern force to crumble and flee across the Potomac, but the victory was a costly one; in the course of the fighting, Lee's ablest general, Stonewall Jackson, had his arm shot off by a nervous Confederate sentry. The arm is buried at nearby Ellwood Manor. Ask a ranger for directions. The wound was patched, but Jackson went on to contract a fatal dose of pneumonia. He was taken to what is now the next stop on this tour: the **Jackson Death Site** (nps.gov/frsp) in nearby Guinea Station. In a small white cabin set against attractive Virginia horse-country, overrun with sprays of purple flowers and daisy fields, Jackson uttered a series of prolonged ramblings. Then he fell silent, whispered, 'Let us cross over the river and rest in the shade of the trees,' and died.

THE DRIVE
You can get here via I-95, which you take to I-295S (then take exit 34A), which takes 50 minutes. Or, for a back road experience (one hour, 10 minutes), take VA-2S south for 35 miles until it connects to VA-643/Rural Point Rd. Stay on VA-643 until it becomes VA-156/Cold Harbor Rd, which leads to the battlefield.

06 COLD HARBOR BATTLEFIELD
By 1864, Union General Ulysses Grant was ready to take the battle into Virginia. His subsequent invasion, dubbed the Overland (or Wilderness) Campaign, was one of the bloodiest of the war. It reached a violent climax at Cold Harbor, just north of Richmond.

At the site now known as **Cold Harbor Battlefield** (nps.gov/rich), Grant threw his men into a full frontal assault; the resultant casualties were horrendous, and a precursor to WWI trench warfare. The area has now reverted to a forest and field checkerboard overseen by the NPS. Ask a local ranger to direct you to the Third Turnout, a series of Union earthworks from where you can look out at the most preserved section of the fight: the long, low field Northern soldiers charged across.

THE DRIVE:
From Cold Harbor, head north on VA-156/Cold Harbor Rd for about 3 miles until it intersects Creighton Rd. Turn left and follow it for 6 miles into downtown Richmond

07 RICHMOND
The **American Civil War Museum** (acwm.org) manages two sites in Richmond: the **White House of the Confederacy** and the **American Civil War Museum at Historic Tredegar**. Guided tours explore the White House, which was occupied by Confederate President Jefferson Davis and his family during the war. The mansion today is surrounded by Virginia Commonwealth University Medical Center.

Located inside the old Tredegar ironworks building, the American Civil War Museum is home to hundreds of artifacts. Exhibits trace the history of the war. The ironworks, which overlook the James River, produced cannons for the Confederacy. Enslaved laborers made up about half of the workforce during the war.

THE DRIVE
Take Rte 95 southbound for about 23 miles and get on exit 52. Turn onto 301 (Wythe St) and follow it until it becomes Washington St, and eventually VA-35/Oaklawn Dr. Look for signs to the battlefield park from here.

WHAT'S IN A NAME?

Although the Civil War is the widely accepted label for the conflict covered in this trip, you'll still hear die-hard Southern boosters refer to the period as the 'War Between the States.' What's the difference? Well, a Civil War implies an armed insurrection against a ruling power that never lost its privilege to govern, whereas the name 'War Between the States' suggests said states always had (and still have) a right to secession from the Republic.

One of the more annoying naming conventions of the war goes thus: while the North preferred to name battles for defining geographic terms (Bull Run, Antietam), Southern officers named them for nearby towns (Manassas, Sharpsburg). Although most Americans refer to battles by their Northern names, in some areas folks know Manassas as in 'the Battle of,' not as the strip mall with a good Waffle House.

08 PETERSBURG

Petersburg, just south of Richmond, is the blue-collar sibling city to the Virginia capital, its center gutted by white flight following desegregation. **Petersburg National Battlefield Park** (nps.gov/pete) marks the spot where Northern and Southern soldiers spent almost a quarter of the war in a protracted, trench-induced standoff. The Battle of the Crater, made well-known in Charles Frazier's *Cold Mountain*, was an attempt by Union soldiers to break this stalemate by tunneling under the Confederate lines and blowing up their fortifications.

THE DRIVE

Drive south of Petersburg, then west through a skein of back roads to follow Lee's last retreat. There's an excellent map available at www.civilwartraveler.com; we prefer taking VA-460 west from Petersburg, then connecting to VA-635, which leads to Appomattox via VA-24.

09 APPOMATTOX COURT HOUSE NATIONAL HISTORICAL PARK

About 92 miles west of Petersburg is **Appomattox Court House National Historical Park** (nps.gov/apco), where the Confederacy finally surrendered. There are several marker stones dedicated to the surrendering Confederates, and the most touching one marks the spot where Robert E Lee rode back from Appomattox after surrendering to Union General

EWY MEDIA/SHUTTERSTOCK ©

Stonewall Jackson Shrine

Ulysses Grant. Lee's soldiers stood on either side of the field waiting for the return of their commander. When Lee rode into sight, he doffed his hat; the troops surged toward him, some saying goodbye while others, too overcome with emotion to speak, passed their hands over the white flanks of Lee's horse, Traveller.

24

BEST FOR

☑

NATURE
LOVERS
Hiking the
forested loop
of the Smart
View Trail.

The Crooked Road

DURATION	DISTANCE	GREAT FOR
3-4 days	260 miles / 418km	History & Culture

BEST TIME TO GO	Visit from May to October for great weather and a packed concert schedule.

Smart View Recreational Area

The place where Kentucky, Tennessee and Virginia kiss is a veritable hotbed of American roots music history, thanks to the vibrant cultural folkways of the Scots-Irish who settled the area in the 18th century. The state-created Crooked Rd carves a winding path through the Blue Ridge Mountains into the Appalachians and the heart of this way of life.

Link your trip

22 Across the Appalachian Trail

Head 30 miles east from Abingdon to reach Mt Rogers and the deep Appalachian mountains.

25 Blue Ridge Parkway

From Roanoke, you can set out north to the Blue Ridge Mountains.

01 ROANOKE

This trip begins in Roanoke, the main urban hub of Southwest Virginia, and continues along the Blue Ridge Pkwy, explored in Trip 25. Roanoke is steadily becoming a regional cultural center, perhaps best exemplified by the presence of the **Taubman Museum of Art** (taubmanmuseum. org). The museum is set in a futuristic glass-and-steel structure inspired by the valley's natural beauty. Inside you'll find a wonderful collection of classic and modern art. The permanent collection includes extensive galleries of American, folk and contempo-

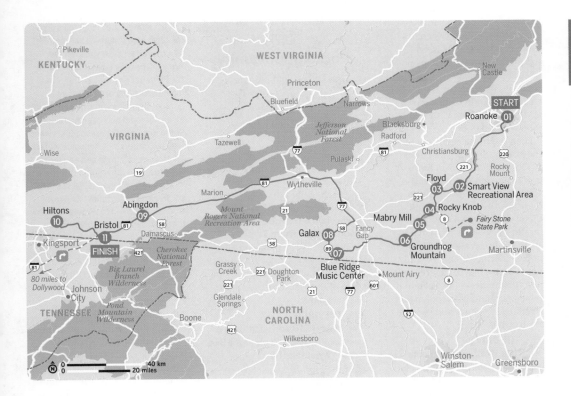

rary Southern art, complemented by frequently rotating guest exhibitions whose thematic content spans the globe.

Before you leave, make sure to check out one of the finest farmers markets in the region. The **Historic City Market** (downtownroanoke.org/city-market) is a sumptuous affair spread out over several city blocks, loaded with temptations even for those with no access to a kitchen.

THE DRIVE

Get onto US 220 southbound in Roanoke and follow signs to the Blue Ridge Pkwy. It's about 33.5 miles from where US 220 hits the parkway to get to the Smart View Recreational Area.

02 SMART VIEW RECREATIONAL AREA

The aptly named Smart View Recreational Area sits at an elevation of 2500ft with commanding vistas of the surrounding valleys. The area is a birder's paradise, rife with trails that cut into hardwood, broadleaf forest that teems with brown thrashers, great-crested flycatchers and Kentucky warblers, among many, many other species.

The **Smart View Trail** is a moderately difficult 2.6-mile loop that shows off the best of this area. If you're not in the mood (or don't have the time) to complete the entire circuit, the paths near the main parking pull-off for this area offer similar landscapes.

THE DRIVE

Continue along the Blue Ridge Pkwy for 4 miles, then turn right onto State Route 860/Shooting Creek Rd. After about a mile, turn left onto State Route 681/Franklin Pike. Follow it for 2 miles, then turn left on Floyd Hwy.

03 FLOYD

Tiny Floyd is a surprising blend of rural conservatives and slightly New Age artisans. Grab a double espresso from a bohemian coffeehouse, then peruse farm tools in the hardware store.

The highlight of this curious town is the jamboree at the **Floyd Country Store** (floydcountrystore.com). Every Friday night, this little store in a clapboard building clears out its inventory and lines up rows of chairs around a dance floor. Around 6:30pm the first musicians on the bill play their hearts out on the stage. Pretty soon the room's filled with locals and visitors hootin' and hollerin' along with the fiddles and banjos.

Then the music spills out onto the streets. Several jam bands twiddle their fiddles in little groups up and down the main road. Listeners cluster round their favorite bands, parking themselves in lawn chairs right on the sidewalk or along the curb. Motorists stare at the scene in bewilderment. There's really nothing else like it. Just remember: this tradition has been maintained as a family-friendly affair. Drinking, smoking and swearing are frowned upon.

 THE DRIVE
Take VA-8/Locust St southbound for 6 miles back to the Blue Ridge Pkwy. Then it's a little over 1½ miles to Rocky Knob. If you follow VA-8, you can detour to Fairy Stone State Park.

 04 **ROCKY KNOB**
At Rocky Knob, almost 1000ft higher than Smart View, rangers have carved out a 4800-acre area that blends natural beauty with landscaped amenities, including picnic areas and comfortable cabins.

If you're really looking to punish yourself and simultaneously soak up the best the Blue Ridge Mountains have to offer, set out on the **Rock Castle Gorge Trail**, a hard-going, 10.8-mile trail that descends deep into the shadowed buttresses of Rock Castle Gorge before clambering out of the dark

Photo opportunity
The Friday night bluegrass-palooza in 'downtown' Floyd.

woods back into the sunlit slopes of Rocky Knob.

A much easier option is covering a small portion of the above via the 0.8 mile **Hardwood Cove Nature Trail**, which follows the beginning of the Rock Castle Gorge Trail and cuts under the dense canopies of some of the oldest forests in the Appalachians.

 THE DRIVE
Mabry Mill is only a little over 3 miles south of Rocky Knob via the Blue Ridge Pkwy, at Mile 176.

DETOUR
Fairy Stone State Park
Start: 04 Rocky Knob

From the Rocky Knob portion of the Blue Ridge Pkwy, head east for about 30 miles. You'll be passing through the upcountry region of Virginia that blends between the Blue Ridge Mountains and the Southside, one of the most rural, least-developed parts of the Commonwealth. Marking the border between these regions is **Fairy Stone State Park** (dcr.virginia.gov/state_parks/fai.shtml).

What's in a name? Well, the park grounds contain silly amounts of staurolite, a mineral that crystallizes at 60- or 90-degree angles, giving it a cross-like structure. Legend has it the cruciform rocks are the tears shed by fairies who learned of the death of Christ.

What else is here? Most folks come for 2880-acre **Philpott Lake**, created as a byproduct reservoir after the Army Corps of Engineers completed the Philpott Dam back in 1952. The mountain waters of the lake are a popular spot for swimming and fishing for smallmouth and largemouth bass. Some 10 miles of multi-use trails wend their way around the dark blue waters. There's also camping and cabins if you want to spend the night.

Get here by taking SR-758 south to US 58 eastbound; follow for 11 miles to VA-8. Take VA-8 to VA-57 and follow that road eastbound to Fairy Stone State Park.

05 **MABRY MILL**
Here's where things go from picturesque Blue Ridge bucolic-ness to 'Oh, c'mon. Too cute.' Built in 1910, Mabry Mill is a working water-wheel-driven grist mill. Its wooden construction has distressed over the years to a state of wonderful entropy; the structure looks like it just fell out of a historical romance novel, except you won't find a strapping young couple in a state of dramatic embrace in front of this building. The mill is managed by **Mabry Mill Restaurant** (mabrymillrestaurant.com), which happens to whip up some of the better breakfasts along the Blue Ridge Pkwy. It has three kinds of specialty pancakes – cornmeal, buckwheat and sweet potato. Throw in a biscuit with Virginia ham and it's a perfect way to start the day.

Three miles down the road, at Mile 179, the half-mile **Round Meadow Creek Loop Trail** leads trekkers through a lovely forest cut through by an achingly attractive stream.

THE DRIVE
Groundhog Mountain is 12 miles south of Mabry Mill on the parkway at Mile 188.

06 GROUNDHOG MOUNTAIN

A split-rail fence and a rickety wooden observation tower overlook the lip of a grassy field that curves over a sky-blue vista onto the Blue Ridge Mountains and Piedmont plateau. Flowering laurel and galax flurry over the greenery in white bursts, framing a picture-perfect picnic spot. This, in any case, is the immediate impression one gets upon arriving at **Groundhog Mountain**, one of the more attractive parking overlooks in this stretch of the Blue Ridge Pkwy. Note that the aforementioned observation tower is built

in the style of local historical tobacco barns.

A mile down the road is the log-and-daub **Puckett Cabin** (nps.gov/blri), last home of local midwife Orleana Hawks Puckett (1844–1939). The site of the property is dotted with exhibitions on the folkways and traditions of local mountain and valley folk.

 THE DRIVE
Continue along the parkway for about 23 miles to the Blue Ridge Music Center, at Mile 213.

07 BLUE RIDGE MUSIC CENTER

As you head closer to the Tennessee border, you'll come across a large, grassy outdoor amphitheater. This is the **Blue Ridge Music Center** (blueridgemusiccenter.net), an arts and music hub for the region that

offers programming that focuses on local musicians carrying on the traditions of Appalachian music. Performances are mostly on weekends and occasionally during the week. Bring a lawn chair and sit yourself down for an afternoon or evening performance. At night you can watch the fireflies glimmer in the darkness.

There are two trails in the vicinity as well – the easy, flat High Creek (1.35 miles) and moderate Fisher Peak (2.24 miles), which slopes up a small mountain peak.

 THE DRIVE
Take VA-89 north for about 7 miles to reach downtown Galax. You'll pass working farms, some of which have quite the hardscrabble aesthetic – very different from the estate farms and stables of northern Virginia and the Shenandoah Valley.

08 GALAX

In Galax's historic downtown, look for the neon marquee of the **Rex Theater** (rextheatergalax.com). This is a big old grande dame theater, with a Friday night show called *Blue Ridge Backroads*. Even if you can't make it to the theater at 8pm, you can listen to the two-hour show broadcast live to surrounding counties on 89.1 FM.

Galax hosts the **Smoke on the Mountain Barbecue Championship** (smokeonthemountainva.com) on the second weekend in July. Teams from all over crowd the streets of downtown with their tricked-out mobile BBQ units.

If you think you've got what it takes to play, poke your head into **Barr's Fiddle Shop** (barrsfiddleshop.com). This little music shop has a big selection of homemade and vintage fiddles and banjos along with mandolins,

Puckett Cabin, Groundhog Mountain

autoharps and harmonicas. You can get a lesson if you have time to hang around, or just admire the fine instruments that hang all over the walls.

 THE DRIVE
Take US 221/US 58 east for 11 miles and hop on I-77 northbound. Take 77 for 17 miles, then follow I-81 southbound for 65 miles.

09 ABINGDON

The gorgeous town of Abingdon anchors Virginia's southwesterly corner. Here, like a mirage in the desert, is the best hotel for hundreds of miles in any direction. The Martha Washington Inn (themartha. com) resides inside a regal, gigantic brick mansion built for General Francis Preston in 1832. Pulling up after a long day's drive is like arriving at heaven's gates. You can almost hear the angels sing as you climb the grand stairs to the huge porch with views framed by columns.

The **Barter Theatre** (barter theatre.com), across the street, is the big man on Main St in its historic red-brick building. This regional theater company puts on its own productions of brand-name plays.

 THE DRIVE
Take I-81 south from Abingdon for about 16 miles, then turn onto US 421 north/US 58 west; follow for about 20 miles to reach Hiltons.

10 HILTONS

Another star attraction on the Crooked Rd is about 30 miles and a rural world away from Abingdon in the microscopic town of Hiltons. Here

at Clinch Mountain, subject of countless bluegrass and country ballads, you will find the **Carter Family Fold** (carterfamilyfold. org), which has live music every Saturday night. At the time of research, the Fold was overseen by Rita Forrester, granddaughter of AP and Sara Carter, who, along with sister-in-law Maybelle, formed the core Carter group, a bedrock lineage of American country music (June Carter Cash was Maybelle's daughter). The music starts at 7:30pm in the big wooden music hall. In the summer there is outdoor seating too. The hall has replaced the original locale, AP's store, which now houses a museum dedicated to Carter family history. Also: there's amateur clog dancing!

 THE DRIVE
Come back the way you came on US 421/US 58 and drive about 20 miles to reach the Tennessee border and the town of Bristol.

11 BRISTOL

In Bristol you can attend the **Bristol Motor Speedway** (bristolmotorspeed

way.com), which runs lots of NASCAR events. If they're not racing, you can still tour the 'world's fastest half-mile' and check out 'The Bristol Experience' in the adjacent museum. Oooh.

Ready to head back home? Pop in one of the CDs you picked up along the way and thrill to old-time music one last time as you ease back to modern life, keeping the wistful memories of banjos and bluegrass tucked safely inside your heart so nobody don't break it again.

 DETOUR
Dollywood
Start: 11 **Bristol**

Across the Tennessee border, about two hours southwest of Bristol, is the legendary Dolly Parton's personal theme park **Dollywood** (dollywood. com). The Smoky Mountains come alive with lots of music and roller coasters. Fans will enjoy going through Dolly's Closet. To take this detour, take I-81 south for 75 miles, then take exit 407 and follow the signs to Dollywood.

25

BEST FOR

☑

CULTURE
Staunton is an arts oasis.

Blue Ridge Parkway

DURATION	DISTANCE	GREAT FOR
3 days	185 miles / 300km	History & Culture

BEST TIME TO GO	Visit June through October for great weather and open amenities.

Woodrow Wilson's childhood home, Staunton

Running through Virginia and North Carolina, the Blue Ridge National Scenic Byway is the most visited area of national parkland in the USA, attracting almost 20 million road trippers a year. 'America's Favorite Drive' meanders through quintessentially bucolic pasturelands and imposing Appalachian vistas, past college towns and mountain hamlets. This trip threads into and off the parkway, exploring all of the above and some back roads in between.

Link your trip

24 The Crooked Road

In Roanoke, slip on dancing clogs and explore regional folkways and back roads.

26 Peninsula to the Piedmont

Head east to Charlottesville and the green hills of the Piedmont.

01 ### STAUNTON

Our trip starts in a place we'd like to end. End up retiring, that is. There are some towns in the USA that just, for lack of a better term, nail it, and Staunton is one of those towns. Luckily, it can serve as a good base for exploring the upper parkway.

So what's here? A pedestrian-friendly and handsome center; more than 200 of the town's buildings were designed by noted Victorian architect TJ Collins, hence Staunton's attractive uniformity. There's

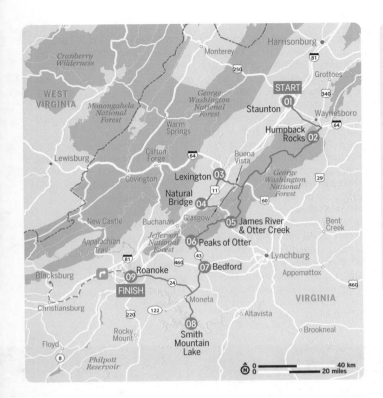

WHY I LOVE THIS TRIP

Amy C Balfour, writer

The Blue Ridge Mountains once marked the start of the western frontier, and Colonial-era statesmen like George Washington and Thomas Jefferson had ties to the region. Part of the Appalachian mountain chain, the Blue Ridge today is a buffer between the Mid-Atlantic and the South, and it separates the cities of the coastal plain from the rural villages of the mountains. As a result, this is a fascinating transition space between cultures, with distinct folkways across the mountain region. The views are darn nice, too.

an artsy yet unpretentious bohemian vibe thanks to the presence of two things: Mary Baldwin, a small women's liberal arts college, and the gem of the Shenandoah mountains: **American Shakespeare Center** (americanshakespearecenter.com). This is the world's only recreation of Shakespeare's original indoor theater. The facility hosts the immensely talented American Shakespeare Center company, which puts on performances throughout the year. See a show here. It will do you good.

History buffs should check out the **Woodrow Wilson Presidential Library** (woodrowwilson.org) across town. Stop by and tour the hilltop Greek Revival

house where Wilson grew up, which has been faithfully restored to its original 1856 appearance.

By this point you'll probably be dreaming of ditching your 9-to-5 job and moving to the country. A good way to snap yourself out of this fantasy is by visiting the **Frontier Culture Museum** (frontiermuseum.org). The hard work of farming comes to life via the familiar Virginia trope of employing historically costumed interpreters. The museum has Irish, German and English farms to explore.

 THE DRIVE

From Staunton, take I-64E toward Richmond for about 15 miles. Take exit 99 to merge onto US 250/ Three Notched Mountain Hwy head-

ing east toward Afton, then follow the signs onto the Blue Ridge Pkwy. Humpback Rocks is at Mile 5.8

02 **HUMPBACK ROCKS**
Had enough great culture and small-town hospitality? No? Tough, because we're moving on to the main event: the Blue Ridge Pkwy. Now, we need to be honest with you: this is a weird trip. We're asking you to drive along the parkway, which slowly snakes across the peaks of the Appalachians, but every now and then we're going to ask you to detour off this scenic mountain road to, well, other scenic roads.

We start at **Humpback Rocks** (nps.gov/blri), the entrance to the Virginia portion of the parkway

(252 miles of the 469-mile parkway are in NC). You can tour 19th-century farm buildings or take the steep trail to the namesake Humpback Rocks, which offer spectacular 360-degree views across the mountains. The on-site visitor center is a good primer for the rest of your parkway experience.

THE DRIVE
The next stretch of the trip is 39 miles on the parkway. Follow signs for US 60, then follow that road west for 10 miles to Lexington.

03 LEXINGTON
What? Another attractive university town set amid the forested mountains of the lower Shenandoah Valley? Well, why not.

In fact, while Staunton moderately revolves around Mary Bald-win, Lexington positively centers, geographically and culturally, around two schools: the **Virginia Military Institute** (VMI; vmi. edu) and **Washington & Lee University** (wlu.edu). VMI is the oldest state-supported military academy in the country, dedicated to producing the classical ideal of citizen-soldiers; the ideals of this institution, and the history of its cadet-students, is explored at the **VMI Museum** (vmi.edu). While graduates do not have to become enlisted officers within the US military, the vast majority do so.

VMI cadets can often be seen jogging around Lexington, perhaps casting a glance at the students at Washington & Lee, a decidedly less structured but no less academically respected school. The W&L campus includes the **University Chapel** (my.wlu.edu/university-chapel-and-galleries), where the school's namesake, patron and Confederate General Robert E Lee is buried. Lee's beloved horse, Traveller, is buried outside, and visitors often leave pennies as a sign of respect.

Just a few miles north on Rte 11 is **Hull's Drive-In movie theater** (hullsdrivein.com). This totally hardcore artifact of the golden age of automobiles is a living museum to the road trips your parents remember.

THE DRIVE
Take US 11 southbound for about 12 miles to get to Natural Bridge (you can take I-81 as well, but it's not nearly as scenic and takes just as long).

Humpback Rocks (p175)

04 NATURAL BRIDGE

Before we send you back to the Blue Ridge Pkwy, stop by the gorgeous **Natural Bridge State Park** (dcr.virginia.gov) and its wonderful potpourri of amusements. Natural Bridge is a legitimate natural wonder – and is even claimed to be one of the Seven Natural Wonders of the World, though just who put that list together remains unclear. Soaring 200ft in the air, this centuries-old rock formation lives up to the hype. Those who aren't afraid of a little religion should hang around for the 'Drama of Creation' light show that plays nightly underneath and around the bridge. Natural Bridge, formerly privately owned, became a state park in 2016.

Photo opportunity

A panorama of the Blue Ridge Mountains from Sharp Top, Peaks of Otter.

 THE DRIVE

Head back to the Blue Ridge Pkwy using US 60 and get on at Buena Vista. Drive about 13 miles south to the James River area near Mile 63.

05 JAMES RIVER & OTTER CREEK

The next portion of the Blue Ridge Pkwy overlooks the road that leads to Lynchburg. Part of the reason for that town's proximity is the James River, which marks the parkway's lowest elevation (650ft above sea level); the course of the river was the original transportation route through the mountains.

This area is rife with hiking and sightseeing opportunities. The **Otter Creek Trail** begins at a local campsite and runs for a moderately strenuous 3.5 miles; you can access it at different points from overlooks at Mile 61.4, Mile 62.5 and Mile 63.1.

If you're in the mood for a really easy jaunt, head to the **James River Visitor Center** at Mile 63.6 and take the 0.2-mile **James River Trail** to the restored James River and Kanawha Canal lock, built between 1845–51. The visitor center has information on the history of the canal and its importance to local transportation. From here you can follow the **Trail of Trees**, which goes a half

mile to a wonderful overlook on the James River.

 THE DRIVE

It's about 20 miles from here to Peaks of Otter along the Blue Ridge Pkwy. At Mile 74.7, the very easy, 0.1-mile Thunder Ridge Trail leads to a pretty valley view. The tough 1.2-mile Apple Orchard Falls trail leads can be accessed at Mile 78.4.

06 PEAKS OF OTTER

The three Peaks of Otter – Sharp Top, Flat Top and Harkening Hill – were once dubbed the highest mountains in North America by Thomas Jefferson. He was decidedly wrong in that assessment, but the peaks are undeniably dramatic, dominating the landscape for miles around.

There's a visitor center at Mile 86; from here you can take the steep 1.5-mile **Sharp Top Trail** (one-way) which summits the eponymous mountain (3875ft). The **Flat Top Trail** goes higher and further (5.4 miles roundtrip), but at a considerably less demanding incline. You'll end at the Peaks Picnic area (say that three times fast). If you're pressed for time, the 0.8-mile **Elk Run Trail** is an easy self-guided loop and nature tour.

At Mile 83.1, just before the visitor center, the **Fallingwater Cascades Trail** is a 1.5-mile loop that wanders past deep-carved ravines to a snowy-white waterfall. The Peaks of Otter Lodge sits prettily beside a lake at the base of the peaks.

 THE DRIVE

Get on VA-43 south, also known as Peaks Rd, from the Blue Ridge Pkwy. It's about an 11-mile drive along this road to Bedford.

DAVID CARLIEY/SHUTTERSTOCK ©

PARKWAY PRACTICALITIES

Most facilities along the the Blue Ridge Pkwy, including picnic areas, visitor centers and museum-style exhibits, such as the historic farms at Humpback Rocks, officially open on Memorial Day weekend (the last weekend in May). With that said, some facilities are open year-round and private concessionaires along the parkway maintain their own hours. You can also check on updated opening hours and facility renovations at nps.gov/blri. During winter, portions of the parkway may be snowed out; check the aforementioned website for updates.

Distances in the park are delineated by mileposts (MPs). The countdown starts around Mile 1 in Virginia, near Waynesboro, and continues all the way to Mile 469 near Cherokee, North Carolina.

There are numerous private camping sites, and four public **campgrounds** (recreation.gov), located at Mile 60.8, Mile 85.6, Mile 120.4 and Mile 161.1, on the Virginia side of the Blue Ridge Pkwy.

Campgrounds along the parkway are open from May to October, with a per-night charge. Use the aforementioned reservations website to book these sites. Demand is higher on weekends and holidays. While there are no electrical hookups at parkway campsites, you will find restrooms, potable water and picnic tables. You're often at a pretty high elevation (over 2500ft high), so even during summer you may want to bring some extra layers, as it can get chilly up here.

The Blue Ridge Pkwy can feel crowded in spring and summer, when thousands of motorists crowd the road, but there are so many pull-offs and picnic areas you rarely feel too hemmed in. Just remember this is a scenic route; don't be the jerk who tailgates on the parkway. Expect people to drive slowly up here. Honestly, it's a good idea to follow suit; this road has lots of narrow twists and turns.

You can take your RV on the parkway. The lowest tunnel clearance is 10ft 6in near the park's terminus in Cherokee, NC.

07 BEDFORD

Tiny Bedford suffered the most casualties per capita during WWII, and hence was chosen to host the **National D-Day Memorial** (dday.org). Among its towering arch and flower garden is a cast of bronze figures reenacting the storming of the beach, complete with bursts of water symbolizing the hail of bullets the soldiers faced.

The surrounding countryside is speckled with vineyards, including an outfit that specializes in the juice of apples, pears, peaches and chili peppers. **Peaks of Otter Winery** (peaksofotterwinery.com) stands out from other viticulture tourism spots with its focus on producing fruit wines (the chili pepper wine is, by the way, 'better for basting than tasting' according to management).

You can learn more about the many vineyards in this area via the **Bottled in Bedford Craft Beverage Trail** (destination bedfordva.com/experiences/beer-wine).

THE DRIVE

Take VA-122 (Burks Hill Rd) southbound for about 13.5 miles. In Moneta, take a left onto State Rte 608 and drive for 6 miles, then turn right onto Smith Mountain Lake Pkwy. Go 2 miles and you're at the park.

08 SMITH MOUNTAIN LAKE

This enormous, 32-square-mile reservoir is one of the most popular recreation spots in southwestern Virginia and the largest lake contained entirely within the borders of the Commonwealth. Vacation rentals and water activities abound, as does development, and there are portions of this picturesque dollop that have been overwhelmed with rental units. Most lake access is via private property only.

This isn't the case at **Smith Mountain Lake State Park** (dcr. virginia.gov/state_parks/smi. shtml), located on the north shore of the lake. Don't get us wrong – there are lots of facilities here if you need them, including a boat ramp, picnic tables, fishing piers, an amphitheater, camping sites and cabin rentals. But in general, the area within the state park preserves the natural beauty of this area. Thirteen hiking trails wind through the surrounding forests.

The nearby **Hickory Hill Winery** (smlwine.com), anchored by a charming 1923 farmhouse, is a lovely spot to lounge about sipping on Merlot either before or after your adventures on the lake.

THE DRIVE

Head back toward Bedford on VA-122 and take a left on State Rte 801/Stony Fork Rd. Follow this to VA-24/Stewartsville Rd and take that road west about 20 miles to Roanoke.

09 ROANOKE

Roanoke is the largest city and commercial hub of Southwest Virginia. It's not quite as picturesque as other towns, but it's a good logistical base. The busy **Center in the Square** (centerinthesquare.org) is the city's cultural heartbeat, with a science museum and planetarium, local history museum and theater. The striking Taubman Museum of Art (p168) a few blocks away has great special exhibits, often spotlighting southern artists.

DETOUR
Blacksburg
Start: 09 Roanoke

Located about 42 miles west of Roanoke, Blacksburg is another higher education–centered community in the mountains of highland Virginia. But this is no small, liberal arts college town. Blacksburg is the home of the largest university in Virginia: the Virginia Polytechnical Institute, better known as **Virginia Tech**, V-Tech or just Tech. The local, odd mascot? That would be 'Hokies,' also known as the Hokie Bird. It's basically a turkey. Sort of. Well...

The word 'hokie' comes from VT's nonsensical fight song, chanted at all university athletic events and many a Blacksburg bar. It has nothing to do with turkeys, but a wild turkey was the team's mascot for much of the 20th century. Said turkeys were the reason the team was nicknamed the 'Fighting Gobblers': 'Gobbler' is North American slang for a turkey, but it has some, well, pejorative connotations, so the university amended the name to 'Hokie Bird,' invoking the school's fight song. Now, go enjoy pub trivia, or feel free to look around the green 2600-acre campus; a good place to start is the **visitor center** (visit.vt.edu).

Blacksburg as a town basically revolves around Tech. We highly recommend a drive on **Catawba Road** (Virginia Rte 785), which rolls past stunning murals of farmland, streams and forestscape.

To take this detour, take I-81 westbound, then exit at 118B to get on US 460; follow this road westbound to Blacksburg.

Roanoke

26

Peninsula to the Piedmont

DURATION	DISTANCE	GREAT FOR
3 days	158 miles / 254km	History & Culture

BEST TIME TO GO	April to July, to soak up sun and American patriotism.

BEST FOR

☑

FAMILIES
A day exploring Colonial Williamsburg (p182).

Yorktown Battlefield

You stand on the cusp of Monticello and look out. There: the Blue Ridge Mountains, and there: the Piedmont plateau meandering off to a topographic pancake intercut by the squiggly blue waters of the Elizabeth and James Rivers. And spread over all of this: the place where America was founded (well, by the British). Where it governed from, and where it won independence.

Link your trip

25 Blue Ridge Parkway

In Charlottesville, head west for 40 miles to reach Staunton and the mountains of the Blue Ridge.

27 Bracketing the Bay

From Williamsburg, head southeast for 20 miles to Newport News, Hampton Roads and shores of the Chesapeake Bay.

01 **YORKTOWN**
Virginia's Historic Triangle consists of the towns of Yorktown, Jamestown and Williamsburg, all arranged in a rough triangular shape on the wooded Virginia peninsula, a geographic appendage known for tidal inlets and marshes, if not the originality of its name.

Yorktown was the site of the American victory of George Washington over the British Lord Cornwallis. The event was more of a whimper than a bang; Cornwallis's forces had endured weeks of siege and faulty supply lines in the fight against the Americans,

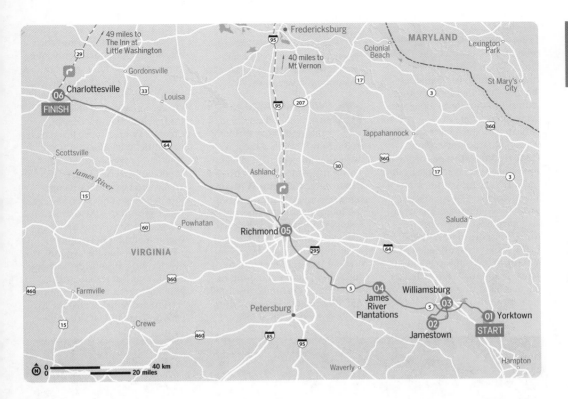

and the Chesapeake Bay, their source of resupply, was blockaded by the French Navy.

There are two ways of experiencing Yorktown's charms. One is the **American Revolution Museum at Yorktown** (historyisfun. org). The park is an interactive, living-history museum that focuses on reconstruction, reenactment and the Revolution's impact on the people who lived through it. It caters a little more to kids, but its cuteness is certainly balanced by an effort to have a candid conversation about the course of the battle and the motivations of the revolutionaries.

Yorktown Battlefield (nps. gov/york), run by the NPS, is the site of the last major battle of the American Revolution. Start your tour at the visitor center and check out the orientation film and the display of Washington's original tent. The 7-mile Battlefield Rd Tour takes you past the major highlights. Don't miss a walk through the last British defensive sites, Redoubts 9 and 10.

THE DRIVE
Get on Colonial National Historic Pkwy and take it 7 miles west. Turn onto SR-641, which becomes VA-199, and follow it for 6 miles, then turn left onto Jamestown Rd. Drive on this for 5 miles and keep an eye out for signs to Jamestown.

JAMESTOWN
02 Jamestown was the first permanent English settlement in North America, although permanent is a relative term. The colony was founded in 1607 on a marshy spit of malaria-stricken wetlands; the settlers included aristocrats and tradesmen, but no farmers. During the 'starving times' of 1609-10, only 61 out of 500 colonists survived; forensic evidence indicates some settlers resorted to cannibalism. Future waves of colonists proved more competent, and turned to tobacco as a profitable cash crop.

Again, there are two areas to explore here. More child-friendly and entertaining, the state-run **Jamestown Settlement** (history isfun.org) reconstructs the 1607 James Fort, a Native American village and full-scale replicas of the first ships that brought the settlers to Jamestown, along with living-history fun.

Located on the former site of the actual Jamestown colony, **Historic Jamestowne** (historic jamestowne.org) is less flashy and far more reflective; if the settlement feels like a living-history park, this comes off as an engaging, quiet archaeology lecture. You're welcome to wander the grassy ruins of the original city of Jamestown, which was abandoned in 1699 as Williamsburg's star ascended, and spend time by the interpretive signage.

 THE DRIVE
Return to the Colonial National Historic Pkwy, then turn right onto Jamestown Rd and follow for 5.5 miles to downtown Williamsburg.

03 **WILLIAMSBURG**
The restored capital of England's largest colony in the New World is a must-see attraction for visitors of all ages. This is not some cheesy, fenced-in theme park; **Colonial Williamsburg** (colonialwilliamsburg.org) is a living, breathing, working history museum that transports visitors back to the 1700s.

The 301-acre area contains 88 original 18th-century buildings and several hundred faithful reproductions. Costumed townsfolk and 'interpreters' in period dress go about their colonial jobs as

blacksmiths, apothecaries, printers, barmaids, soldiers and patriots, breaking character only long enough to pose for a snapshot.

Costumed patriots like Patrick Henry and Thomas Jefferson still deliver impassioned speeches for freedom, but to its credit, Colonial Williamsburg has grown up a little. Where once it was all about projecting a rah-rah version of American-heck-yeah in a powdered wig, today reenactors debate and question slavery, women's suffrage, the rights of indigenous Americans and the very moral right of revolution.

Walking around the historic district and patronizing the shops and taverns is free, but entry to building tours and most exhibits is restricted to ticket holders. To park and purchase tickets, follow

College of William & Mary, Williamsburg

signs to the visitor center, north of the historic district between Hwy 132 and Colonial Pkwy, where kids can hire out period costumes. Most day activities are included with the admission price. Evening events (ghost walks, witch trials, chamber recitals) cost extra.

Parking is free; shuttle buses run frequently to and from the historic district, or walk along the tree-lined footpath.

Colonial Williamsburg isn't the only sight to see in Williamsburg. Chartered in 1693, the **College of William & Mary** (wm.edu) is the second-oldest college in the country and retains the oldest academic building in continuous use in the USA, the Sir Christopher Wren Building. The school's alumni include Thomas Jefferson, James Monroe and comedian Jon Stewart. The campus is green, attractive, filled with historic buildings and worth a wander.

THE DRIVE
Take the Jamestown Rd out of Williamsburg to VA-199, then turn right. Follow for about 2 miles, then turn left on VA-5 and follow it west for about 18 miles to reach Sherwood Forest in the James River Plantations.

04 JAMES RIVER PLANTATIONS

The grand homes of Virginia's enslaving aristocracy were a clear sign of the era's class divisions. A string of them line scenic Hwy 5 on the north side of the river. The ones listed here run from east to west.

Sherwood Forest (sherwoodforest.org), the longest frame house in the country, was the home of 10th US president, John Tyler. The grounds (and a touching pet cemetery) are open to self-guided tours.

Berkeley (berkeleyplantation.com) was the site of the first official Thanksgiving in 1619. It was the birthplace and home of Benjamin Harrison V, a signatory of the Declaration of Independence, and his son William Henry Harrison, ninth US president.

Shirley (shirleyplantation.com), situated picturesquely on the river, is Virginia's oldest plantation (1613) and perhaps the best example of how a British-model plantation actually appeared, with its tidy row of brick service and trade houses – tool barn, ice house, laundry etc – leading up to the big house. There's a very popular wine-tasting room and restaurant.

THE DRIVE
Continue west on VA-5 for abut 31 miles – you'll follow this road right into downtown Richmond. Alternatively, you may want to take VA-5 for 27 miles to I-895; take that road westbound, then take I-95 northbound. Take exit 74A to reach downtown Richmond.

05 RICHMOND

Virginia's capital is a handsome town, full of red-brick and brownstone rowhouses that leave a softer impression than their sometimes staid Northeastern counterparts. History is ubiquitous and sometimes uncomfortable; this was where patriot Patrick Henry gave his famous 'Give me Liberty, or give me Death!' speech, and where the enslaving Southern Confederate States placed their capital.

Designed by Thomas Jefferson, the **Virginia State Capitol** (virginiacapitol.gov) was completed in 1788. Free tours are offered throughout the week.

The **Virginia Museum of Fine Arts** (VMFA; vmfa.museum) has a remarkable collection of European works, sacred Himalayan art and one of the largest Fabergé egg collections on display outside Russia. It also hosts excellent temporary exhibitions (admission free to $20). Out the front of the museum is *Rumors of War*, a statue by Kehinde Wiley. It is a modern take on the Confederate statues that used to line Monument Avenue.

THE DRIVE
Take I-64 westbound for 63 miles, then take exit 124 to follow US 250 westbound. Follow 250 for 2 miles, then turn left onto High St to reach downtown Charlottesville

DETOUR
Mount Vernon
Start: 05 **Richmond**

Well, we hit the homes of two founding fathers on this trip – why not shoot for a threesome? So drive to the outskirts of Washington, DC, and the home of George and Martha Washington: **Mount Vernon** (mountvernon.org).

A visit here is an easy escape from the city – one that the president himself enjoyed. It's also a journey through history: the country estate of this quintessential gentleman has been meticulously restored and affords a glimpse of rural gentility from a time long gone. On the Potomac banks, the 19-room mansion displays George and Martha's colonial tastes, while the outbuildings and quarters for enslaved people show what was needed for the functioning of the estate.

George and Martha are both buried here, as requested by the first president in his will. The modern Ford Orientation Center, also on the grounds, is a must-see. It features a 20-minute film that shows Washington's courage under fire, including his

KRISTI BLOKHIN/SHUTTERSTOCK ©

Blue Mountain Brewery

BREWERIES & WINERIES OF THE PIEDMONT

Small- and medium-scale winemaking and beer brewing is rapidly growing in the Piedmont. The following are all in Charlottesville or the surrounding vicinity.

Blenheim Vineyards (blenheimvineyards.com) Blenheim is owned by musician Dave Matthews (of the Dave Matthews band), who in some ways – what with his folkie-preppie vibe and eternal gap-year sunniness and sense of discovery and the fact that he owns a vineyard – is the Platonic ideal of a University of Virginia student. Trust us, the album *Crash* is as popular on campus as it was in 1998. Anyway, the wines are great and the setting is sheer bucolic joy.

Blue Mountain Brewery (bluemountainbrewery.com) Located 20 miles from Charlottesville near the high slopes of Skyline Dr, Blue Mountain Brewery is some kind of wonderful. These guys are dedicated to their craft and their craft beers, which include a crisp Bavarian-style wheat beer that is all kinds of good in the hot summer swelter, and the muscular Full Nelson, brewed with local hops.

Pippin Hill (pippinhillfarm.com) Wonderful views over the rolling plateau of the Piedmont greet you at Pippin Hill, which is located in a bar that just about screams rustic hipster paradise. Pippin Hill leads the way in practicing sustainable viticulture.

pivotal crossing of the Delaware River (the do-or-die moment of the Revolutionary War). Another highlight is the sleek Reynolds Museum and Education Center. Home to galleries and theaters, it gives more insight into Washington's life using interactive displays, short films produced by the cable TV History Channel and three life-size models of Washington himself. The museum also features period furnishings, clothing and jewelry (Martha was quite taken with finery) and George's unusual dentures.

To visit, take I-95 northbound for 85 miles, then take exit 161 and follow US 1 northbound. Drive for about 9 miles, then follow the signs to Mount Vernon.

06 **CHARLOTTESVILLE**
Set in the shadow of the Blue Ridge Mountains, Charlottesville is regularly ranked as one of the country's best places to live. This culturally rich town of 45,000 is home to the **University of Virginia** (UVA), which attracts Southern aristocracy and artsy bohemians in equal proportion. The UVA's centerpiece is the Thomas Jefferson–designed **Rotunda** (rotunda.virginia.edu), a scale replica of Rome's Pantheon. Free, student-led tours of the Rotunda meet inside the main entrance daily at 10am, 11am, 2pm, 3pm and 4pm. UVA's **Fralin Art Museum** (uvafralinartmuseum. virginia.edu) has an eclectic and interesting collection of American, European and Asian arts.

The main attraction is just outside of 'C-ville': **Monticello** (monticello.org), an architectural masterpiece designed and inhabited by Thomas Jefferson, founding father and third US president. Today it is the only home in the US designated a UN

World Heritage site. Built in Roman neoclassical style, the house was the centerpiece of a 5000-acre plantation tended by 150 enslaved people. Monticello today does not gloss over the complicated past of the man who declared that 'all men are created equal' in the Declaration of Independence. Jefferson, an enslaver, is thought to have fathered children with the enslaved Sally Hemings. Jefferson and his family are buried in a small wooded plot near the home.

🏁 DETOUR
The Inn at Little Washington
Start: 06 Charlottesville

Feeling hungry? Not just 'I could use a sandwich' hungry but 'In the mood for a rustic five-star gastronomic head-explosion' hungry?

Then head 60 miles northeast toward Washington (the town, not the

Photo opportunity

Monticello set against the sunset.

capital) and settle in at the **Inn at Little Washington** (theinnatlittlewashington. com), a sacred destination on the epicurean trail. Founded more than 30 years ago by Patrick O'Connell and his partner, it was named one of the '10 Best Restaurants in the World' by the *International Herald Tribune*. The inn's pleasures come at a price, but it is worth every cent.

First of all the service is, unsurprisingly, impeccable, and the food hits all the grace notes. For the first course

you might try the beet fantasia or the eggs in an egg (once prepared for the Queen of England on her visit to American shores). Next, you could try the pecan-crusted soft-shell crab tempura with Italian mustard fruit. The 'pepper crusted tuna pretending to be a filet mignon capped with seared duck fois gras on charred onions with a burgundy butter sauce' is a good example of what's happening in the kitchen; namely, taking the finest ingredients and turning them into a global medley, a sort of international gastronomic carnival.

So, yeah, any questions? Go. Toss your credit score to the wind and just go. To really make the evening count, reserve one of the achingly perfect rooms at the adjacent inn from which the restaurant gets its name.

EUROBANKS/SHUTTERSTOCK ©

Monticello, Charlottesville

27

Bracketing the Bay

DURATION	DISTANCE	GREAT FOR
2 days	275 miles / 442km	Families

BEST TIME TO GO	Visit from June to September to enjoy the best of the beaches.

Virginia is blessed with three coasts, and you'll experience them all on this trip. From the golden sands of Virginia Beach to the quiet forests that line the rivers of the Northern Neck, to the gentle marsh country lining the Chesapeake Bay and the skinny Virginia Eastern Shore, there's always water at your fingertips, and all the leisure and seafood that the watery geography promises.

Link your trip

19 Delmarva

From Chincoteague Island, head north into the marshes and beaches fronting the Atlantic Ocean.

26 Peninsula to the Piedmont

Go west from Hampton Roads into the rolling farmland and living history museums of Virginia's Historic Triangle.

01 **NORTHERN NECK**
About 85 miles south of Washington, DC via I-95 and VA-3 is the Northern Neck, a peninsula of land sandwiched between the Potomac and Rappahannock Rivers. **Colonial Beach** is a small resort town on the Potomac, with a pretty public beach and some decent dining and lodging options. But the main draw to this area is of a more historical bent.

Eleven miles southeast of Colonial Beach, at the point where Pope's Creek flows into the Potomac River, is a rustic patchwork of tobacco fields, wheat

George Washington Birthplace National Monument

plots, broadleaf forest and waterfront views over the bluffs of the Northern Neck. This is where John Washington – great-grandfather of the first president – settled in 1657. Washington carved out a plantation here, where his most famed descendant was born in 1732.

An obelisk fashioned from Vermont marble, a one-tenth replica of the Washington Monument in Washington, DC, greets visitors to the **George Washington Birthplace National Monument** (nps.gov/gewa), run by the National Park Service. The site is interesting enough as Washington's birthplace, but it's more engaging as a peek into the lifestyle of the plantation owners who formed Virginia's original aristocracy, a class of essentially large-land-owning gentry, which stood in contrast to the small plot farmers and mercantile class of Northern colonies like New York and Massachusetts.

🚗 **THE DRIVE**
Take VA-205E out of Colonial Beach for 6 miles to VA-3. Head east on VA-3 for about 41 miles, then turn right onto VA-354 (River Rd). Follow signs to State Rd 683/Belle Isle Rd, which leads to Belle Isle State Park.

02 **BELLE ISLE STATE PARK**
Belle Isle State Park (dcr. virginia.gov/state_parks/ bel.shtml) beckons travelers who want a full menu of outdoor activ-ities to pick from. This is a small state park, yet it boasts picnic areas, boat launches, hiking and biking trails and a host of other well-maintained amenities. Keep an eye out for numerous bald eagles patrolling this marsh and forest habitat.

The entire park is built around a Georgian mansion – the **Belle Isle Mansion** – that feels like a dictionary illustration that might hang next to the word 'mansion.' It was built around 1760 by Raleigh Downman and restored in the 1940s by Thomas Tileston Waterman, the first director of the Historic American Buildings Survey; today the mansion can be admired from afar, but the big building itself is owned by a private family.

Another historic property, the **Bel Air House**, is available for overnight rentals. It's almost always booked every weekend in summer for weddings months in advance, but if you're interested, call 800-933-7275, or go to reserveamerica.com.

 THE DRIVE
Take Belle Isle Rd (VA-354S) for 3 miles to VA-201. Turn left onto 201 and take it to VA-3E. Follow VA-3E through hills and woodlands for 42 miles until it runs into US 17S. Take US 17 south for 25 miles to reach Newport News.

Photo opportunity

George Washington's birthplace (p187) set against woods and water.

03 **NEWPORT NEWS**
Newport News is the first town you'll come across in the Hampton Roads. Almost everything you encounter in these parts is either tied to the water or the military in some way (and often, both). So why is the area called Hampton 'Roads'? The term 'roads' comes from roadstead, an old nautical term for an area where a ship can be at anchor that is not as sheltered as a harbor – other examples include Castle Roads in Bermuda and Brest Roads in France.

What about Newport News? That's up for a lot more debate. What seems most probable is 'News' derives from 'Ness,' an old mariner's term for 'point.'

The area's connection to the water and the military is exemplified by the **Mariners' Museum** (marinersmuseum.org), one of the largest maritime museums in the country. Exhibits include an intimidatingly comprehensive collection of miniature boats depicting the evolution of shipbuilding from the ancient world

Virginia Beach

to modern navies; displays on the Chesapeake Bay; and the USS *Monitor* exhibit, which contains the remains of one of the world's first ironclad warships, dredged from the waters of Hampton Roads.

The **Virginia Living Museum** (thevlm.org) is an educational extravaganza that comprises a petting zoo, planetarium and other interactive science-y stuff. The best exhibits feature native wildlife in their natural habitats, including three beautiful, extremely rare red wolves.

THE DRIVE
Take I-64E for about 19 miles across the Elizabeth River. Get off in Norfolk on Exit 277 onto Tidewater Blvd.

04 NORFOLK
Norfolk is the home of **Naval Station Norfolk** (cnrma.cnic.navy.mil), the largest naval base in the world. Even if you're not into boats, it's hard not to feel awed by the sight of the stunningly enormous warships at berth here. Depending on which ships are in, you might see aircraft carriers, destroyers, frigates, amphibious assault ships and submarines. The 45-minute bus tours are conducted by naval personnel and must be booked in advance (hours vary).

Nauticus (nauticus.org) is a massive interactive maritime-themed museum that has exhibits on undersea exploration, the aquatic life of the Chesapeake Bay and US Naval lore. Clambering around the decks and inner corridors of the USS *Wisconsin* is a definite highlight.

Norfolk's excellent **Chrysler Museum of Art** (chrysler.org) hosts eclectic exhibitions, as well as demos and workshops in its glassmaking studio.

THE DRIVE
In Norfolk, hop on I-264E and follow the highway about 16 miles east to downtown Virginia Beach.

DETOUR
The Great Dismal Swamp
Start: 4 Norfolk

About 30 miles southwest of Norfolk, straddling the Virginia and North Carolina border, is more than 1 million acres of morass, rivers, lakes, flooded forests and mudflats. Here, the water runs red, brown and black as it leaches highly concentrated tannins from a veritable jungle's worth of vegetation, including bald cypress, tupelo and pine trees.

This is the **Great Dismal Swamp**, and here on the Virginia side of the border one can find the **Great Dismal Swamp National Wildlife Refuge** (fws.gov/refuge/great_dismal_swamp). There are some 112,000 acres of protected land here, a wet home for bobcats, black bears, red foxes, coyotes and over 200 species of birds. In late April, the refuge hosts an annual birding festival (see website for details) that coincides with the biggest migratory period of the year; during past festivals, birders have seen the extremely secretive Wayne's warbler. Disclosure: we're not sure how big a deal this is, but when we told a birding friend, they practically cried.

The Great Dismal Swamp is not just a home for animals. Native Americans may have first settled here a full 13,000 years ago, and for centuries, escaped enslaved Africans known as maroons hid in the swamp's shadowy depths.

There are miles of hiking trails within the swamp, almost all of which are quite flat. Contact the park headquarters to speak with rangers about local fishing opportunities.

05 VIRGINIA BEACH
The largest city in Virginia. The longest pleasure beach in the world. A location along the Chesapeake Bay Bridge-Tunnel, the longest bridge-tunnel complex in the world.

There's a lot of superlatives going on in Virginia Beach, which sprawls in several directions and consists of several distinct areas. The **resort beach** is the main strip of golden sand, with a 3-mile boardwalk and loads of beach games, greasy food and amusement park tat.

The **Chesapeake Bay Beaches** line Shore Dr on the northern side of the city. These are calmer, more nature-oriented beaches,

A PENINSULA APART

Delmarva – the Eastern Shore of Maryland, made up of the nine counties in the state that lie on the east side of the Chesapeake Bay, the Eastern Shore of Virginia, which consists of Accomack and Northampton counties, and the entire state of Delaware – is decidedly off the radar. Not just the tourist radar either; Delmarva residents have a sense of separation from the rest of the country that is both a source of pride and sporadic resentment.

The former derives from a cultural legacy passed through generations of small-town traditions and connection to a unique geography; the latter manifests in occasional insularity, although the growth of the tourism industry is discouraging this sort of behavior.

So why is this region so distinct, when it seems so close to some of the nation's biggest metropolitan areas? The answer lies in the question, because said cities and their culture were historically cut off by the Chesapeake Bay. The Bay Bridge wasn't built until 1952; the Hampton Roads Bridge–Tunnel wasn't completed until 1957 (and traffic wasn't flowing in both directions until 1976). Until then, the only way out of here was by boat or twisting back roads.

While the highway, the internet and the shrinking small-scale commercial fishing industry have contributed to the homogenization of the region, this area still feels set apart from the rest of the Eastern seaboard. It's a flat land that's not quite Mid-Atlantic, not quite Southern yet also all of the above, where Philly pizza shares space on the menu with Maryland fried chicken and Virginia ham. Southern Delaware, Maryland's Eastern Shore and Virginia's Eastern Shore – the 'Del', 'Mar' and 'Va' of DelMarVa – may be divided between three states east of the Chesapeake Bay, but in practice they form one cohesive cultural unit.

See p134 for a trip through Delmarva.

for those who prefer waterfront forest to sandy coast. South of the resort beaches, along Sandbridge Rd, is **Sandbridge Beach**. This is a more upscale area of vacation rentals and seasonal condos.

Just north of Sandbridge is the **Virginia Aquarium & Marine Science Center** (virginia aquarium.com). If you want to see an aquarium done right, head here. The harbor seals and komodo dragons are a lot of fun, and there's an IMAX cinema onsite.

THE DRIVE
Follow signs north to US 13N and the Chesapeake Bay Bridge-Tunnel. You'll pay toll to cross 23 miles of bridge and tunnel, one of the most impressive engineering feats anywhere. US 13 runs the length of the Virginia Eastern Shore.

06 VIRGINIA EASTERN SHORE

This long, flat peninsula is separated from Virginia by the Chesapeake Bay, culture and history. The main town for eating and lodging is Chincoteague Island, at the other end of the peninsula, some 68 miles north by the Maryland border, covered in our Delmarva trip (p134).

Wild dunescapes are a disappearing feature of the American landscape – they're often swallowed by developments or erosion. The 300-acre **Savage Neck Dunes Natural Area Preserve** (dcr.virginia.gov) protects a small patch of dusty headland, all windblown umbrella sedge and tiny dwarf burhead.

The main pleasure on the Shore is just poking around back roads out to the waterfront(s) – either the rough Atlantic or placid Chesapeake Bay. The best way to access the water is by small craft like kayaks, and if you're gonna get in a kayak, you might as well have a buzz, right? So hook up with **Southeast Expeditions** (southeastexpeditions.net), which leads a Paddle Your Glass Off kayak winery tour to some local vineyards. It's a lot of fun. Southeast offers plenty of sober, nature-oriented kayak tours as well.

Arriving

Most major cities in New York and the Mid-Atlantic are served by an international airport. The key international airports in the region are John F Kennedy International (NY), Ronald Reagan Washington National Airport (DC) and Dulles International Airport (DC). Amtrak trains run regularly between major cities on the eastern seaboard; Union Station in DC is a major hub.

Car Rental at Airports

Most airports will have at least one on-site car rental agency, but it is best to pre-book. Daily rates may be slightly higher when renting at the airport than from an off-site rental company thanks to airport fees. On the other hand, car shortages and unexpected unavailability are less likely at airports since they maintain large fleets. At larger airports you will likely need to ride a free shuttle to and from the rental agency. At smaller airports you can typically walk from the terminal to the rental office and parking lot.

Airports in larger cities may also have rentals available through a car-sharing network like Turo, which offers competitive prices and interesting car models – like a 2017 Lamborghini at Dulles International! For Turo rentals, read the details carefully regarding pick-up and drop-off locations, who pays for tolls and what type of insurance is needed.

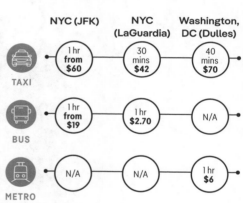

	NYC (JFK)	NYC (LaGuardia)	Washington, DC (Dulles)
TAXI	1 hr from $60	30 mins $42	40 mins $70
BUS	1 hr from $19	1 hr $2.70	N/A
METRO	N/A	N/A	1 hr $6

VISAS

Generally not required for stays of 90 days or less for citizens of the Visa Waiver Program countries, following ESTA approval (esta.cbp.dhs.gov). Apply for ESTA authorization at least 72 hours in advance.

MONEY

ATMs are widely available, but credit cards are required for car and hotel reservations. Tipping in the US is customary, not optional.

CELL PHONES

Cell phone coverage is typically available across the region, but service may drop occasionally in mountainous places or more isolated rural areas. Coverage comes and goes on Skyline Drive and the Blue Ridge Parkway.

FUEL

Gas stations, open late or 24 hours, are easy to find in large urban centers and along major interstates. They may be infrequent or have limited hours in more rural areas.

Getting Around

ROAD RULES

» When emergency vehicles (eg police, fire or ambulance) approach from either direction, pull off to the side of the road.

» It is usually illegal to talk or text on a handheld phone while driving; use a hands-free device or pull over to take your call.

» The blood-alcohol limit for drivers is 0.08%. Penalties are severe for driving under the influence (DUI) of alcohol and/or drugs.

DRIVING INFO

Drive on the right.

70

Top speed limit is 70mph on some highways.

Use of seat belts and child safety seats is required.

TIP

The busiest driving corridors in the region tend to be federal interstates and state highways, although local streets can be frustratingly crowded in urban and suburban areas during rush hour.

Driver's License

All drivers must carry a driver's license, car registration and proof of insurance. If your license is not in English, you will need an official translation or an International Driving Permit (IDP).

Insurance

All drivers are required to obtain a minimum amount of liability insurance, which covers the damage that you might cause to other people and property in an accident. Liability insurance can be purchased from rental car companies for about $16 per day.

Border Crossing

Crossing the US–Canada border at Niagara Falls, the St Lawrence Seaway or on Hwy 87 north of Champlain, NY, is generally straightforward, although lines can be a hassle. All travelers entering the US are required to carry a passport.

Parking

Public parking in large cities can be extremely challenging. Private garages are expensive and metered rules confusing. Read them carefully. In rural areas, parking is generally free and easy to find, but double-check for signage.

TRAVEL COSTS

Rental
From $51/day

Gas
Approx $3.50/gal

EV charging
$0–$0.70/kWh

Skyline Drive
$30

LEFT: IMAGINEERINC/SHUTTERSTOCK ©, RIGHT: NOAH SAUVE/SHUTTERSTOCK ©

Accommodations

GLAMPING

More and more glamping destinations are popping up across the country, with canvas tents, yurts, Airstreams and tiny homes among the options. Many lean high-end, with luxury linens and organic bath products, and they may offer activities like yoga and movie nights. Others are simply a few steps up from camping. Check listings at Glamping Hub (glampinghub.com), HipCamp (hipcamp. com), AutoCamp (autocamp.com) and Under Canvas (undercanvas.com). The atmosphere at the trendier spots tends to be communal, with guests gathering around firepits and in common areas.

HOW MUCH FOR A NIGHT IN A...

B&B or Inn
From $139/day

Public Campground
Free to $30/day

Mom & Pop Motel
From $79/day

National & State Park Campgrounds

On public lands, primitive campgrounds are the cheapest but have no facilities; basic campgrounds may have toilets, drinking water and picnic tables. Developed campgrounds have more amenities and RV sites with hookups. Reserve national park and other federal campsites through recreation.gov. For some state park campgrounds, you can book through ReserveAmerica (reserveamerica.com).

Private Campgrounds

Private campgrounds cater to RVs (recreational vehicles) with full electrical and water hookups plus dump stations. Tent sites may be sparse and uninviting. Hot showers and coin-op laundry are usually available, along with a pool, wif-fi and camping cabins. Many places are family friendly, especially Kampground of America (KOA), and may offer planned activities and bike or canoe rentals.

Hotels

Hotels typically include cable TV, wi-fi, private baths and a continental breakfast. Many midrange properties provide microwaves, hairdryers and swimming pools, while top-end hotels add concierge services, fitness and business centers, spas, restaurants and bars. Many hotels in larger cities charge a hefty overnight parking fee. Scope out nearby garages or street parking to save money.

Motels

Motels have rooms that open onto a parking lot, and they tend to cluster around interstate exits and along main routes into town. Many are inexpensive mom-and-pop operations. Breakfast is rare or minimal. Amenities might top out at wi-fi and a TV. Although most motel rooms won't win any style awards, they can be clean, comfortable and good value.

B&BS & INNS

These accommodations vary from small, comfy houses with shared baths to romantic, antique-filled historic homes with private baths. Those focusing on upscale romance may discourage children. Inns and B&Bs often require a minimum stay of two or three days on weekends, and reservations are essential. Always call ahead to confirm bathroom arrangements and policies regarding kids, pets, smoking etc.

Cars

HOW MUCH TO HIRE...

An Economy Car

From $35/ day

An EV

From $48/ day

A Campervan

From $90/ day

Car Rental

To rent a car you typically need to be at least 25 years old, hold a valid driver's license and have a major credit card. Some companies will rent to drivers between the ages of 21 and 24 for an additional charge.

Economy-sized vehicles currently range from about $51 to $88 per day. Child safety seats are compulsory (reserve ahead) and cost about $15 per day.

Car Rental Express (carrentalexpress. com) rates and compares independent agencies in US cities; it's particularly useful for searching

out cheaper long-term rentals. Autoslash (autoslash.com) compares rates and incorporates discounts you may have from various auto clubs and other memberships.

Be aware that one-way rentals tend to be more expensive.

RVs & Campervans

While it's fairly easy to find an RV rental agency across New York and the Mid-Atlantic, it can be harder to find a company specializing in campervans. Expect daily prices from $150 to $332 depending on the make.

Cruise America (cruiseamerica.com) rents RVs in Virginia, Maryland, New Jersey, New York and Pennsylvania. Depending on the size, their vehicles can sleep from four to seven people. Escape Campervans rents colorful vans from its office in Jersey City, just south of NYC. Beyond New York, consider a peer-to-peer campervan rental, which means renting from a private owner. Try Outdoorsy (outdoorsy.com) or GoCamp (gocamp.com). Both offer RVs and campervans.

EVs & HYBRIDS

Some rental companies, including Turo, offer EVs and hybrids. Though the daily rental fee for an EV may be higher, you may see greater savings over the course of your trip.

Look for cars with more than 200 miles of driving range. Apps like abetterrouteplanner.com, plugshare.com and chargepoint.com can help with itinerary planning.

Health & Safe Travel

Ticks

Ticks are present across most parks in the Mid-Atlantic, so check yourself carefully after hiking and camping. Since some ticks carry Lyme disease or trigger alpha-gal syndrome (AGS) and other nasty things, you want to avoid them if possible. DEET repellent and appropriate dress (long pants, a hat) will minimize the risk of a tick biting you.

HEALTH INSURANCE

The United States offers possibly the finest health care in the world – the problem is that it can be prohibitively expensive. It's essential to purchase travel health insurance if your home policy doesn't cover you for medical expenses abroad. Find out in advance if your insurance plan will make payments directly to providers or reimburse you later for overseas health expenditures.

Environmental Hazards

Cold exposure can be a problem, especially in the mountains. Keep all body surfaces covered, including the head and neck. Watch for the 'umbles' – stumbles, mumbles, fumbles and grumbles – which are signs of impending hypothermia.

Dehydration is the main contributor to heat exhaustion. Symptoms include feeling weak, headache, nausea and sweaty skin.

Tap Water

Tap water is safe to drink everywhere in the Mid-Atlantic, except in some state or national parks where it is clearly indicated that tap water is not potable. There are also some roadside rest areas along interstates in Virginia noting that the tap water is not potable.

BREAKDOWNS

If your car breaks down, pull off the road as far from traffic as possible. Turn on your hazard lights if you're on the side of the road. Once you're in a safe place, call the roadside emergency assistance number of your car-rental company or, if you're driving your own car, your automobile association.

Responsible Travel

Climate Change

It's impossible to ignore the impact we have when travelling, and the importance of making changes where we can. Lonely Planet urges all travellers to engage with their travel carbon footprint. There are many carbon calculators online that allow travellers to estimate the carbon emissions generated by their journey; try resurgence.org/resources/carbon-calculator.html. Many airlines and booking sites offer travelers the option of offsetting the impact of greenhouse gas emissions by contributing to climate-friendly initiatives around the world. We continue to offset the carbon footprint of all Lonely Planet staff travel, while recognising this is a mitigation more than a solution.

---

appalachiantrail.org

Protects the Appalachian Trail.

lnt.org

Leave No Trace site shares insights into no-impact travel.

nationalparks.org

Official partner of the National Park Service.

FARMERS MARKETS

Fresh produce from farms is a regional highlight, particularly from late spring through early fall. Most cities have a weekly outdoor farmers market, with produce and arts and crafts for sale. Check with tourism offices for dates.

USED GEAR

Save money and resources by buying name-brand secondhand gear at outdoor consignment shops, typically found in mountain towns and some larger cities. Noteworthy stores include 3 Rivers Outdoors in Pittsburgh and Play It Again Sports in New Jersey and New York.

STARGAZING

Urban light pollution diminishes the number of stars visible along much of the East Coast, but stargazing is still decent in a few spots. Virginia leads the pack among the Mid-Atlantic states with five International Dark Skies Parks. For a full list, visit darksky.org.

Nuts & Bolts

CURRENCY: US DOLLAR ($)

Credit Cards

Major credit cards are almost universally accepted. In fact, it is almost impossible to rent a car, book a hotel room or buy tickets without one. A credit card may also be vital in emergencies. Visa, Mastercard and American Express are the most widely accepted credit cards.

Debit Cards

When using debit cards to rent a car, be mindful of the fact that most major rental companies will charge a hefty additional deposit, sometimes equalling the cost of the entire rental. If the car is returned in good shape, the extra funds should be released in a day or two.

Tipping

Tipping in the US is not optional. Only withhold a tip in the case of outrageously bad service.

Restaurant servers Tip 15% to 20%.

Bartenders Tip 15% to 20% per round; minimum $1 per drink.

Guided trips Not required but recommended. A good start is $20 per day.

Speeding Tickets

If you are pulled over by the police, there is no system of paying traffic tickets on the spot. There is usually a 30-day period to pay by mail.

Toilets

Visitor centers, libraries and many parks have public restrooms. Pit toilets are often located near major trailheads.

Drones

Flying drones at national parks and most state parks is illegal. Beaches often have more lenient restrictions.

ELECTRICITY 120V/60HZ

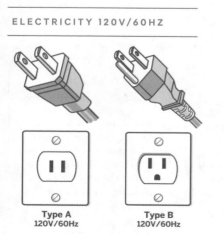

Type A
120V/60Hz

Type B
120V/60Hz

HOW MUCH FOR...

entry to the Blue Ridge Parkway
free

museum admission
free–$36

a half-day tour
from $50

Index

Map Pages 000

Map Pages 000

Map Pages 000

THE WRITERS

This is the 5th edition of Lonely Planet's *Best Road Trips New York & the Mid-Atlantic* guidebook, updated with new material by Amy C Balfour. Writers on previous editions whose work also appears in this book are included below.

Amy C Balfour

Amy grew up in Richmond, Virginia, and now lives in the Shenandoah Valley in the foothills of the Blue Ridge Mountains. A few of her favorite places between the Atlantic and the Appalachians include Sharp Top Mountain, Lexington, VA, Berlin, MD, and the New River Gorge. Top escapes? Scott's Addition in Richmond, VA, downtown Staunton, VA, Chincoteague Island and Frederick, MD. Amy has authored or co-authored more than 60 books for Lonely Planet, including *USA*, *Eastern USA* and *Florida & the South's Best Trips*. Her stories have appeared in *Backpacker*, *Sierra*, *Southern Living* and *Women's Health*.

Contributing writers

Ray Bartlett, Michael Grosberg, Brian Kluepfel, Simon Richmond, Karla Zimmerman

SEND US YOUR FEEDBACK

We love to hear from travelers – your comments keep us on our toes and help make our books better. Our well-travelled team reads every word on what you loved or loathed about this book. Although we cannot reply individually to your submissions, we always guarantee that your feedback goes straight to the appropriate writers, in time for the next edition. Each person who sends us information is thanked in the next edition.

Visit **lonelyplanet.com/contact** to submit your updates and suggestions or to ask for help. Our award-winning website also features inspirational travel stories and news.

Note: We may edit, reproduce and incorporate your comments in Lonely Planet products such as guidebooks, websites and digital products, so let us know if you are happy to have your name acknowledged. For a copy of our privacy policy visit **lonelyplanet.com/legal**.

BEHIND THE SCENES

This book was produced by the following:

Commissioning Editor
Caroline Trefler

Production Editor
Barbara Delissen

Book Designer
Clara Monitto

Cartographer
Daniela Machová

Assisting Editors
Christopher Pitts

Cover Researcher
Kat Marsh

Thanks to
James Appleton, Natalie Butler, Melanie Dankel, Saralinda Turner

Product Development
Amy Lynch, Marc Backwell, Katerina Pavkova, Fergal Condon, Ania Bartoszek

ACKNOWLEDGMENTS

Cover photograph
Popolopen Bridge, near Fort Montgomery State Historic Site; Nancy Kennedy/Shutterstock ©